The Courage to Doubt

THE
COURAGE TO DOUBT

Exploring an Old Testament Theme

ROBERT DAVIDSON

SCM PRESS LTD

334 01957 5

First published 1983
by SCM Press Ltd
26–30 Tottenham Road, London N1

Phototypeset by Input Typesetting Ltd
and printed in Great Britain by
Richard Clay Ltd (The Chaucer Press)
Bungay, Suffolk

CONTENTS

PREFACE

Chapters 1–8 were the basis of the Kerr Lectures delivered in the University of Glasgow in 1981. I am grateful to the Trustees of the Kerr Lectureship for the invitation to deliver the lectures. It provided me with the incentive to explore further a theme in which I have long been interested. The willingness of my Glasgow colleagues Professor John Macdonald, Dr Robert P. Carroll and Mr Alastair G. Hunter to accept additional teaching and administrative responsibilities made possible the study leave necessary for the preparation of the lectures. I am indebted to Mrs Jean Johnston for secretarial assistance and to my research student Gerrit Singgih for help with proof-reading. I offer this book as an inadequate tribute to Robert Dobbie, sometime Professor of Old Testament in Emmanuel College Toronto – scholar, teacher, saint and friend – who many years ago in St Mary's College, St Andrews, first provoked me into having 'The Courage to Doubt'.

Glasgow 1983   Robert Davidson

INTRODUCTION

Most good Presbyterian sermons, and many bad ones, take as their starting point a text. As a loyal Scottish Presbyterian let me offer as a text for this study Isaiah 45.15 which the RSV renders:

> Truly, thou art a God who hidest thyself,
> O God of Israel, the Saviour.

and which the Good News Bible, less pretentiously and less poetically renders:

> The God of Israel who saves his people
> is a god who conceals himself

Like most biblical texts, this one is capable of more than one interpretation. If we look at it in context there are, broadly speaking, two approaches to it which make sense. It occurs in a passage which depicts other nations coming humbly one day to Israel to acknowledge that Israel's knowledge of God is the only true knowledge.

(a) The first line of interpretation would see verse 15 as the natural continuation of the confession on the lips of these other nations, a confession which begins in the second half of verse 14. The confession thus contains four elements:

1. God is among you (i.e. Israel).
2. There is no other god.
3. God has until now been hidden from us other peoples.
4. We now recognize his true nature as made known in Israel – he is the one who delivers.

If this is the true interpretation then such other nations were in for something of a rude awakening. The clouds of God's hiddenness would not immediately disperse through contact with Israel. At least this was not Israel's own experience. The author of Isaiah 40–55 himself bears eloquent witness to the fact that they were many perplexed people in Israel (cf. 40.27). Israel, as God's servant was herself often blind and deaf (cf. 42.18ff.).

(b) We may take the nations' confession as having only two elements – 'God is among you' and 'There is no other god' – and as ending at verse 14. Verse 15 then contains the prophet's reflection upon the mystery which is involved in such a confession; the mystery of a God who is not self-evidently accessible, who at one and the same time may be hidden and yet known. The experience of the nations in this respect is an illustration of something which is true of Israel's own experience. If this interpretation is correct then we are in touch with a paradox which runs widely and deeply through the faith of Israel. On the one hand God is known. He has chosen to reveal himself. Certain things can be said about the way he acts, and from the way he acts, e.g. in the exodus, certain conclusions may be drawn about his character. On the other hand there always remains an element of hiddenness in God, the something which lies beyond human comprehension.

There are two ways in which we may seek to resolve this paradox:

(i) The way which is presupposed in the New English Bible translation of the verse:

> How then canst thou be a god that hidest thyself,
> O God of Israel, the deliverer.

This translation, which I believe to be erroneous, seems to say that once people have confessed their faith in a God who is known as saviour, that is that. God *is* known and there is no longer any meaningful way in which we can go on talking about God as 'hidden'.

(ii) The other way may be indicated by parodying the NEB translation as follows:

> How then canst thou be a god that delivers,
> O God of Israel, the hidden one.

In this case we so stress the hiddenness, the mystery, the unknowability of God that we end up hedging all our theological bets concerning what may be said with any certainty about God.

The essence of a paradox, however, is that it must not be resolved; that it holds together two truths which at first sight may seem logically contradictory, but which need each other and interact upon each other. The Old Testament, I believe, bears continuing witness to such a paradox, holding together the knowability and the hiddenness of God. Men were often caught in the tension of this paradox. Sometimes they were led to rebel against and to question what was being confidently affirmed about God in order to retain faith in God. The prophet Malachi accuses his contemporaries of violating the covenant with God by being blind to moral issues and by asking, 'Where is the God of justice?' (Mal. 2.17). But that same question, which is in Malachi an expression of faithlessness, may also be wrung from someone agonizingly trying to hold on to a realistic faith. What is offered here is a study in a particular aspect of Old Testament spirituality, an aspect which may have more than a passing relevence today, when many, even within the believing community, find themselves forced to question and doubt, and often do so with an unnecessarily guilty conscience.

1

WORSHIP AND QUESTIONING

One of the things which modern Old Testament scholarship has made abundantly clear is that in the Old Testament we are in touch, not with one monolithic theology, but with a series of traditions which often coexist side by side and interact upon one another, and which are each capable of being adapted, expanded and reshaped.[1] These traditions gave the community of Israel its identity and enabled it to respond creatively – or negatively – to situations of crisis. If we ask how and in what circles these traditions were handed on from generation to generation there is no one answer. There would, however, be a fair measure of agreement that one of the most important bearers of tradition in ancient Israel was the cult and the community gathered for worship. The cult has been well described as 'the fertile soil in which ideas were born – and lived. There ancient traditions were given their form and handed down to posterity: there the psalms were composed and used. In it the hope, the joy, the fear, the anxiety and the desperation of the people were expressed: in it Yahweh's answers came to them. The cult was nothing accidental: it was the living core in the relationship between Yahweh and the people.'[2]

It is as true of Israel – as it is of most religious communities – that if we would try to understand its faith we must look at how and why the community worshipped. We must not be misled by the pungent criticisms that were made of cultic practices by the eighth- and seventh-century prophets in Israel, criticisms which may tempt us to adopt a negative attitude towards, or underestimate the value of worship in Israel. The greatest threat to the continuing vitality of a religion usually comes from within.[3] The

tradition may become fossilized, worship stereotyped and for-
malized until in the name of God it blinds people to God and the
radical claims he makes on their lives. There is no more effective
immunization against God than the means of grace – misunder-
stood. The prophets' attack is not on the cult *per se*, but on such
misunderstanding. Both Isaiah and Micah have harsh things to
say about the false security generated by worship in their day
(e.g. Isa. 1.10–15; Micah 3.11), but side by side with such criticisms
there is to be found in both books a common oracle which looks
for the consummation of God's purposes for all peoples in terms
of that knowledge of God and God's will which centres upon
Jerusalem and the temple.

> In days to come
> the mountain of the Lord's house
> shall be set over all other mountains
> lifted high above the hills.
> All the nations shall come streaming to it,
> and many peoples shall come and say,
> 'Come, let us climb up on to the mountain of the Lord,
> to the house of the God of Jacob,
> that he may teach us his ways
> and we may walk in his paths.'
> For instruction issues from Zion,
> and out of Jerusalem comes the word of the Lord;
> he will be judge between the nations,
> arbiter among many peoples.
> They shall beat their swords into mattocks
> and their spears into pruning-knives;
> nation shall not lift sword against nation
> nor ever again be trained for war (Isa. 2.2–4; Micah 4.1–3).

The prophets criticize the cult, as they criticize so much else in
contemporary society, including many of the religious traditions
society professes, but they do so with a purpose. Prophetic
preaching 'shatters and transforms tradition in order to announce
the approach of the Living One'.[4] Institutionalized worship
needed to listen to the corrective and critical prophetic word, but
it was in the context of worship that much of this prophetic
challenge was to be transmitted to future generations, and there
is every reason to believe that it was through worship that most
Israelites in all ages were open to the approach of the Living One.

'No historian of Hebrew religion can permit himself to relegate the themes of worship to some appendage on institutions . . . It may be said that in Israel there would have been no knowledge of God without the service of God. Theology was bred in celebration.'[5] But what kind of knowledge of God is it that we see reflected in the service and worship of God? What varied themes are concealed in this word celebration?

Let us begin by looking at the psalms in the light of such questions, and looking at them with one basic assumption. Whatever difficulties and differences there may be in detail in classifying the psalms into distinct categories, the only sound approach to understanding the psalms is in terms of 'form criticism'.[6] The psalms as a whole fall into clearly discernible types, each with characteristic structure, language and content. Further, most of these types of psalms find their natural context in different acts of worship in Israel. This remains true even when we cannot be sure as to what particular religious festival or act of worship lies behind certain psalms; whether, for example, there was an annual New Year festival in the Jerusalem temple celebrating the kingship of Yahweh or a royal Zion festival.

There are psalms which may be classified as *hymns*. It is characteristic of such hymns that they express adoration. In them we find the community humbling itself before, and looking at its life in the light of, the majesty, the mystery and the wonder of God. Thus Psalm 8 has as its key opening and closing refrain;

> O Lord our sovereign,
> how glorious is thy name in all the earth.

In between there is the recognition, based on the creation hymn in Genesis 1, of the pivotal role of man in the world;

> . . . thou has made him a little less than a god,
> crowning him with glory and honour (v. 5).

Yet this is man surrounded by a question mark when set within the context of the mystery and immensity of God's universe;

> what is man that thou shouldst remember him,
> mortal man that thou shouldst care for him? (v. 4)

Psalm 100 opens with an urgent and joyful invitation;

> Acclaim the Lord, all men on earth,
> worship the Lord in gladness;
> enter his presence with songs of exultation. (vv. 1–2)

It continues in true hymnic style to specify the reasons for such acclaim, reasons rooted in the known character of God. So Psalm 136 celebrates the expression in creation (vv. 3–9) in history (vv. 10–22) and in continuing human experience (vv. 23–25), of that bed-rock of Israel's faith, the unchanging dependability, the steadfast love of the God who is acclaimed as the 'God of gods' and the 'Lord of lords' (vv. 23–25). It is in such hymns that we find Israel's echoing 'Hallelujah', 'praise the Lord'. The shortest psalm is one such perfect miniature hymn, universal in its outlook:

> Praise the Lord, all nations,
> extol him all you peoples;
> for his love protecting us is strong,
> the Lord's constancy is everlasting.
> Praise the Lord. (Ps. 117)

Roughly one in five of all the psalms fall into this category.[7] They express the rich assurance, the deep-welling joy of the community's faith.

Corresponding to the hymns are *Psalms of Personal Thanksgiving*. Such psalms often speak of a situation of crisis in a man's life, but it is a crisis which is passed. The psalmist has been delivered, his prayers answered. Very often at the beginning and end of such psalms the worshipper gives voice to a personal word of thanks. Thus Psalm 30 begins:

> I will exalt thee, O Lord;
> thou has lifted me up
> and hast not let my enemies make merry over me.

And ends:

> Thou has turned my laments into dancing;
> thou has stripped off my sackcloth and clothed me with joy,
> that my spirit may sing psalms to thee and never cease,
> I will confess thee for ever, O Lord my God.

Similarly Psalm 34 opens with a joyful expression of thanks:

> I will bless the Lord continually;
> his praise shall always be on my lips.

In the Lord I will glory;
    the humble shall hear and be glad.
O glorify the Lord with me,
    and let us exalt his name together.
I sought the Lord's help and he answered me;
    he set me free from all my terrors.

It ends on a note of confident faith:

The Lord ransoms the lives of his servants,
    and none who seek refuge in him are brought to ruin.[8]

Closely allied to such psalms of personal thanksgiving is another group of psalms not always clearly distinguished from them, *Psalms of Confidence*. They radiate the same kind of trust and quiet confidence without necessarily expressing these in thanksgiving. Psalms 23 and 27 are classic examples of this type of psalm. Such confidence is also the dominant note in certain other groups of psalms. Thus there are psalms usually called 'the songs of Zion', because they celebrate Jerusalem as 'the city of God', and the temple on Mount Zion as 'the house of the Lord' whose continuing security is guaranteed by the powerful, mystic presence of God in her midst. Psalm 48, for example, after lovingly describing the city, the senseless futility of any attempt to destroy it, the constant praise of God offered by his worshipping people in the temple, ends with an invitation:

Make the round of Zion in procession,
    count the number of her towers,
        and take good note of her ramparts,
    pass her palaces in review,
        that you may tell generations yet to come:
Such is God,
    our God for ever and ever;
        he shall be our guide eternally (Ps. 48.12–14).[9]

Likewise there is a group of psalms – Psalms 47, 93, 95–99 – usually designated *Psalms of the Kingship of Yahweh*. The thematic phrase which recurs in them is 'Yahweh (the Lord) is king'. Whether such psalms are to be assigned to a particular festival in the Jerusalem religious calendar is largely irrelevant for our purpose. More to the point is it to notice that they all celebrate the kingly supremacy of Yahweh, past, present and future, his control over all the forces of nature and history, his greatness which reduces to impotence all the gods of other peoples, and leads his worshippers to celebrate in a song of joy and thanksgiving:

> Sing a new song to the Lord:
>> since to the Lord, all men on earth.
> Sing to the Lord and bless his name,
>> proclaim his triumph day by day.
> Declare his glory among the nations,
>> his marvellous deeds among all peoples (Ps. 96.1–3).

In all of this there is nothing theologically surprising. Israel's life was dominated by belief in the good news of a God who had brought order out of chaos, who had delivered his people from oppression in the past, and who would remain for ever true to his own character. Worship, as response to such a God, could hardly do other than express itself in terms of adoration, praise, thanksgiving and confidence. Somewhere between one third and one half of the psalms give voice to such feelings. Indeed it is hard to see how any faith could lastingly survive unless it were able to provide its devotees with grounds for such joyful celebration. Yet the fact that fewer than one half of the psalms are expressive of such feelings ought to give us pause for thought. What remains and why?

Corresponding to the hymns, in which the community celebrated the wonder, majesty and goodness of God, are the *Community Laments*. Such laments spring out of and relive some crisis in the life of the nation. Psalm 74 is a good example. Although it is not always possible to be certain of the original crisis situation which gave birth to the lament – and interpretations which do not link the lament to any specific historical event have been offered – Psalm 74 would be particularly appropriate as a response to the Babylonian destruction of Jerusalem and its temple in 587 BC. It vividly describes the desolation of city and temple and, in the light of this, typically asks two questions: 'why?' and 'how long?'.

> Why hast thou cast us off, O God? Is it for ever?
> Why art thou so stern, so angry with the sheep of thy flock?
>> (v. 1)

> How long, O God, will the enemy taunt thee?
> Will the adversary pour scorn on thy name for ever? (v. 10)

Why dost thou hold back thy hand,
why keep thy right hand within thy bosom? (v. 11)

Why, in other words, in face of the humiliation and tragedy of
your people do you sit twiddling your thumbs and doing nothing?
The psalmist then recounts the tradition of faith in which the
community has been nurtured, a tradition which celebrates the
universal power of Israel's God (vv. 12–17); he calls on this God to
remember (vv. 2, 18) and urges him to do something consistent
with his own interests and character:

> Rise up, O God, maintain thy own cause;
>> remember how brutal men taunt thee all day long.
> Ignore no longer the cries of thy assailants,
>> the mounting clamour of those who defy thee (v. 23).

Psalm 44 explores similar themes. It begins by recalling the clear
witness of the past to the mighty deeds of God;

> O God, we have heard for ourselves,
>> our fathers have told us,
> all the deeds which thou didst in their days,
>> all the work of thy hand in days of old (v. 1).

The story which the present has to tell, however, is very different:

> But now thou hast rejected and humbled us
>> and dost no longer lead our armies into battle.
> Thou has hurled us back before the enemy,
>> and our foes plunder us as they will (vv. 10–11).

For this enigma the psalmist can find no obvious explanation,
certainly not in any theology of judgment on human sinfulness:

> All this has fallen us, but we do not forget thee
>> and have not betrayed thy covenant;
> we have not gone back on our purpose
>> nor have our feet strayed from thy path (vv. 17–18).

Faced with apparently meaningless suffering the community can
only appeal to God to wake up:

> Bestir thyself, Lord, why dost thou sleep?
>> Awake, do not reject us for ever.
> Why dost thou hide thy face,
>> heedless of our misery and our sufferings?
> For we sink down to the dust

and lie prone on the earth.
Arise and come to our help;
    for thy love's sake set us free (vv. 23–26).

It is important to grasp the tensions within this psalm: the tension
between what the past affirms to be true and what the present
seems to deny; the tension between believing that the key to
God's nature is to be found in the idea of love and facing a
situation in which there are no evident signs of such love. If you
have been brought up to affirm that God is a powerful, active,
living God and live through an experience which seems to speak
only of the triumph of ruthless and arrogant evil, how do you
explain it? Is God asleep? Nor is the immediate sharpness of this
question blunted by asserting that the psalmist's language here is
metaphorical and that he is only asserting that God *seems* to be
asleep. It is too convenient quickly to dismiss as metaphorical all
language about God which is disturbing. One of the *Psalms of
Confidence* asserts:

> The guardian of Israel never slumbers, never sleeps
> (Ps. 121.4).

This lament can only ask God 'why dost thou sleep?'
    Such community laments – and there are many examples of
them among the psalms [10] – are never content merely to note the
meaninglessness of the present crisis, nor do they show any
passive acceptance of it. They are characterized by protest and
they have nowhere to take their protest except to God.[11] The
harsh reality of life has forced the community to ask probing
questions about its faith – and to these questions there are no
immediate or easy answers.
    If community laments are well represented in the Psalter, even
more numerous are the *Individual* or *Personal Laments*. Psalm 13 is
typical of such laments. Four times in the first two verses the cry
goes up 'How long?'.

> How long, O Lord, wilt thou forget me?
>   How long wilt thou hide thy face from me?
> How long must I suffer anguish in my soul,
>   grief in my heart, day and night?
> How long shall my enemy lord it over me?

The psalm then moves into an appeal to God:

Look now and answer me, O Lord my God (v. 3).

It ends by expressing confidence that the answer will come, with the psalmist joyfully anticipating the reversal of his present plight (vv. 5–6). Like many of the personal laments this is a psalm of transition, of movement from darkness to light, from pain-wracked questions to joyous hope. And it is precisely the fact of transition which is interesting. Worship, for this psalmist, is concerned not merely with the end of his journey but equally with its beginning. If there is a darkness, it is darkness which demands to be faced in God's presence; if there are perplexing questions, they are questions which are poured out to God in worship.

Psalm 38 is the lament of a man in the grip of severe personal suffering. He feels himself to be on the receiving end of God's anger, wounded by God's arrows (vv. 1–2). Tormented by pain, his strength ebbing, shunned by his friends and family, an object of derision to gloating enemies, he turns to God to make an urgent plea:

> Lord, do not forsake me:
>   keep not far from me, my God,
> Hasten to my help, O lord of my salvation (vv. 21–22).

Although we may see continuing trust in this appeal to God – indeed worship assumes some such continuing trust – the God to whom he makes his plea is the God who is the source of his trouble, the God who wounds. No indication is given in this psalm as to whether or how his plea is answered.

Psalm 109 introduces us to another element which appears not infrequently in the personal laments. It begins with a plea to God to break his silence, to speak to a situation in which the psalmist feels helpless in the face of the hatred and the attacks of men whom he describes as 'the wicked' who

> . . . have repaid me evil for good,
> and hatred in return for my love (v. 5).

The wicked in this psalm are probably personal enemies who are prepared to commit perjury by using the due processes of law to have the psalmist condemned on the basis of false accusations (cf. vv. 6, 20). As he thinks of these venomous accusers the psalmist breaks into a bitter and extended curse (vv. 8–20). There are several examples of such 'Old Testament unevangelical prayers',[12] as they have been called, and numerous attempts to explain them away or to provide them with at least minimal theological respectability. It is possible, however, to become so obsessed either with dismissing such curses as spiritually defective or with providing justification for them, that we fail to recognize that such curses have a recognized place in the total thought pattern of several of the psalms of lament. From cursing, the psalmist turns to contrast himself 'downtrodden and poor' (v. 22) making his plea to God:

> Help me, O Lord my God;
>   save me, by thy unfailing love,
> that men may know this is thy doing
>   and thou alone, O Lord, hast done it (vv. 26–27)

with his accusers for whom he prays:

> May my accusers be clothed with dishonour,
>   wrapped in their shame as in a cloak (v. 29).

The psalm ends with the confident assertion that God

> . . . stands at the poor man's right side
> to save him from his adversaries (v. 31).

We find in this psalm a grim recognition of the power and the apparent success of 'the wicked' and a raw honesty which sees nothing incongruous in an explosion of vengeance as part of an act of worship.

There have been many attempts to identify the situations out of which the psalms of personal lament spring, many theories as to the identity of 'the wicked' who frequently feature in such psalms, many reconstructions of particular cultic acts which provide them with a natural setting. No one explanation is feasible or likely.[13] In any society there are many circumstances which may threaten a person's security and cause physical, mental and spiritual anguish. Some of these circumstances, e.g. pain and death, are basic human experiences, others may be more culturally defined, but whatever the circumstances which give rise to them, it is noteworthy that psalms of personal lament occur with greater frequency in the Old Testament than any other type of psalm.

The very number and variety of such personal lament psalms raise questions for the interpreter.[14] Are they, for example, all on the same level of theological sensitivity or is it possible to distinguish between questions and protests which are potentially creative, the stepping stones to a more mature and realistic faith, and questions and protests which are simply sterile, the fruit of nothing other than human blindness and unfaithfulness? Can we differentiate between the darkness which stems from serious unresolved theological difficulties and the darkness which is nothing other than the reflection of emotional self-indulgence? Only by a depth analysis which sought, in each psalm, to enter into the psalmist's experience could we begin to provide answers to such questions. Is such a depth analysis possible? If we approach a psalm – or indeed any biblical text – asking 'What did this psalm originally mean? What was in the mind of the author when he wrote it?', we may have to confess that we do not really know. All that we have is the text as it now lies before us. Even after we have analysed it with all the critical tools at our disposal, it is no easy matter to jump from the text into the mind of the author, particularly when we are dealing with a text which comes to us from an ancient culture, radically different in many respects from our own in terms of its social and intellectual presuppositions. I am not claiming that we should not ask 'What did this psalm originally mean?', I am only saying that that question may not be as easy to answer as we think and that we may have to settle for something far less than certainty. Furthermore, 'What did this psalm originally mean?' may not be the most important or the most profitable question to ask. It may be equally important and more realistic to ask 'How was this psalm understood by successive generations of worshippers in Israel and in the Christian church? What theological meaning or meanings did it convey to later interpreters?' It is particularly true that the language of worship is often flexible, capable of conveying many different shades of meaning and of speaking differently to people in differing circumstances. Thus if we revert for a moment to Psalm 74, one of the laments of the community, it may have come originally out of a particular moment of historical crisis in the life of the community such as the destruction of Jerusalem by the Babylonians in 587 BC, but as has been wisely said: '. . . even if Psalm 74 and others like it derive their present form in part at least from some historical moment . . . their significance is not limited to that moment; it has meaning for other situations, less outwardly drastic but nevertheless serious for the continuing religious life and well-being of the community'.[15]

This has a two-fold consequence for our understanding of the psalms of lament:

1. Such psalms found a lasting place in the hymn book of ancient Israel and were continuingly used and useful because both the community and individuals within the community found across the centuries that serious threats to the integrity of their religious experience had to be faced. In every age faith involved a struggle, a struggle to understand the ways of the God whose presence was celebrated in worship, but who often seemed strangely absent. 'Why?' and 'How long?' were repeatedly discovered to be as authentic cries as 'Hallelujah'.

2. Granted the reality of this element of struggle in faith and the perplexity born of the apparent absence or unconcern of God, such psalms of lament could be given an interpretation which would take them far beyond their original terms of reference. Thus the wicked, who in many cases in such psalms may have been quite literal enemies whether foreigners, unscrupulous power manipulators within Israel or false accusers, could become the symbol of any threat to faith.

The psalms of lament, therefore, suggest that among the many traditions which found expression in worship in ancient Israel and were handed on to the future through worship, there was one which we might describe as 'the courage to doubt', using doubt in the widest sense to indicate any questioning of, or protest against the adequacy of inherited faith.

In the light of the central place which such psalms of lament occupy in worship in ancient Israel, I want to raise a question about the hymn books we use today. Let us analyse *The Church Hymnary, Third Edition* (1973) now commonly in use in the Church of Scotland and in certain other latter day Presbyterian temples in the British Isles. One of the innovations in this Hymn Book was that, instead of printing the Scottish Metrical Psalms separately and in their entirety, it incorporated a selection of psalms into the body of the hymn book. Fifty eight of the one hundred and fifty psalms in the Old Testament appear as hymns in this book. I have no objection to selection *per se*, particularly selection from the Scottish Metrical Psalms which at worse sink to the level of religious doggerel – and religious doggerel is no more uplifting than any other form of doggerel. The principles which underlie the selection, however, do raise questions. The declared intention of the selection was 'to promote a fuller use of the riches of the psalter and that the range of selection may be widened'.[16] It is arguable that what has been retained does not reflect the riches of the psalter but is evidence rather of a theologically determined emasculation of the psalter which virtually eliminates some of its most characteristic features.

Of the psalms which express adoration, praise, thanksgiving, confidence the majority have been retained, twenty four out of a possible thirty eight, approximately sixty-four per cent.[17] When we turn to the psalms of lament the picture is very different. Of the community laments only four out of fourteen are retained – in part. I say in part because the selectivity process goes on internally within these psalms. Of the four community laments two, Psalms 85 and 130, remain in full. When we look at Psalm 90, however, we find that only verses 1 and 2, 14 and 16 survive. The effect of this is to eliminate all those elements which refer to human frailty and weakness, to the suffering of the community, to the disturbing anger of God, and to ignore the characteristic question 'How long, O Lord?' (v. 13). Thus by a process of selection a community lament is converted into a hymn of praise. Precisely the same happens to Psalm 106, with the same effect, when only verses 1–5 and 48 remain. The situation is even more striking in the case of the psalms of personal lament. One of a classification which includes forty-one psalms in this category, only ten are represented in the hymn book, and again only in part. In Psalm 9, which may originally have formed one psalm with what is now Psalm 10, only verses 7–11 remain, thus eliminating any reference to the gap between what faith expects and experience seems to teach. In themselves these verses form an unexceptional hymn of praise. Most of Psalm 22 remains – verses 1–9, 11, 15–19, 22–24, 27, 30, 31. The verses omitted, probably purely on literary grounds, do not in this case alter the character of the psalm; but we may at least wonder whether the psalm would have been retained in this form had it not been hallowed in Christian tradition by its opening words being on the lips of Jesus as he was crucified. In the case of Psalm 25 only verses 4, 5a, 6–10 are retained. Thus all references to the psalmists enemies, triumphant and numerous (vv. 2, 10) are eliminated; as is the description of the psalmists plight 'lonely and oppressed' (v. 16), in misery and trouble (cf. vv. 17–18). What remains becomes a very pious hymn of confession. Of Psalm 26 only verses 6–8 are retained to become one of the hymns appropriate to Holy Communion, the lament element totally eliminated. Psalm 42 has been treated less drastically, only verses 6 and 7 being omitted. The lament element which is expressed at its strongest in verses 9–11 remains intact, but again the language in this section particularly verse 10; 'My enemies taunt me, jeering at my misfortune' finds natural echoes in the passion narrative, particularly in its Matthean and Lucan forms, and the psalm is thus naturally incorporated into the hymns dealing with 'Christ's Passion and Cross'. Psalm 43 is a brief psalm, five verses in all; yet verses 1–2 have been eliminated, thus effectively ignoring what is the crux of the psalmist's problem, the fact that he has been attacked by 'malignant men and liars' (v. 1), by enemies who oppress him (v. 2), and feels rejected by God (v. 2). The traditional Hebrew title of Psalm 102 is 'A prayer of the afflicted when he is overwhelmed, and pours out his complaint to God'; less accurately the early church regarded it as one of the penitential psalms. By retaining only verses 13–18 the hymnary makes the process of misunderstanding complete. A powerful lament e.g. verses 2–4,

> Listen to my prayer
>   and, when I call, answer me soon;
> for my days vanish like smoke,
>   my body is burnt up as in an oven.
> I am stricken, withered like grass:
>   I cannot find the strength to eat.

is turned into one of the songs of Zion, looking forward to God revealing again his glory in a restored temple on Mount Zion. Psalm 139 appears in the attractive form of an adaptation from the New English Bible by Ian Pitt Watson, the adaptation drawing material from verses 1–12, 23 and 24. This ignores *inter alia* all references in the psalm to 'the wicked', the 'men of blood' (v. 19); it suppresses the intense expression of hatred which the psalmist directs against his enemies (vv. 19–24). By retaining only verses, 1, 6 and 8 of Psalm 143, all the typical elements of the lament, – the enemies, the psalmist's darkness and despair, his urgent pleas to God – have disappeared. The net result of all this is that out of forty-one psalms of personal lament only two remain with the lament element intact, both of them because of christological associations. The compilers of *The Church Hymnary, Third Edition*, therefore, seem to be saying that the lament element which is so prominent in the Old Testament psalms has no point of contact with the experience or need of the worshipper today. Their approach to the riches of the psalms is highly selective. Psalms which affirm the greatness and majesty of God and which incorporate the people's response of confident praise are well represented: psalms which give voice to the questions which threaten faith, which explore the darkness of human despair and crippling meaninglessness, which show men reacting bitterly against the forces of evil in the world, are virtually eliminated.

Nor are there hymns, not based on the psalter, which express this disappearing element in most contemporary hymn books. Thus *The Church Hymnary, Third Edition* in dealing with the 'Responses to the Word of God' lists: Adoration and Thanksgiving, Affirmation, Dedication and Discipleship, Stewardship and Service, Witness and Encouragement, Intercession, The Church Triumphant. Most of these themes find their parallels in the Psalms – although intercession has low priority – but nothing here remotely approaches the lament element. For that we would have to include a section entitled 'Questioning and Protest'. Similarly in the joint Hymn Book of the Anglican and United Church of Canada, the few psalms which are retained show the same imbalance, and the worshippers are invited to respond to God, by affirming our faith, by giving thanks, by remembering the world etc., by bringing our requests, among them requests for help in daily living, for guidance. . . . We have only to look at this request section, however, (Hymns 258–270) to see how far removed they are from many of the requests found in the psalms. To echo the psalms we would need a section in which we respond to God 'by affirming our doubts', 'by bringing our unanswered questions and our despair'. There is no hymn book known to me in current use which questions faith so seriously and consistently as the psalms; no hymn book which so openly encourages people to live through, in the context of worship, the dark night of their soul. Why is it, in the words of Claus Westermann that '. . . in Western Christendom the lament has been totally excluded from man's relationship with God, with the result that it has completely disappeared above all from prayer and worship'?[8] Is it that the tradition of faith in which we are nurtured is so radically different from that of the psalmist that this is an element in Israel's hymn book to which, in the light of Christ, the Christian says an emphatic 'no'? Why then is it that it is the words of just such a lament that we find on the lips of Jesus on the cross? Why is it that there are many people in the church today who seem near to the psalmists in their need, people who have radical doubts about some of the traditional certainties, people crushed by the bitter reality of evil in their lives, people who find it far from easy to affirm the living presence of God in their experience, people who have long since ceased to pray since their prayers seemed to go out into an unanswering silence, people who are asking in terms of our age the same questions which haunted psalmists 'why'? and 'how long'?

It is, of course, true, as J. M. Powis Smith noted, that hymn books need constant revision 'to meet the needs of our own souls and accord with the aesthetic and theological standards of our own day'.[19] Few people today could sing with any vestige of solemnity the verse of a seventeenth-century hymn which he quotes:

> Ye monsters of the briny deep,
>   Your Maker's praises spout;
> Up from the deep ye codlings peep,
>   And wag your tails about.

There is, however, a real danger that 'the aesthetic and theological standards of our own day' – which may indeed lead us to recoil from the raw vigour of some of the psalms – may at the same time mislead us into neglecting continuingly important aspects of the tradition of faith we inherit. Smith himself, I think, is in danger of doing precisely this when, after noting what he calls an orthodox attitude to life and suffering in Psalm 1, he comments: 'This orthodoxy is scarcely questioned in the psalter. The legitimate function of doubt, inquiry and investigation finds no recognition. This is, of course, natural in view of the purpose and function of the psalter in Judaism. We do not hymn our doubts and our problems in the great congregation. We come together to strengthen one another by our common enthusiasms and loyalties, not to disturb and weaken by adding new troubles to those already possessed'.[20] But the psalmists *do* hymn their doubts and openly voice their troubles. Nor is it obvious that the sharing of doubts and the voicing of troubles necessarily lead to the disturbance or the weakening of faith. The psalms have a wholesome catholicity which recognizes that '. . . life as it comes along is beset by hurt, betrayal. . . . It may be suggested that the one-sided liturgical renewal of today has in effect driven the hurtful side of experience either into obscure corners of faith practice or completely out of Christian worship into various forms of psychotherapy and growth groups'.[21] It is appropriate then that a psychotherapist should warn of the dangers in this for the Christian faith. 'For the most part the Churches have not yet learned that the best way to pass from defensive rationalisations to secure faith is to let doubts, inconsistencies, confusions and rebellions come out into the open instead of using various forms of spiritual coercion to keep them hidden or to draw them from awareness altogether.'[22] One of the most effective ways of bringing them out into the open is, like the psalms, to give them their place in worship; otherwise worship can become only too easily a subtle form of spiritual coercion.

2

WORSHIP AND THE SEARCH FOR ENLIGHTENMENT

There will still be priests to guide us, still wise men to advise, still prophets to proclaim the word (Jer. 18.18).

Thus, within the context of a plot to discredit the prophet Jeremiah and his message, we find a statement of the three most important channels of tradition in the life of ancient Israel:

1. The priest, who carries out a teaching ministry based on *tôrāh*, instruction, guidance given in the light of the community's religious inheritance, guidance covering all aspects of the community's life, social and ethical as well as cultic, guidance given often in the context of worship.

2. The wise man, who is concerned with *'ēṣāh*, counsel, advice drawing widely upon observation of human experience; whether political counsel offered to king and court or more general advice and comment on the prudent as opposed to the foolish, the successful as opposed to the disastrous life.

3. The prophet, who is the messenger of the *dābhār*, the word of Yahweh, a word which claims authoritatively and self-authenticatingly to speak to the contemporary situation in the life of the community.

This classification is useful and convenient provided we remember that we are not talking about channels which flow in isolation from one another. Priests, wise men and prophets in their activity and in their teaching touch one another at many points. There are books attributed to prophets, e.g. Habakkuk, which far from containing the prophetic 'Thus says the Lord' are built up from liturgical material, laments and hymns, which may seem more closely related to priestly material. There are psalms in which, in response to the people's praise or petition, God addresses the congregation, e.g. Psalm 75.2ff. and it is a reasonable assumption that at this, and at other points, in the psalms we are in touch with the activity of prophets functioning within the cult.[1] Prophets and wise men often found themselves dealing, from their different standpoints, with the same situation of crisis in the life of the nation.[2]

Among the psalms there are several which have been classified as 'Wisdom Psalms' or 'didactic songs or poems'. It is hardly surprising that it has been difficult to decide what precisely makes a psalm into a 'Wisdom Psalm', since attempts to define wisdom or the wisdom literature or the wisdom tradition are equally problematic.[3] Whatever the formal problems of definition there are psalms which deal with some of the characteristic concerns of the wise men in Israel. They speak of a knowledge which claims to come from observation and experience. They use some of the typical language which we find in the wisdom tradition in the book of Proverbs – the doctrine of the two ways in life, the contrast in fortune and character between the righteous and the wicked. They also begin to probe into some of the problems raised by wisdom teaching and its neat distinctions. In many cases such psalms are not addressed to God, either in praise or protest; they are in the form of poetic meditations on certain features of life. Even when such a psalm, as is the case with Psalm 112, begins with a call to worship, 'Hallelujah', 'O Praise the Lord', this call, in spite of its communal liturgical significance, does not influence the content of, nor does it seem to stand in any organic relationship to, the rest of the psalm. Before we begin to analyse the teaching about life and the wrestling with some of life's anomalies which we find in such psalms, it is important to recognize that we have no right to expect to find in these psalms one wholly consistent response. They share a common framework, but within this framework they often go their separate ways. It is notorious, of course, that such inconsistencies exist side by side in any hymn book. Unreconciled, and sometimes irreconcilable, theologies are cheerfully sung today by untroubled congregations. Thus Paraphrase 2, Hymn 72 in *The Church Hymnary Third Edition*, 'O God of Bethel' describes life as 'this weary pilgrimage' and talks about 'each perplexing path of life' while Hymn 367 invites us to celebrate 'the beauty of the earth, the beauty of the skies', 'the beauty of each hour', 'the joy of ear and eye . . . the heart and minds delight', 'the joy of human love' – a catalogue of experiences which could hardly be labelled as 'this weary pilgrimage'. Yet I have heard both these hymns sung by the same congregation in the course of one act of worship. We must not look for consistency where none is necessarily to be found, nor should we underestimate people's ability to live with the irreconcilable.

Psalm 1, generally believed to be a late psalm, serves in its present context as a prologue to the entire collection of psalms. It thus focusses attention upon some of the major themes which in one form or another are to be reiterated throughout the collection. It draws a sharp contrast between two types of men:

(*a*) The man whose attitude is described negatively as rejecting the influence of 'the wicked', 'sinners' and 'the scornful', and positively in terms of the delight which comes from centring life upon *tôrāh*, the instruction, the law of the Lord. Such a positive, joyful attitude to *tôrāh* finds expression in many psalms, not least in Psalm 119, e.g. vv. 44–48

> I will heed thy law continually, for ever and ever;
>> I walk in freedom wherever I will,
>>> because I have studied thy precepts.
> I will speak of thy instruction before kings
>> and will not be ashamed;
>>> in thy commandments I find continuing delight;
> I love them with all my heart.
> I welcome thy commandments
>> and will meditate on thy statutes.

The man who thus states his priorities and commitment is one of 'the righteous' (vv. 5, 6). The 'righteous' man, *ṣaddîq* in the psalms, is not the man who claims arrogantly to be sinless or perfect. He is the man who believes that he is living in a right relationship with God, gladly ordering his life in the light of God's *tôrāh*. He belongs to the faithful within the community.

(*b*) The wicked, whose attitude throughout this psalm is assumed to be the opposite of righteous.

Attitude decides fortune. The righteous man not only knows a happiness which comes from his relationship with God, but he is likened to a fruitful, vigorous tree planted by a water channel; 'in all that he does he prospers' (v. 3). The wicked, *per contra*, are 'like chaff driven by the wind', a simile probably intended to underline the chronic instability and insecurity which surrounds everything they do. Between the two there is inevitable separation. The 'way of the righteous', the whole tenor of his life, is watched over by the Lord (v. 6); it is rooted in God and leads to God; but the way of the wicked leads nowhere, except to doom and destruction. There is no reason to assume that the psalmist at this point has in mind the thought of any final judgment beyond this present life;[4] rather he is talking about how he believes things work out in our present experience.

The didactic purpose of Psalm 1, therefore, is to remind the worshipper that life involves choice, the choice between two contrasting ways, and to spell out the inevitable consequences which are bound up with such choice. To speak of choice is one thing; to describe the relationship between choice and what is believed to be certain of its consequences is another. What is Psalm 1 claiming when it describes the righteous man as one who 'in all that he does he prospers' (v. 3)?[5]

Whatever its precise etymology the Hebrew word *ṣlḥ*, here translated 'prospers' usually has in the Old Testament the connotation of success in some particular sphere of human activity. Very commonly it is used of military success (e.g. I Kings 22.12, 15; Jer. 2.37; 32.5; II Chron. 13.12; 20.20; 24.20; 26.5; 31.21). It may describe success in a particular mission, e.g. the finding of a suitable wife for Isaac (Gen. 24.21, 40, 42, 56) or in the search for new land in which to settle (Judg. 18.5); the successful completion of ambitious building projects (I Chron. 22.11; II Chron. 7.11; 14.6) or the successful upholding of the cause of the orphan (Jer. 5.8). It is used to describe Joseph as the successful entrepreneur both in his master's household and in prison (Gen. 39.2, 3, 23). In terms of God's activity it is used to indicate God's word successfully accomplishing its purpose in the world (Isa. 55.11), and the servant of the Lord successfully carrying through his God-given mission (Isa. 53.10). Apart from one general wisdom saying in Proverbs 28.13, that open confession of faults is a healthy exercise, there is little evidence that the word is used in any generalized or spiritual sense. There is therefore a strong presupposition that in Psalm 1 the word will similarly be used to indicate specific, tangible, success. The link between such success and obedience to God's known commandments is stressed in several of the passages which employ this verb. Thus in I Chron. 22.13, David warns Solomon that success depends upon him being 'careful to observe the decrees and the ordinances which the Lord enjoined upon Moses for Israel' (cf. II Chron. 13.12); while in the Joseph narratives on each occasion Joseph's success is linked to the fact that 'the Lord was with him' (Gen. 39.2, 3, 23).

That godliness and material prosperity are but two sides of the one coin is the claim of a strong and continuing tradition in Proverbs (e.g. Prov. 3.9–16) and in the dialogue throughout the book of Job. There is a success factor in life which claims to rest upon a man's relationship with God. The appeal to such a success factor has been repeatedly made by religious movements within and outwith the Judaeo-Christian tradition.[6] Psalm 1 is but one of several wisdom psalms which reflect this tradition. Psalm 112 focusses attention upon the happiness of the man 'who fears the Lord' (v. 1). Such happiness is seen in character traits which are sympathetically delineated in verses 4–9. Here is a 'good' man, gracious, compassionate, generous with strong inner resources. For us the only jarring note is that 'in the end he will gloat over his enemies' (v. 8). But the fear of the Lord pays dividends of a different kind, tangible, material dividends which society recognizes and respects. Here is a man who will father an influential and powerful family (v. 2), whose 'house shall be full of wealth and riches' (v. 3). This picture is confirmed by Psalm 128 which promises a full life, long and prosperous to 'all who fear the Lord' (v. 1). Psalm 34 is an alphabetic acrostic poem which contains an address by a wisdom teacher to his children, an address which while admitting that a good man must be prepared to meet misfortune, nevertheless strongly and confidently contrasts the righteous and the wicked in terms of their attitude and their fate (vv. 11–22). Psalm 144, a royal psalm, ends by describing the powerful blessing which flows from the king to a nation which worships Yahweh:

> Happy are we whose sons in their early prime stand like tall towers,
>> Our daughters like sculptured pillars at the corners of a palace.
> Our barns are full and furnish plentiful provisions;
>> our sheep bear lambs in thousands upon thousands;
>>> the oxen in our fields are fat and sleek;
> there is no miscarriage or untimely birth,
>> no cries of distress in our public places.

Happy are the people in such a case as ours;
   happy the people who have the Lord for their God
      (Ps. 144.12–15).

If it be true that such words must be placed within the setting of a religious festival where 'The earthly wealth of a healthy rising generation, endowed with vital energy, the blessings of a rich harvest, fecundity of the flocks and peace both in country and in town are the visible signs of the blessings imparted by divine grace',[7] then it must be wondered how often and to how many people in ancient Israel such divine grace was visible. Nor is the problem resolved by regarding such statements as 'primarily a statement of faith rather than the result of the observation of human fortunes'.[8] Statements of faith do normally claim to find some verification in human experience. Indeed the stronger the faith, the greater the temptation to make the move from 'this is what I believe' to 'this is in fact how life operates'. Nevertheless neither blinkered theological optimism nor dogmatic confidence are in themselves adequate to explain the tenacity with which many in Israel held to what may be described as the traditional view[9] concerning the inevitable retribution which would befall the wicked and the fullness of life which would be the lot of the righteous. There must always have been *some* people who, in their own experience, found that piety and prosperity coexisted harmoniously, and who could therefore personally identify with Psalm 1, untroubled by the fact that it had nothing to say either about the difficulties and the suffering of the righteous or about the evident success of the wicked.

Many of the agonized 'whys' and 'how longs', which we find in the lament psalms, are witness to the fact that for many of the faithful in Israel's life did not follow this script. In the face of this, the lament psalms seek to help the worshipper to live through the darkness of their experience. They make urgent appeal to God, but they do not claim either to understand or to explain the apparent irrationality of what has happened. In some of the wisdom psalms, however, we hear the voice of men who felt compelled not only to acknowledge the irrationality but to seek some understanding of it, and in particular to wrestle with the problem raised by the continuing prosperity and success of the wicked. For them continuing faith was only possible once they had faced the fact that the anomalies of life had broken the neat tidiness of the traditional view.

In some ways, the most tentative approach to the problem is to be found in Psalm 37, an acrostic poem of twenty two proverbial statements whose inner connection is not always clear. The opening words of the psalm – although they are immediately qualified by a theological comment – reveal the psalmist's difficulty:

> Do not strive to outdo the evildoers
> or emulate those who do wrong.

It is evident from this, and from other references in the psalm, that there were evildoers in the community who, contrary to expectation, were doing extremely well for themselves and succeeding to such a degree that others were envious of their success. Power, ruthlessly used, (v. 14) and great wealth (v. 16) were at the disposal of the wicked. The righteous, *per contra*, have to live in comparative poverty, facing difficulties and times of trouble, vulnerable to the attacks of the wicked (vv. 16, 24, 32, 35). To this extent the psalm is realistic; but how far does the realism go in its handling of the problem posed by the success of the wicked? The problem is attacked from two angles:

(*a*) At several points the psalm is concerned to affirm that the success of the wicked is transient:

> For like grass they soon wither,
> and fade like the green of spring (v. 2).

> A little while and the wicked will be no more;
> look well and you will find their place is empty (v. 10).

> The Lord shall laugh at them,
> for he sees that their time is coming (v. 13).

> I have watched a wicked man at his work,
> rank as a spreading tree in its native soil.
> I passed by one day, and he was gone;
> I searched for him but he could not be found (vv. 35–36).

Here today . . . but gone tomorrow; such is this psalmist's verdict on the wicked. He believes that by very nature the success of the wicked is built on shifting sand. In a God ordered world it is necessarily temporary – as events, he claims, always prove. In other words he is inviting us to see the prosperity of the wicked as no more than a temporary aberration.

(*b*) He tries to undermine any feelings of envy at the prosperity of the wicked by claiming;

> Better is the little which the righteous has
> than the great wealth of the wicked (v. 16).

Even if wealth may be regarded as a sign of God's approval, that verdict cannot be extended to ill-gotten wealth. Better in this case a little, better because it lasts (v. 18), and better because it goes hand in hand with a quality of life which is acceptable to God; a life of generosity (vv. 21, 26), of wisdom and fair dealing (v. 30), a life which is steady because it is directed by the law of God (v. 31).

There are lines of thought here capable of profound development, but the overall impression we receive from the psalm is that the author remains trapped within the traditional framework he has inherited, noting deviations from it, yet unwilling to break radically from it. The deviations were temporary deviations, no more; the solid framework of a divinely ordered world of reward and retribution remains unquestioned. Thus

> The wicked watch for the righteous man,
> and seek to take his life;
> but the Lord will not leave him in their power
> nor let him be condemned before his judges (vv. 32–33).

Is this a realistic observation on the way in which society operated in ancient Israel? Were the innocent never found guilty through the manipulation of the due processes of law? The repeated prophetic attacks upon the perversion of justice (e.g. Amos 2.4; 5.12; Isa. 1.17) the numerous warnings in the law against the dangers or bribery and the need to protect the legal rights of those at risk in society (e.g. Exod. 23.2, 6–8; Deut. 16.18–20) tell a very different story. It is hard to escape the conclusion that what in religious terms ought to be has coloured the psalmist's description of what in fact is. Or take verse 25

> I have been young and am now grown old,
> and never have I seen a righteous man abandoned,
> or his children begging for bread.[10]

We may, of course, try to take the sting out of this statement by spiritualizing the word 'abandoned', but the psalmist has in his mind such material and physical consequences of being abandoned by God as 'his children begging for bread'. Yet the world of ancient Israel was in certain respects little different from the world we know. It was a world where men were often manipulated and crushed by power structures which the ruthless and the ambitious used for their own purposes; a world in which children, good and evil alike, died or were crippled by poverty, disease and malnutrition.

The realism of Psalm 37 must be severely qualified. The psalmist is aware that life does not quite follow the religious script he has been handed; but instead of being prepared to rewrite the script he decides merely to add a few explanatory footnotes. Meanwhile he repeatedly calls upon his people to 'trust', to commit their life to the Lord (vv. 3, 5), to hold fast to their faith in a God who will help, deliver and save (v. 40). This may in certain circumstances be effective pastoral counselling but it leaves many questions not only unanswered, but virtually unasked. Let us not underestimate the ability of people to live with unanswered questions. There are always those who are aware of questions which they can neither handle nor resolve, but are content to remain in the situation of saying 'Yes I can see the difficulty, but I still believe'. Perhaps we all do this at some point; the crunch comes when we try to decide at what point and for what reasons this is a tenable position.

Psalm 49 begins, in characteristic style, with an appeal to men to listen, while the wisdom teacher attempts through a piece of wisdom instruction (*māshāl*) to come to terms with a riddle or perplexing problem (*ḥîdāh*) which he believes to be of general human interest and concern. The problem, outlined briefly in verses 5–6, is a personal problem, acutely perplexing, given the tendency to equate righteousness with prosperity. How is the psalmist to deal with the evident success story of evil men, treacherous foes

> who trust in their riches
> and boast of their great wealth (v. 6)

and use that wealth and the power which comes from it to the detriment of others? The lynch-pin of the psalmist's answers is to be found in a refrain which occurs at verses 12 and 20, a refrain which points to the inevitable boundary within which all human pretensions must be set. Although the refrain raises certain critical problems its central thrust is hardly in doubt. In verse 12 the

Hebrew textual tradition may be rendered quite literally as in the RSV:

> Man cannot abide in his pomp,
> he is like the beasts that perish.

In verse 20, the Hebrew textual tradition – and the Greek tradition at verse 12 – has a variant in the first line: 'Man in his pomp has no understanding', i.e. blinded by the wealth in which he puts his trust, man has no real insight into what life is all about. The New English Bible adopting a slight conjectural emendation to the traditional text renders both at verses 12 and 20:

> For men are like oxen whose life cannot last,
> they are like cattle whose time is short.[11]

Both the RSV and the NEB eliminate the variation between verses 12 and 20 but there is little reason for so doing. The second refrain in the Hebrew tradition echoes and builds upon the first. Men, claims the psalmist, may throw their weight about for a time, but sooner or later they come face to face with the one certainty in life – death, death the inescapable leveller, whom no amount of money can buy off. A price tag may be put on many things, but not on the duration of life. Any attempt to evaluate life which does not take this fact into account can only be misleading. At death men are herded like sheep 'into Sheol, the land of Death' (v. 14) where all human pretensions and distinction are obliterated.

Since death and what may or may not lie beyond it play an important part in the thinking of several of the Old Testament books with which we shall be concerned, let us digress for a moment to take a closer look at this concept of 'Sheol, the land of Death'. For those for whom religion is primarily concerned with death and the life hereafter the Old Testament must be a very disappointing book. During the Old Testament period death seems for most Hebrews to have been neither a preoccupation nor a problem. It was simply a fact to be accepted. They seem to have inherited and accepted without much questioning, an attitude to death which we find widely documented elsewhere in the world of the Ancient Near East, particularly in Mesopotamia. Death is the god-decreed and inevitable lot of mankind, one of the most important factors which differentiate man from the gods. The point is well made in the Epic of Gilgamesh, where the hero

Gilgamesh, distraught by the death of his friend Enkidu, sets out on his travels in search of the secret or everlasting life and comes one day to an inn where 'mine hostess' gives him words of sound advice:

> The life thou pursuest thou shalt not find,
>   When the gods created mankind,
> Death for mankind they set aside,
> Life in their own hands remaining.[12]

The only sensible course of action is to accept the duties and pleasures which each day brings. Mortality on this view is not something to be regretted or to be challenged; it is merely part of the definition of what it means to be human. The anthropology with which Genesis 2–3 works is instructive in this context. Life is acknowledged to be God's gift. God breathes into man what is termed 'the breath of life' and man becomes 'a living personality', as opposed to some dead and inanimate pieces of sculpture (Gen. 2.7). This gift of life is something which, within the providence of God, man shares with other living creatures, birds, fish, animals, etc. At death God takes back this 'breath of life' and man returns to being the basic, earthly, raw material from which his outer frame was fashioned:

> Dust you are and to dust you shall return (Gen. 3.19; cf. Job 34.14).

The classic statement of this position in the Old Testament is to be found in Ecclesiastes 3.19–20 which the New English Bible, in one of its more inspired moments, translates:

> For man is a creature of chance, and the beasts are creatures of chance, and one mischance awaits them all: death comes to all alike. They all draw the same breath. Men have no advantage over the beasts. . . . All go to the same place: all came from the dust, and to the dust all return.

These are not merely the words of a latter day sceptic in Israel; they are the words of a man restating age-old certainties at a time when some other people were asking 'is this all that can be said?'. For most Hebrews there was no tragedy in the death of a man who had lived life to the full and reached a ripe old age, surrounded by his family, particularly his sons in whom the family name would live on after his death. In such circumstances a man,

without regret, will be 'gathered to his people and buried alongside his forefathers' in the family tomb (cf. Gen. 49.29). The first
oracle of Balaam in Numbers 23.7–10 ends:

> Who can count the host of Jacob
> or number the hordes of Israel?
> Let me die as men die who are righteous,
> grant that my end may be as theirs!

For all men a 'righteous', appropriate, fitting end would be to die
like Jacob at a ripe old age, surrounded by many descendants. If
there be tragedy in death, it is the tragedy of premature death
with life's potentialities unfulfilled; particularly tragic being the
death of a sonless man for this would effectively mark the end of
the family – hence, *inter alia*, the custom of the levirate marriage
(cf. Gen. 38; Ruth; Deut. 25.5–10).

But what was believed to happen to a man when the customary
mourning rites had been performed and the body deposited in
the family tomb? Popular Hebrew thinking seems to have
accepted unquestioningly belief in the existence of a vague shadowy netherworld to which a man went down at death (e.g. Gen.
37.35; I Sam. 2.6). This shadowy netherworld was commonly
called *Sheol*. Various synonyms for Sheol are to be found in the
Old Testament, most of them having a decidedly bleak or negative
connotation: thus the 'Pit' (e.g. Ps. 16.10), 'Abaddon' (destruction,
Prov. 15.11; 27.20; Ps. 88.11), 'the darkness', 'the land of oblivion'
(e.g. Ps. 88.12). Two passages from Job vividly sketch in the
bleakness of Sheol. In Job 10.21–22 Sheol is described as:

> . . . a land of gloom,
> a land of deep darkness . . .
> a land of gathering shadows, of deepening darkness,
> lit by no ray of light, dark upon dark.

This land of gloom is a land utterly devoid of hope.

> If I measure Sheol for my house,
> if I spread my couch in the darkness,
> if I call the grave my father
> and the worm my mother or my sister,
> where, then, will my hope be,
> and who will take account of my piety?
> I cannot take them down to Sheol with me,
> nor can they descend with me into the earth (Job. 17.13–16).

Sheol represents the negation of everything which makes life meaningful, including the possibility of any real contact with God. In a prayer attributed to King Hezekiah after his recovery from a serious illness, Hezekiah thanks God for bringing him back from the very gates of death since:

> Sheol cannot confess thee,
> Death cannot praise thee,
> nor can they who go down to the abyss
>   hope for thy truth,
> The living, the living alone confess thee
>   as I do this day (Isa. 38.18–20).

Centuries later the same sentiments are echoed by Ben Sirach:

> Who in the nether world can glorify the Most High,
>   in place of the living who offer their praise?
> No more can the dead give praise than those who have never
>   lived:
> they glorify the Lord who are alive and well (Ecclus.
>   17.22–23).

One of the lament psalms, the words of a man for whom life seems to have been unrelieved despair and gloom, asks a series of rhetorical questions all of which expect the answer no;

> Dost thou work wonders for the dead?
>   Shall their company rise up and praise thee?
> Will they speak of thy faithful love in the grave
>   of thy sure help in the place of Destruction?
> Will thy wonders be known in the dark,
>   thy victories in the land of oblivion? (Ps. 88.10–12)

All that makes life distinctive and worthwhile, piety, honour, wealth, status and function in society disappear into a grey twilight. Only the now of present experience can give any positive connotation.

> Give, take and treat yourself well,
>   for in the nether world there are no joys to seek.
> All flesh grows old, like a garment;
>   the age-old law is 'All must die' (Ecclus. 14.16–17).[13]

This is the traditional theology, or rather lack of theology, of death against which we must evaluate Psalm 49. However confidently evil men may

> trust in their riches
> and boast of their great wealth (v. 6)

they are on a journey which ends in Sheol, and there is nothing they can do about it. Using legal terminology, the language of 'ransom' (*pādāh*), the payment which in certain circumstances is acceptable as substitution or in exchange for something else, sometimes in exchange for a life which would be forfeit for a capital offence (e.g. Exod. 21.30), the psalmist insists that there is nothing a man can pay, no matter how wealthy he may be, which could secure him an eternal season ticket for this present life, no price he could ever pay to secure his release from the clutches of death;

> their flesh must rot away
> and their bodies be wasted by Sheol,
> stripped of all honour (v. 14).

Then comes the unexpected affirmation of faith:

> But God will ransom my life,
> he will take me from the power of Sheol (v. 15).

If we try to penetrate behind these words into the psalmist's mind to ask how precisely he thought God would take him from the power of Sheol, there can be little certainty. Has he reached the point of stating a belief in some form of personal immortality and eternal communion with God? The language of verse 16 is consistent with some such belief, but can hardly be taken to demonstrate it.[14] We may be formulating the wrong question when we seek to put the issue in these terms. As A. Weiser has well put it: 'The religious certitude of which he speaks is for him not so much a knowing what is going to happen, but rather a power which sustains him and enables him to procede steadily even when he cannot see clearly the course which his life is going to take.'[15] He is stating, and stating with unquestionable clarity and conviction that there is a power greater than the power of Sheol, i.e. God, and that those who trust this God have access to a hope that money can never buy.

In Psalm 49, therefore, we find a man having the courage to call into question the traditional teaching which had nurtured him, and to do so on several different levels.

1. He makes no attempt to defend in any way the thesis that in God's providence righteousness and prosperity must walk hand

in hand. He is only too painfully and bitterly aware that success comes to evil men, and that the wealthiest and most powerful men in society are often corrupt and godless. Unlike the author of Psalm 37 he shows no signs of trying to salvage from the fire of his experience the ashes of the traditional teaching.

2. He invites men to take seriously the relevance to the problem of theodicy of the boundary placed on human life and thought by death and the traditional picture of Sheol. He goes further in this respect than Psalm 37. The success of the wicked is no longer to be dismissed as a temporary aberration in an otherwise moral universe. Having dispensed with the traditional framework, he no longer thinks in terms of aberrations, but of the fundamental question mark which death places alongside all human pretensions. He is taking what is already there in the religious tradition he inherits, the concept of Sheol, and giving it new and urgent theological relevance.

3. Having used the traditional picture of Sheol as a limiting factor in the discussion of the problem of reward and retribution, he then has the courage to question whether the traditional picture of Sheol has the last word to say; whether there may not be the need to introduce a limiting factor into the concept of Sheol, i.e. God. This step is possible only because of his sense of relationship with God. What drives him to journey beyond the frontiers of the normal understanding of this relationship is the realism of his struggle to come to terms with the inadequacy of the traditional motif of retribution. He journeys further than the author of Psalm 37 because he questions more radically.

We turn now to Psalm 73. Although there are grounds for classifying Psalm 73 as a thanksgiving psalm rather than a wisdom psalm,[16] there is no doubt that it deals with a wisdom theme, basically the same theme as Psalm 49. From verse 2 onwards the psalm graphically describes a problem, the success of the wicked, which poses a serious threat to the psalmist's faith. This is prefaced, however, by a statement of faith:

> How good God is to Israel!
> How good to those who are pure in heart.[17]

What is the relationship between these opening words and the rest of the psalm? There are three possibilities.

1. These words are the theological starting point of the psalmist's difficulties. As such they must be taken as a summary of

the faith in which the psalmist had been nurtured. Yes, says the psalmist, I know what I ought to believe; God's goodness is always demonstrated to his own faithful people. But my experience of life – the experience he begins to recount in verses 2ff. – points in a very different direction. Out of this tension between inherited belief and personal experience his spiritual agony unfolds.

2. The opening words of the psalm may be taken as the end product of the experience which the rest of the psalm describes; as if the psalmist were saying, 'Listen, God is indeed good to his faithful people, I know . . . this was what I discovered as I struggled to make sense of life'.

3. These words represent *both* the starting point of the psalmist's experience *and* the end product of his experience. They can be both because in between the psalmist has been led to redefine what God's goodness means. Although strong arguments can be urged in favour of any of these views, the third approach makes most sense since it is in this process of redefinition that much of the interest of the psalm lies.

When we turn to the psalmist's problem we find that in essence it is the same problem as lies behind Psalm 49, though it is described in greater detail and in different terms. Isaiah 48.22 neatly summarizes much Old Testament teaching:

There shall be no *shālôm* for the wicked, says the Lord.

Although *shālôm* is conventionally translated 'peace' it has a much wider and richer range of meaning than what is normally conveyed by peace. It has been defined as 'a completeness, a success, a maturity, a situation which is both prosperous and secure withal, a state of wellbeing which is the direct result of the beneficent Presence of God'.[18] By very definition, therefore, the wicked who disregard God's presence cannot enjoy *shālôm*. But they do, protests the author of Psalm 73. I look around me and I see the *shālôm* of the wicked. It makes me green with envy (v. 3). The wicked openly boast of their success. They are healthy, carefree well fed. They enjoy wielding power to the detriment of others. Sneers and slander are their stock in trade. They are popular; they openly snap their fingers at God, assuming that he neither knows nor cares what goes on in the world. Not only do they defy God, but their godless arrogance pays handsome dividends. For the psalmist, however, the only reward for being faithful to God was suffering (v. 14). Faced with this situation the author of Psalm 73, instead of asking the obvious question 'why do the wicked prosper?' raises a far more fundamental question 'What is the meaning of faith?' Is there any point in continuing to believe and trying to pursue a godly life when all that it seems to lead to is suffering? Would it not make more sense to assume that the world makes no sense and to renounce faith in God? (vv. 13–14). Then he hesitates:

> Yet had I let myself talk on in this fashion,
> I should have betrayed the family of God (v. 15).

It is as if the full implications of what he has been thinking come home to him. If faith is pointless then it means that the whole tradition in which he has been nurtured is a fraud, and that the people with whom he worships and in whose company he seeks to serve God are wholly deluded. This conclusion he is not prepared to draw. His personal doubts, troubling as they are, are held in check by the faith of the community. Many people could echo this psalmist's experience that in time of perplexity the faith of others has kept them from spiritual bankruptcy. It is one of the compelling reasons for belonging to a believing community. The other side of the same coin is stressed in Psalm 69 where the plea to God to answer the psalmist's prayer is urged partly on the grounds that if there is no answer it will have an adverse effect on others who look to God for help (cf. Ps. 69.6). The sense of being upheld by the faith of the community, however, does not solve the psalmist's problem. It still remains, puzzling, hard to understand:

> until I went into God's sacred courts (v. 17).

It was in the temple, through some experience which came to him in worship, that the psalmist saw himself and his problem in a new light. There have been many attempts to define more precisely what particular festive occasion or ritual act lies behind the psalmist's words. None is capable of proof.[19] All we have is the text which points to two convictions which came to the psalmist through worship:

(a) The conviction of the fragile transience of the wicked. They may seem secure and successful, but the truth is quite otherwise. They are as insubstantial as a dream which vanishes as soon as you wake up; their stability illusory, destined to crumble suddenly in face of God-sent disaster and terror (vv. 18–20); whether the 'end' and the 'terrors' associated with death or some other awesome confrontation with the reality of God's judgment in this life, is not clear. This conviction, which closely parallels Psalm 49, without using the concept of Sheol, is a negative conviction which in itself does not penetrate to the core of the psalmist's personal spiritual problem.

(*b*) More positively – and this is where Psalm 73 breaks new ground – the psalmist is forced to recognize that the problem lies not simply or indeed mainly in the fact that the wicked prosper. The problem centres upon his own inadequate understanding of what faith means. Why had he been envious of the wicked? Did this not presuppose that he too believed that faith ought to pay tangible, material dividends? He is being driven to face the truth to which Martin Buber pointed when in a different context he declared 'Always and everywhere in the history of religion the fact that God is identified with success is the greatest obstacle to a steadfast religious life'.[20] But what is the essence of faith? In verses 23–26 he describes the reality which gripped him as he worshipped.

> Yet I am always with thee,
>   thou holdest my right hand;
> thou dost guide me by thy counsel
>   and afterwards wilt receive me with glory.
> Whom have I in heaven but thee?
>   and having thee, I desire nothing else on earth.
> Though body and heart fail,
>   yet God is my possession for ever.

Considerable discussion has centred upon the meaning of the words in v. 24b:

> and afterwards wilt receive me with (or 'in') glory.

Does 'afterwards' mean after this present life, and does 'glory' refer to some heavenly existence beyond the frontier of death; or is the psalmist simply saying that after all the suffering and spiritual agony he has experienced God will restore him to honour in this life?[21] As in the case of Ps. 49.15 the arguments are inconclusive and for the same reason. Nor for our present purposes is it important to try to decide the issue either way. Beyond all the uncertainties of interpretation, the passage speaks of a transforming two-fold certainty which came to the psalmist;

1. that faith did not depend on his grasp of God, but on God's grasp of him;

2. that the essence of faith is a relationship with God which nothing can break and in the light of which everything else pales into insignificance.

The psalmist has reached the point of being able to see that the problem of the success of the wicked is an irrelevance. Even if the wicked do flourish, says the psalmist, I have something, the one thing of supreme value, which they can never have, my relationship with God. As has been well said Psalm 73 'began a song on the issue of theodicy and ended it on a credo of the eternal presence'.[22]

But it is not merely the psalmist's conclusion which is interesting, it is why he reached this conclusion. If he had never been compelled by a clear-headed analysis of experience to question the traditional teaching which nurtured him; if he had not been driven to doubt whether faith had any value at all, he would never have broken through to a deeper faith. It was his doubts, his unanswered questions, and his honest and agonizing attempt to deal with them, which proved to be spiritually productive. For this man doubt, far from being destructive of faith, was the midwife at the birth of a more compelling faith. His doubts about the traditional teaching on reward and punishment are no more radical than those in Psalm 49, but in the light of such doubts he asks different, more searching, questions which unlock the door to a more intense inner conflict. For this reason Psalm 73 'occupies a foremost place among the mature fruits borne by the struggles through which Old Testament faith had to pass'.[23]

Our consideration of some of the wisdom and wisdom-related psalms has revealed no one attitude to the traditional thesis that the righteous flourish and the wicked do not. Some psalms are content to state and to remain within the traditional framework – thus Psalms 1, 34, 112, 128. Others are aware of a problem yet believe that, with qualifications, the traditional teaching remains intact – thus Psalm 37. Psalm 49 makes no attempt to defend the tradition but seeks to press the relevance of the limiting factor of death, and the meaning of faith when confronted with this limiting factor. Psalm 73 journeys further in exploring the meaning of faith. It is not possible to argue convincingly for any chronological development linking these different responses. The different stances are closely related to the different dimensions of the psalmists' spiritual experience, and such different dimensions may coexist.[24] Within the hymn book of ancient Israel there was room for many attitudes, from quiet acceptance to the search for new understanding, and such a search whether tentative or radical, was as authentic a part of Israel's worship as quiet acceptance. Because of this, people of very varied spiritual needs and insight have been able to find in the psalms throughout the ages 'a mirror for their own identity'.[25]

If worship is – as we have claimed – a sensitive indicator of a community's religion, then it will be surprising if we do not find the same themes and concerns – protest and questioning, the search for enlightenment, a willingness to move beyond accepted teaching – reflected in other areas of Israel's literary traditions. It has been customary to recognize the presence of such themes, powerfully expressed, in certain books of the Old Testament, notably Job and Ecclesiastes. What has not been adequately investigated is the extent to which such themes are more widely represented in the literary and theological traditions contained within the Old Testament.

3

FAITH ON PILGRIMAGE – THE
PATRIARCHAL TRADITIONS

If worship is one of the most important guides to the beliefs of a community, so also are the stories it remembers and tells about its origins, and the characteristics it ascribes to its founding fathers. It is in this context that we turn to examine some aspects of the patriarchal traditions in Genesis 12–50, particularly some of the stories associated with Abraham, Isaac and Jacob. There is still considerable divergence of opinion in scholarly circles as to the way in which these narratives should be handled. To what extent, for example, are we entitled to claim historicity for them?[1] In one sense such issues are irrelevant for our purposes. Only one comment is needed. However much or however little we may wish to assign historicity to the narratives, they were not remembered or handed on in ancient Israel merely because of a belief that they contained valid historical memories. With the exception of Genesis 14, a chapter which raises complex questions, the narratives are not concerned with history in the sense of significant public events in the life of a community or nation. The narratives focus upon the commonplace, the trivialities if you like of family life, upon domestic tensions, love and hatred, quarrels and reconciliations, upon the hopes and fears of ordinary people. We may call the stories about Abraham 'the Abraham Saga', in much the same way as we talk about Galsworthy's 'Forsyte Saga', the story of a family extended over several generations, although this 'Abraham Saga' is much more disjointed, full of all kinds of loose ends which a novelist would wish to tie together. Many of the stories are of very varied character. There are explanations, sometimes different explanations, of place names (e.g. the two explanations of the name Beersheba in Gen. 21.31 and 26.33) and of personal names (e.g. Gen. 17.5; 17.15; 32.28). Other stories explain why a certain place was an important centre for worship (e.g. Gen. 28.10–22) or why there was that well-known cairn of stones east of the Jordan (Gen. 31.45–54). If our modern under-standing of the way in which traditions develop is anywhere near the mark, many of these stories must have existed at one time in isolation from one another. Attempts to probe behind the present form of narrative, however, raise complex issues which have yielded little in the way of generally accepted results. The various rivulets, different in point of origin and flowing for a time through different terrain, have coalesced into the main stream of the patriarchal traditions as they now lie before us in Genesis. It is one of the marks of much contemporary Old Testament scholar-ship that it is again beginning to take seriously the final form of the narratives both in terms of literary appreciation and theological significance.[2]

In their present form the patriarchal traditions tell the story of a pilgrim faith, a faith summed up in the opening words of Genesis 12:

> The Lord said to Abram, 'Leave your own country, your kinsmen, and your father's house, and go to a country that I will show you. I will make you into a great nation, I will bless you. . . .'

a theme echoed in the dying words of Joseph:

> I am dying; but God will not fail to come to your aid and take you from here to the land which he promises on oath to Abraham, Isaac and Jacob (Gen. 50.24).

The whole of Genesis 12–50 is in the form of a confession of faith in the mystery of God's initiative – he comes, he calls – and in the promises he makes to his people. In essence this was to be Israel's faith across the centuries. We cannot understand the patriarchal narratives unless we recognize that what was remembered and told about the patriarchs was, in the main, only that which was of lasting significance to men of faith in Israel in later generations. They identified with Abraham, Isaac and Jacob. They too jour-neyed in faith; they lived in the light of promises given and promises unfulfilled. Like Jacob, who was Israel, they lied,

cheated and wrestled with God. This was their story, the continuing story of what faith meant in ancient Israel. From this
standpoint I want to direct your attention to one or two interesting
features in the narratives.

There is always the temptation to make biblical characters more
pious than they are in the earliest form of the tradition. This is a
tendency which has gone on across the centuries. It features in
many a pulpit. It thrives particularly on trying to answer questions
which the narratives themselves leave unanswered. If, for example, Genesis 12.1ff. asserts that the Lord called Abram to leave
his country and promised him a blessing, then later tradition
wants to know why the Lord called, and why he fastened upon
this man Abram instead of upon some other person. Many stories
were current in various circles in the post-biblical Jewish community in an attempt to answer such questions.[3] In his mother's
womb and at birth he had been providentially saved from the
murderous intentions of a king who had been forewarned that
there was to be born in his kingdom one who would challenge his
divine authority and give the lie to his religion. At the precocious
age of twenty days he was carrying on a theological conversation
with his mother. He grew up to ridicule the idolatry in the midst
of which he lived, and in spite of attempts to silence him, he
became the missionary of the one true God, in which task he was
zealously supported by his wife Sarah. Thus before the Lord said
to Abram 'Leave . . .', he had already proved himself the model
believer, the friend of God. What in Genesis 12.1ff. is left unex-
plained, hidden in the mystery of God's initiative and grace, is
later justified by the previous track record of Abram. But this is
not merely a post-biblical phenomenon; the same process can be
traced with the biblical tradition itself.

Within Genesis 12–50 there are two stories which speak of
Abram being involved in a situation in which he passes off his
wife Sarai as his sister, once in Egypt (Gen. 12.10–20) and once in
the Philistine town of Gerar (Gen. 20). There is much to be said for
regarding these as variant versions of one basic theme story told
about the patriarchs, a story told and retold in different circles. A
similar story is in fact told about another of the patriarchs, Isaac,
in Genesis 26. However we explain the relationship between the
narratives it is instructive to compare Genesis, 12.10–20 with
Genesis 20. In Genesis 12, which in literary critical terms is usually
assigned to the earliest strand in the narrative, the 'J' source,

probably as early as the tenth century BC, the story is told briefly, without much in the way of comment or detail. No attempt is made either to defend or to explain Abram's action in passing off Sarai as his sister. Indeed Sarai's entry into Pharaoh's harem proves a sound investment for Abram; sheep and cattle, male and female slaves, asses and camels, are the price Pharaoh is prepared to pay to Sarai's 'brother'.[4] In the whole story there is but one reference to the Lord; he strikes 'Pharaoh and his household with grave diseases on account of Abram's wife Sarai' (v. 17). Nothing is said, however, to indicate how Pharaoh knew that the troubles which befell his household were linked to the presence of Sarai in his harem. When we turn to Genesis 20 the story is much more circumstantial and detailed. In this version, usually assigned to the 'E' source of the eighth century BC, moral and religious issues predominate. Two dialogues, one between God and Abimelech, king of Gerar (Gen. 20.3–7) the other between Abimelech and Abraham (Gen. 20.9–13) take up more than half of the story and set the tone. In the first dialogue God exonerates Abimelech of all responsibility for what happened; he had acted 'with a clear conscience and in all innocence' (v. 5). Abraham is described by God to Abimelech as 'a prophet' who will 'intercede on your behalf' (v. 7). In the second dialogue Abraham proceeds to justify his action to Abimelech on several grounds:

(*a*) He was living as an alien in what he believed to be a God-less community. A beautiful wife was therefore an unnecessary additional hazard.

(*b*) He had not strictly told a lie; 'She is in fact my sister, she is my father's daughter though not by the same mother' (v. 12), an argument which in later Israel would have landed Abraham in serious trouble since it is a direct violation of the legislation in Leviticus 18.9.

(*c*) Sarah herself, as a dutiful wife, had agreed to connive at the stratagem. The overall effect is on the one hand to underline the providential aspect of what happened, and on the other make Abraham's attitude appear in a much more favourable light. This inner biblical development continues in later extra biblical material. In the retelling of the story in the Aramaic document, commonly called the Genesis Apocryphon, to be dated around 100 BC,[5] Abraham is forewarned in a dream – a common biblical motif – a dream which he recounts and interprets to Sarah, that in Egypt his life is going to be in danger on account of Sarah. Sarah,

whose dazzling beauty is described at length, is forcibly taken
from Abraham one night while Abraham tearfully prays to God
and asks for God's judgment to fall upon Pharaoh and his people.
The plagues come. Pharaoh's physicians and magicians are powerless to do anything to stop them. An Egyptian emissary arrives
beseeching Abraham to pray for the afflicted people, that the
plagues may be withdrawn. Lot insists that this will only be
possible on condition that Sarah is restored forthwith to her
rightful husband. Pharaoh complies with the request. Other
legends tell how Abraham – who apparently first discovered
Sarah's 'Miss World' potential on the journey down to Egypt –
aware of the Egyptians' reputation for sensuality, tried to smuggle
her into Egypt in a casket only to be thwarted by suspicious and
efficient custom's officials. A powerful armed force escorts Sarah
to the royal harem, while her heart-broken husband protests to
God. More and more the responsibility for describing the relationship with Abraham as 'sisterly' is placed on Sarah's
shoulders.[6] I draw attention to this expansion and development
of the Abraham-Sarah theme solely to underline the fact that once
a biblical character becomes a key figure in the thinking of the
community, there is a strong tendency to reshape the character to
conform more closely to the ideal which he is supposed to
represent.

If we go on to ask what particular aspect of Abraham's life came
to be regarded as of supreme significance, then the answer, in
part at least, is contained in Genesis 15.6:

> Abraham put his faith in the Lord, and the Lord counted that
> faith to him as righteousness.

Abraham becomes the father of the people of God, the paradigm
of faith, faith not in the sense of intellectual assent to a series of
confessional statements, but faith as personal trust in and commitment to God. Such trust – to paraphrase Genesis 15.6 – receives
the seal of God's approval. The word translated 'counted' or
'reckoned' (RSV) probably comes from a cultic background where
the priest passes a verdict on the acceptability or otherwise of the
offering brought by the worshipper (cf. Lev. 7.18; Num. 18.27,
30). Given that the worshipper and his offering are acceptable to
God he is described as 'righteous', in the right relationship with
God.[7] Thus Abraham is viewed as the model for faith in as much
as he is a man who responds in trust to what God promises, and

on this basis he is in a right relationship with, acceptable to, God.[8] But what are the implications of such 'trust'? It is but a small step to define trust in such a way that it eliminates questions and stills the voice of protest. Evidence for this is already to be found in Targumic tradition where there is added to the end of the verse an explanatory gloss 'because he did not raise any objections (or speak rebelliously) to Him'.[9] This, however, is precisely what we do not find in the Genesis traditions.

Let us first take a closer look at the structure of Genesis 15. Verse 6 is self-evidently the comment of the narrator or the editor of the chapter, a comment full of theological meaning defining, in terms of Abraham, the true attitude to God. This comment has been inserted between two blocks of material, each containing a dialogue between the Lord and Abraham, the one in verses 1–5, the other in verses 7ff. The relationship between these two traditions, the one (vv. 1–5) centring upon the promise of innumerable descendants, the other (vv. 7ff.) centring upon the promise of the land, has been variously explained.[10] We are not concerned with the pre-history of the traditions, however, but only with how they function in their present context in Genesis 15. In the first dialogue Abraham who had refused, according to Genesis 14, to accept any reward from the king of Sodom for defeating the Eastern peril, is promised 'a very great reward' (Gen. 15.1) or following more closely the traditional text, promised that the Lord would be his shield and very great reward. To this Abraham immediately raises an objection. His future is bleak, wholly uncertain. Promised that from him would come 'a great nation' (Gen. 12.2), 'many descendants' (Gen. 13.6) he remains childless. There is no sign of even the possibility of the promise being fulfilled. This objection is countered by a word of reassurance from the Lord (Gen. 15.4–5). The second dialogue begins with the Lord identifying himself by what he had already done for Abraham and by the promise he had made, a promise spelt out this time in terms of the giving of a land to occupy (Gen. 15.7). To this Abraham, whose attitude has just been summed up in terms of faith, trust, immediately responds not with a joyful 'amen' but with a question 'O Lord God, how can I be sure that I will occupy it?' (Gen. 15.7). The possible implications of such a response troubled some Jewish commentators. The Midrash attributes to R. Ḥama b.Ḥanina the comment that Abraham spoke 'not as one who makes a complaint, but he asked "Through what merit will I inherit the land?" God replied "through the merit of the atoning sacrifices which I will institute for thy sons" ', a comment which links Abraham's question closely to the cultic act which follows.[11] It is more natural, however, to see behind the question continuing hesitation and uncertainty. The question is then countered by an assurance which comes in terms of the mysterious covenant rite which links together descendants and land (Gen. 15.9–21). The Midrash Rabbah on Exodus 5.22 reflects a tradition which sees in Abraham's words an expression of doubt. In defence of his words of protest to God 'Why, O Lord, hast thou brought misfortune on the people?' Moses claims to have read Genesis, noting that the generation of the Flood and the people of Sodom were justly punished for their sins. 'But this people, what has it done to be more enslaved than all the preceding generations? Is it because Abraham said "Whereby shall I know that I will possess it?" and Thou didst say unto him "Know of surety that they seed shall be a stranger" '(Gen. XV, 13).[12] When this passage recognizes that Abraham's question contains an expression of doubt, it characteristically assumes that such doubt is sinful, the cause of punishment to Abraham's descendants. In the biblical text, however, *on either side* of the definition of faith the pattern is the same:

(*a*) the Lord speaks;

(*b*) the human response is one of questioning or objection;

(*c*) the objection is met by an assurance which affirms that the objection will prove to be groundless at some unspecified point in the future.

This is a pattern which we shall find in many other contexts in the Old Testament.[13] It has been argued that the phrase translated 'Abraham put his faith in the Lord' should be rendered 'Abraham found security in the Lord'.[14] If this is so we would have to say that such security was not believed to be inconsistent with living with the insecurity of as yet unanswered questions.

Within the Abraham traditions there is a narrative which illustrates clearly that there is not felt to be anything incongruous in trusting God and at the same time raising serious questions as to the way in which God seems to operate in the world; the account in Genesis 18.16–33 of Abraham pleading for Sodom and Gomorrah. Despite certain elements of ambiguity and mystery in the incident – for example the oscillation between the 'men' (v. 16, cf. v. 2), the Lord (vv. 21, 22) and the 'angels' or messengers

(v. 19) – the narrative focusses upon issues which were never far from the centre of Israel's religious thinking:

1. There is the conviction that God's purposes are knowable. He himself chooses to reveal them to certain people. 'Shall I conceal from Abraham what I intend to do?' (v. 17). This echoes the statement in Amos 3.7 a statement basic to the entire prophetic tradition

. . . the Lord God does nothing
without giving to his servants the prophets knowledge of
his plans.

2. Not only are God's purposes knowable, but they are understandable and morally justifiable. There is a strict correlation between what God expects from men and the way in which He himself acts. If conforming to the way of the Lord means for Abraham's descendants 'to do what is right and just' (v. 19), this is so only because the Lord can be depended upon to do what is right and just. This is the assumption of the narrative from beginning to end. In a quaintly anthropomorphic way verses 20–21 depict the Lord as planning a personal legal investigation to find out whether the accusations made concerning the outrageous conduct of Sodom and Gomorrah are valid; the implication being that if judgment is to fall upon the cities of the plain it must be seen to be justified. This becomes the basis of Abraham's objection:

Shall not the judge of all the earth do what is just? (v. 25)

These words presuppose that the God whom Abraham addresses is a god concerned with all human activity, and that he can be depended upon to act in an ordered way which will commend itself to the moral sense of men.[15] They are prefaced by a phrase 'Far be it from you' (*halîlāh lekhā*) which presupposes that any other possibility would be inconceivable, given certain assumptions about the nature of God.

It cannot be claimed without qualification that this conviction was always held by all men at all times in ancient Israel. There are stories preserved which depict Yahweh as acting in an irrational demonic fashion (e.g. Exod. 4.24–26) the apparently unmotivated attack by Yahweh on Moses. Whatever primitive sociological factors may be adduced to provide background to this story it still depicts Yahweh as attacking, with intent to kill, the man whom he has just commissioned to be the leader of his people and his emissary to Pharaoh.[16] In all ages there must have been different levels of understanding within Israel as to precisely what is meant by the claim that God does what is just; which would have been no more surprising than the different levels of understanding of Christian doctrine which coexist within the Christian community today. But for those who shaped and held to what came to be the creative and continuing faith of Israel, there was no going back on the basic conviction expressed in Abraham's question:

Shall not the judge of all the earth do what is just?

And herein lay a problem, since this is not a conviction easy to sustain, particularly if you insist, as Israel tended to do, that the conviction must be capable of empirical verification in human experience. Targumic tradition seems to try to soften the harshness of the issue in this story on the one hand by introducing the thought that the people of Sodom may have acted wickedly not knowing that their conduct was subject to God's scrutiny, and when faced with this knowledge may repent, in which case all will be well; and on the other by featuring the anger of God as the motivating force in his attitude towards Sodom.[17] Some of the deepest crises of faith in ancient Israel, however, were to centre around situations in which the facts of experience seemed to call into question the belief that God does 'what is just'. There would have been much less heartsearching within the Old Testament if religious tradition in Israel had been prepared either to settle for some form of dualism or to compromise on its insistence that God must be just. And world literature would have been deprived of one of its masterpieces, the book of Job.

The particular form in which the problem arises in Genesis 18 has its roots in the emphasis, expressed in many different ways in the Old Testament, that men do not live in isolation as individuals; they belong to communities and community responsibility is accepted as a norm. If an offence is committed against another community or against God, then not only the offender but the group to which he belongs share in the responsibility for his actions and are caught up in its consequences. Thus in the narrative in Joshua 7.10–26 Achan's sin is Israel's sin (v. 11) and Achan's entire household pay the penalty for his offence. Numbers 15.22–26 stipulates that for any inadvertent offence committed by a member of the community the whole community must make an offering so that the community may be forgiven since 'the inadvertence was shared by the whole people' (v. 26). Likewise the main burden of prophetic teaching certainly in pre-exilic Israel, while attacking specific wrongs within the community and often specific sections of the community, assumes realistically that the whole community, the exploited as well as the exploiter, the oppressed and the oppressor, will be involved in the judgment which will engulf the nation. But if community responsibility works negatively, why should it not work in the opposite direction? If the guilt of the wicked spreads like a cancer to destroy the whole body politic, why should not the healing power of innocence be able to restore the community to health? So Abraham poses the question to God:

Wilt thou really sweep away innocent and guilty together? (v. 23)

'Innocent' and 'guilty' are more appropriate translations than the traditional 'righteous' and 'wicked' or the New English Bible 'good' and 'bad'. In this narrative the strongly legal flavour which often attaches to these words ought to be retained. The basis of Abraham's appeal is none other than that the judge of all the earth must do what is just. A judge who gives right decisions cannot condemn both the innocent and the guilty. Suppose there are within the community innocent people who ought not to be condemned or destroyed, will they not save the community from destruction? 'The Yahwist recognises that there is more injustice in the death of a few innocent people than in the sparing of the guilty multitude: his question however is "To what limits is the application of this principle subject?" '[18] Beginning with fifty, Abraham, with ever-increasing boldness, reduces the number . . . forty-five . . . forty . . . thirty . . . twenty . . . ten; and there is clearly no logical reason why he should stop at ten: Why not five . . . or one? The Rabbis suggest various reasons why the cut off point is ten: this is the number needed for a quorum for public prayer; eight had not been enough to save the world at the flood, the eight being Noah and his wife, his three sons and their wives; the ten would consist of Lot and his wife, their four daughters and husbands. At least one Rabbi, however, in the light of Jeremiah 5.1, recognized that the principle could be extended to one man.[19]

The validity of the principle and the limitations within which it may reasonably be expected to operate are not, however, our primary concern. Let us take a closer look at the nature of the dialogue within which the principal is discussed.

1. There is a frank acknowledgment that this is no dialogue between equals. Abraham is conscious that he speaks as a mere man 'dust and ashes that I am' (v. 27). Twice there occurs a phrase which the NEB translates 'May I presume to speak to the Lord' (vv. 27, 31)[20] twice the words 'Please do not be angry, O Lord' (vv. 30, 32). This, as it were, is clearly defining the limitations within which the dialogue takes place; this is creature speaking to creator, dust and ashes speaking to the judge of all the earth, and therefore speaking with limited knowledge.

2. Nevertheless Abraham insists in pushing his questions. The very conviction that God is just means that the questions *must* be pushed, and pushed, with whatever hesitations, to the boundary of human understanding. There is no suggestion that faith expresses itself in silent acquiescence; rather faith compels Abraham to interrogate in a situation where there seems to be a contradiction between a doctrine of God (i.e. he does what is just) and the facts of human experience. A modern Jewish writer, Elie Wiesel, comments that Abraham '. . . did not hesitate for a moment to take God to task as he tried to save two condemned cities from destruction. How can You – who are justice – be unjust? He was the first who dared query God. And God listened and answered. For unlike Job, Abraham was protesting on behalf of others, not of himself. God forgave Abraham everything, including his questions'.[21] But did Abraham need to be forgiven his questions? Nothing in the Genesis narrative suggests such a need; it simply notes that the dialogue ends: 'When the Lord had finished talking with Abraham, he left him, and Abraham returned home' (v. 33). There is, I believe, enough in the Old Testament to suggest that there are occasions when it is silent acquiescence or the sheltering behind well-worn religious platitudes which need to be forgiven rather than urgent questioning.

The dialogue between Abraham and the Lord in Genesis 18.23–32, therefore, discloses a tension between the need to question, the demand to know, and a recognition of the limitations within which such questioning must take place. This tension comes to powerful expression in the book of Job.

Before we leave Genesis 18 there is one other issue worth raising. Why is it that this particular problem emerges at this precise moment in the Genesis narrative? There may well be an important sociological factor involved. The doctrine of shared responsibility and guilt works with reasonable plausibility given a close-knit community such as the family group or clan, but what happens when a man no longer functions as a member of such a homogenous group, but finds himself living as an outsider in a different social grouping, in this case the settled town or city? It is perhaps no accident that the dialogue between Abraham and the Lord takes place in the narrative at a point just after Lot has broken with Abraham, left the family group and gone to live as an alien in Sodom. Certainly we must be prepared to take seriously the sociological context in which certain beliefs are formulated and the way in which a given formulation may be called into question by changing social factors. There was at least one major sociological break – the end of the independent Judean kingdom in 587 BC – which precipitated a crisis of faith in many circles and evoked, as we shall see, a very varied response.[22]

We turn now to Genesis 22.1–18, the so-called *akedah*, the binding of Isaac, a passage which has haunted the conscience of, and been vigorously discussed by, Jews and Christians across the centuries. Here above all the comment which Bruce Vawter makes on the Genesis stories must be taken with full seriousness: 'If we must resist the temptation to read into these stories more than they are intended to say or other than they are intended to say, we must also not succumb to the opposite temptation to hold their meaning to be paltry and parsimonious when they would have it generous'.[23] It is parsimonious to view the narrative as primarily a polemic against child sacrifice. That child sacrifice was practised sporadically in the Ancient Near East we know from both Canaanite and Moabite sources (cf. II Kings 3.27). Even in Israel, though rigorously forbidden in the law (e.g. Deut. 18.10; Lev. 18.21) as being inconsistent with obedience to Yahweh, it was practised in situations of crisis and recrudescent paganism (e.g. II Kings 21.6; Jer. 19.5). The very fact that the narrative depicts Abraham as being willing to sacrifice Isaac at God's demand means that to Abraham the idea of child sacrifice was not unthinkable. At most a move away from child sacrifice may be one of the motifs in the material which lies behind the present form of the narrative. It is paltry, moreover, to see in the story merely a cult legend explaining the origin of some sanctuary not clearly identified in the narrative, but subsequently to be identified in religious tradition as Jerusalem with its temple for sacrifice, blessing and instruction.

The narrative is noteworthy for its restraint, its severe and simple factuality, the total lack of emotional and psychological comment. It tells of the ultimate demand, the sacrifice of the son upon whom the family future depends. Nothing is said about what father and son were thinking as they walked in silence to the place of sacrifice, a silence broken only by a puzzled question from Isaac and an evasive reply from Abraham (vv. 7–8). With chilling matter-of-factness the altar is built, Isaac bound, and the knife raised.[24] Later tradition broke the restraint, and numerous studies and commentaries have sought to answer questions the narrative leaves untouched. Targumic tradition, for example, provides a motivation for the testing in a prior quarrel between Ishmael and Isaac, in the course of which Isaac boasts that he would be prepared to sacrifice anything for God, including himself. The Midrash introduces into Abraham and Isaac's silent walk a loquacious companion, Samuel, the wicked angel, who tries unsuccessfully to deflect both father and son from their intended course of action.[25] In spite of his restraint, however, the narrator makes his intentions quite clear. The key to the understanding of the narrative is contained in the opening words: 'The time came when God put Abraham to the test' (v. 1). The temptation to ask 'why?' is almost irresistible: 'For his own good', say some commentators, or 'to serve as an example to the peoples of the world'; in order, claims Augustine that 'Abraham may discover himself; this testing is none other than a space offered to freedom, it is the way to fulfilment'.[26] Although Rabbinic thought tends to shift the centre of interest in the narrative from Abraham to Isaac and the merits of sacrifice, it is also taken as a classic case of God testing the righteous.

> R. Jonathan said 'A potter does not examine defective vessels, because he cannot give them a single blow without breaking them. What then does he examine? Only the sound vessels, for he will not break them even with many blows. Similarly the Holy One, blessed be He, tests not the wicked but the righteous; as it says "the Lord trieth the righteous" (i.e. Psalm 11.5)'.[27]

There is further a tendency in certain circles to shift responsibility for the testing from God to Satan, thus creating a scenario very similar to that found in the introduction to Job, with Satan in this case insinuating to God that Abraham in his joy at the birth of Isaac had forgotten his creator.

The purpose of this testing, however, is clearly indicated in the narrative at verse 12 where the fatal plunge of Abraham's knife is stopped with the comment: 'for now I know that you fear God'. This 'fear of God' – which is also a prominent motif in the testing of Job, according to the prologue to the book of Job (Job 1.8, 9) is here, as the context shows, synonymous with unqualified obedience to God's demand. Yet we cannot separate the question of this 'fear of God' from the nature of the test demanded. This is not the sacrifice of any child; it is the sacrifice of a particular child – 'your son, your only son, whom you love, Isaac' (v. 2). In this description the phrases become progressively more explicit and fraught with tension: *'your son'* – but Abraham had two sons Ishmael and Isaac, and in the previous chapter Abraham is induced to agree to Sarah's request for the expulsion of Ishmael by the reassuring promise that he will have descendants by Isaac (Gen. 21.12); *your only son* or perhaps better to convey the sense of the underlying Hebrew, 'your one and only son', special, because this was the son born to Abraham and Sarah after long delay and frustration, the child in whom all Abraham's hopes for the future fulfilment of God's promises are concentrated; *Isaac* the only visible sign Abraham had been given of God's trust-worthiness. If Isaac dies, so dies the promise of 'the many descendants', 'the great nation'. When Abraham left Mesopotamia, according to Genesis 12.1, he was sacrificing his past, leaving country and kinsmen, sustained by a promise; now he is being asked to sacrifice the future, the God-promised future. The 'Go' of Genesis 12.1 is in danger of being negated by the 'Go' of Genesis 22.2.[28] Jewish interpretation, both ancient and modern, has rightly fastened upon this as the *sine qua non* in the narrative. The Midrash Rabbah at Genesis 22.5, 'I and the lad will go yonder' draws attention to the word 'yonder', Hebrew *'ad kōh* and attributes to R. Joshua B. Levi the comment 'We will go and see what is to be the eventual outcome of *koh'*, a reference back to the promise in Genesis 15.6 *'koh* (thus) shall thy seed be' i.e. we shall see how that promise can be fulfilled if Isaac dies now. Elie Wiesel comments '. . . by sacrificing his son to obey God's will, Abraham knew he was in fact sacrificing his knowledge of God and his faith in God. If Isaac were to die to whom would the father transmit this faith, this knowledge? The end of Isaac would connote the end of a prodigious adventure: the first (i.e. the first descendant) would become the last'.[29] Abraham is being tested to the point of seeing whether he is prepared to live with God-given hope and faith destroyed, self-destroyed at God's command. He then discovers hope and faith given back in the very moment when they seem to have no future. He is learning that God's promises are renewed (verses 15–18) through what seems to be the very negation of these promises. He serves a God who is beyond all that he has promised or given. This dimension in the narrative only becomes clear when we read it against a background, the background of the story of the outworking of God's purposes, sketched throughout Genesis. As Erich Auerback says of such biblical narratives:

> Doctrine and promise are incarnate in them and inseparable from them. In the story of Isaac it is not only God's intervention at the beginning and the end, but even the factual and psychological elements which come between, that are mysterious, merely touched upon, fraught with background. . . . Since so much in the story is dark and incomplete, and since the reader knows that God is a hidden God, his effort to interpret it constantly finds something new to feed upon.[30]

We have already noted the laconic brevity of the story which leaves no room for any exploration of Abraham's feelings or reactions. But this is not merely Abraham's story, it is Israel's continuing story. She had to learn to live at times stripped of much that she had hitherto regarded as essential to her faith, not least in the experience of national collapse and exile.[31] She had to face 'the paradox of presence in absence. She knew that God hidden is still God. She served a God who forsook her and even stood up against her as an enemy in order to teach her the selflessness of devotion'.[32] If it be argued that the primary purpose of the narrative in its present form is to stress the obedience of Abraham as 'an edifying example of obedience for all subsequent devotees of Yahweh' and as 'an example of Abraham's faith in contrast to this lack of faith depicted in such stories as Genesis 12.10–20 and Genesis 16',[33] it is nevertheless an obedience which has looked into the abyss of a future destroyed, and a faith in a God who seems to demand the end of hope. It speaks, as G. von Rad has put it, of 'a road out into God-forsakenness',[34] a road on which Abraham does not know that God is but testing him. The reader of the story knows. With hindsight, what to the participant is God-forsakenness is seen to be testing. But such hindsight is not comfortingly available to the reader when he faces his own experience of God-forsakenness. In the patriarchal traditions God's first word to Abraham was a challenge to leave the settled security of the past and to go out into the unknown future seeking the fulfilment of a promise; his last word is the renewal of that promise through an experience which threatens to destroy it. For some in Israel this challenge and the experience of God-forsakenness were an inescapable part of obedient faith.

From the traditions which centre upon Abraham we turn now to look at the Jacob traditions, and in particular at one of the strangest and most hauntingly perplexing narratives in the Old Testament, Jacob's nocturnal encounter at the ford of Jabbok as recounted in Genesis 32.22–32. It has been well described as being 'like a mystical poem, barely coherent, barely intelligible, not only to the reader, but even to the protaganists'.[35] Just as such a poem is capable of being interpreted on several different levels, so is it possible to approach this passage with different interests and expectations and find in the darkness of the eerie gorge of Jabbok clues which lead along many and varied paths of meaning. This is all the more possible since the narrative comes to us, not white-hot from one creative mind, but shaped and reshaped across many centuries before it surfaces in its present form in Genesis. The impossibility of fully assimilating into the religious outlook of the narrator elements which can be traced back to earlier, more primitive legends accounts for some of the dislocations and rough edges which are apparent in the narrative. The aetiological element in the story is strong. Here we are told why a certain ford was called 'Wrestling Ford', the name Jabbok being linked with the Hebrew verb 'wrestled' in verses 24–25; why Jacob's name was changed to Israel (v. 28); why a certain sanctuary was called Penuel (v. 30); why a particular food taboo – interestingly not one mentioned elsewhere in the Old Testament – was observed (v. 32). Yet such 'whys', though numerous, are very much on the periphery of the narrative as it lies before us in its present context in the book of Genesis. Let us examine this context more closely. The Jacob traditions are brutally candid. Spoiled son of a doting mother, Jacob was both liar and cheat. Sent away from home for his own safety, he turned out to be adept in the game of one-up-manship at the expense of his father-in-law Laban, himself no mean operator. He returns home to face the brother whom once he had shamelessly cheated. This incident at the Jabbok is placed between the account of Jacob's careful, if somewhat anxious, preparations for his meeting with Esau (Gen. 32.1–12) and the description of that meeting in chapter 33. Anticipating with fear his coming meeting with Esau, Jacob prays (Gen. 32.9–11), the first occasion in the Jacob traditions on which a prayer is attributed to him. This prayer appeals to God on the grounds that it is God who has summoned him back to his homeland, acknowledges that he does not deserve the prosperity he has already received from God, gives voice to his present fears, and pleads 'Save me I pray from my brother Esau' for only thus can the promises God has made for the future be realized. The present context of the incident at Jabbok strongly suggests that it is intended to be the answer, or at least part answer, to this prayer. As such it has a strangely paradoxical character.

This is not the place to attempt to explain or even to explore the significance of all the features in the narrative, but there are three features in it which are central to any understanding of it in its present context:

1. The context of Jacob's prayer in Genesis 32.9–11 assumes that, in Jacob's opinion the threat to his future – a future which he believes to be God-promised – comes from Esau. He therefore appeals to God to remove this threat. In the outcome he finds himself instead involved in a struggle with a mysterious assailant[36] who is never referred to in the narrative as other than 'a man' (v. 25), 'the man' (vv. 26, 28), i.e. someone, but who is assumed in the comments in vv. 28–30 to be none other than God, e.g. in the explanation of the name Peniel as 'I have seen God face to face . . .' (v. 30). The answer to Jacob's prayer comes not through passively waiting for God to do something to remove the threat of Esau, but through his being locked in conflict, wrestling with one whose identity is at first unknown, but who, in the course of the conflict, is identified, with great daring, as God seen face to face. When this unidentified assailant wishes to withdraw from the struggle 'for day is breaking' (v. 26)[37] Jacob replies 'I will not let you go unless you bless me'. Once before Jacob had asked for a blessing . . . from an aged, blind father (Genesis 27). The link with chapter 27 has often been noted. Rashi, for example, comments on the words '(*unless*) *you bless me*' – admit my right to the blessings which my father gave me and to which Esau lays

claim'.[38] But at this point the narrative stands not in continuity with Genesis 27, but in sharp contrast to it. Then Jacob had received a blessing by deceit and by smooth, reassuring and misleading words, but now from God a blessing is only obtained through sharp conflict, through a costly personal struggle from which Jacob emerges limping with a dislocated hip (vv. 25, 32).

2. The blessing which Jacob receives is symbolized by the new name given to him, the name Israel. The significance of this feature in the narrative is only appreciated when we recognize that in the ancient world a name was not merely a convenient identity label. In a person's name there was written something of his character. The new name signifies the change, actual and potential, in Jacob's character. One of the traditions in Genesis links the name Jacob with the way in which he had supplanted or cheated his brother Esau (Gen. 27.35–36), Jacob 'the cheat' now becomes 'Israel'. The meaning of the word Israel is far from certain.[39] Another tradition in Genesis, without offering any explanation of the name, places the name change from Jacob to Israel in a different setting (Gen. 35.10). In strict linguistic terms Israel can hardly mean 'one who strives with God', but this is the meaning given to it in the passage: 'Your name shall no longer be Jacob, but Israel, because you strove with God and with men, and prevailed' (v. 28). There is no reason to assume that the reference to striving with men is anything other than a recalling of Jacob's conflicts with Esau and Laban;[40] but it is not only the memory of human conflict which is handed down across the centuries in the name Israel, it is also the experience of being locked in conflict with God. If such conflict and struggle with God had not been a characteristic feature of Israel's religious experience it is highly unlikely that 'one who strives with God' would ever have been the meaning associated with and preserved in the name Israel.

The tradition of Jacob's wrestling with God appears again in the Old Testament in Hosea 12.4–5. Though this passage is beset with textual difficulties[41] there is little doubt that verses 4–5 reflect a tradition which is very similar to, if not necessarily identical, with Genesis 32.22ff.:

Even in the womb Jacob overreached his brother,
    and in manhood he strove with God.
He overpowered (or strove against) an angel and prevailed,
    he wept and sought his favour. . . .

Beyond all the detailed textual and exegetical difficulties in this
passage there is one major issue of interpretation. Does this
passage speak favourably of Jacob, or does it condemn him? It has
been argued that in Hosea 12.4–5, 'The emphasis lies upon the
mysterious nature of the divine purpose. The contrast and comparison are drawn between the child in the womb who "overtakes" his brother, who then by divine favour wins the priority,
and a man in his maturity who strives with God, overcomes the
angel of God. . . . Contrasted with the indication of divine willingness to bless and protect, exemplified in Israel's ancestor, is
the marked unfaithfulness of the present community. The recall
of the past points to the responsibilities of the present'.[42] On this
view Jacob, in his encounter with God, provides Hosea with an
illustration for a sermon on what the Israel of his own day ought
to be, but sadly is not. This does not, however, seem the most
natural interpretation of Hosea 12. It is probable that here, as
elsewhere, Hosea is using tradition freely and creatively for his
own purposes. The Jacob story in Hosea 12 is set within the
context of an indictment or a charge that the Lord has to bring
against his people. It is prefaced by a statement of the punishment
God will inflict Jacob (i.e. the Israel of the prophet's day) because
of 'his ways' and 'his deeds' (v. 2). We would, therefore, expect
verses 4–5 to illustrate the kind of deeds for which Jacob is to be
condemned. In the light of this charge sheet the people are called
upon to repent in verse 6. If this interpretation is correct the
incident at Penuel is given a condemnatory interpretation by
Hosea. Jacob's overreaching of his brother and his striving with
God are parallel illustrations of his wrong attitude to life. Genesis
32.23ff. is thus given a Promethean meaning; Jacob is condemned
for trying forcibly to obtain from God his own desires. Taken
together Genesis 32 and Hosea 12 thus point us to the ambiguous
nature of this 'striving with God'. It may either illustrate human
pride and self-assertiveness in the face of God, or it may be the
expression of a humble, if desperate, need to struggle for new
understanding.

   3. As a *quid pro quo* Jacob interrogates his unidentified assailant:
'Tell me, I pray you, your name' (v. 29). His question is met by a
question: 'Why do you ask my name?' To be in possession of the
name of a god is not only, for the ancient world, to have insight
into his nature and character, but also to have access to the power
which the deity possesses and thus to be able to use that power

for one's own purposes.[43] Jacob had spent much of his life, according to the Genesis traditions, using other people, their strength and their weaknesses, to serve his own ends. But God was not there so to be used. His presence could be known, yet it remained elusive; his blessing could be received, yet the mystery of his name remained undisclosed. This ultimate and indefinable mystery of God's nature remained to haunt Israel and to call into question the validity of beliefs which threatened too easily to sacrifice this mystery on the altar of a falsely comforting security.

Jacob's enigmatic encounter in the darkness of Jabbok is a paradigm of much that we find elsewhere in the Old Testament; the paradigm of a nation's encounter with God, an encounter which was sometimes to take the form of a turbulent struggle in the darkness of tragedy, exile and persecution, an encounter with enemies whose intentions and purposes seemed destructive, but who in the outcome provided the way through to an authentic and deeper experience of God; the paradigm of many a more personal encounter in the darkness of private despair and threatening meaningless.[44]

The patriarchal narratives, therefore, join hands with the psalms of lament and the wisdom psalms. They reflect a religious tradition in which the experience of God was often costly and ambiguous; where trust in God, far from leading to passivity or unquestioning acquiescence, often demanded that questions be faced; where assurance found its counterpoint in the open expression of doubt; where faith was taken to the point where it contemplated its own demise.

4

THE BURDEN OF LEADERSHIP –
THE MOSAIC TRADITIONS

Of all the human participants in the traditions which centre upon the birth of Israel as the people of God – the Exodus, Mount Sinai and wilderness wandering traditions – Moses alone stands forth with any clearly delineated personality. Compared with Moses, the others, friend and foe alike, Aaron and the nameless Pharaohs, Miriam and Korah, are mere colourless foils. The biblical traditions themselves, however, are far from being unanimous in their assessment of Moses. Outside the Pentateuch there are very few references to Moses in pre-exilic literature,[1] a fact which may tell us more about the provenance and theological interests of that literature than it does about the Mosaic traditions themselves. Within the Pentateuch the assessment varies. To the Deuteronomist Moses, God's servant, is the prophet *par excellence*. As the obituary notice in Deut. 30.10 puts it:

'There has never yet risen in Israel a prophet like Moses whom the Lord knew face to face.'; compare Deut. 18.18 which claims that the true prophetic line in Israel, in contrast to all false prophecy, is that of the prophet like Moses who had the Lord's word in his mouth and declared the Lord's demands to the people. Although the expressions 'he knew him face to face' or 'the Lord spoke to him face to face' are used of no other prophet in the Old Testament and are intended to denote the primary place in prophetic revelation occupied by Moses, nevertheless for the Deuteronomists Moses role is prophetic. The story in Numbers 12, however, of the rebellion of Aaron and Miriam against the authority of Moses, affirms that Moses transcends all normal human categories, including that of prophet:

> If he were your prophet and nothing more,
> I would make myself known to him in a vision,
> I would speak with him in a dream.
> But my servant Moses is not such a prophet;
> he alone is faithful in all my household.
> With him I speak face to face,
> openly and not in riddles.
> He shall see the very form of the Lord.
> How dare you speak against my servant Moses?[2]
>   (Num. 12.6–8)

To Moses, therefore, this passage assigns a unique role of leadership and authority, based upon his faithful relationship with God, and transcending that of prophet.

If Old Testament tradition found it difficult to speak with a united voice about Moses, modern scholarship has compounded the difficulty. The pursuit of the historical Moses led one prominent Old Testament scholar to affirm that the only thing that could be said with any certainty about Moses was that he died and was buried somewhere in Transjordan.[3] Martin Buber,[4] on the other hand, while freely admitting that legendary motifs have filled out the narratives and that later insertions have disfigured some of the primary material, argues that the narratives in Exodus and Numbers put us in touch with an authentic historical figure of towering personality and irreplacable religious significance. Fortunately, as in the case of the patriarchal narratives, we do not need for our purposes to reach a decision on the complex historical and literary questions involved. If, for example, Exodus 3, the account of the theophany to Moses in the burning bush, his commissioning to God's service and his initial objection contains primary material, then we may well admit that in the following chapters there has been added a series of objections 'which allows a variety of divergent traditions to be incorporated within the narrative framework. The questions reflect divergent concerns and point to a development of tradition over a considerable length of time.'[5] The data provided by these different concerns and the particular way in which the tradition developed, however, are just as important for Israel's understanding of the role and character of Moses as the primary material; indeed more import-

ant, since it may always be questionable to what extent we can uncover the primary material. The developed tradition is an essential part of the theological thrust of the text as it existed in Israel from the time of the exile onwards, and as it now lies before us. Even if at this point we adhere to the classical source division of the material into J, E and P, the element of human objection is present in all the sources.

The section of the Exodus narrative which covers the period from the initial theophany at the burning bush up to the moment when Moses sets out to return to Egypt (3.1–4.18) is characterized by a series of objections, five in all, in which Moses seeks to avoid or to postpone the hazards of accepting God's commission to be the leader and deliverer of his people. After the initial theophany (3.1–6) the narrative provides us with an expanded version of the pattern which we encountered in Genesis 15:[6]

The Lord speaks (3.7–10)
　　Moses' first objection (3.11)
Objection countered by a word of assurance backed up by a
　　sign (3.12)
　　Moses' second objection (3.13)
Objection countered in an expanded section (3.14–22)
　　Moses' third objection (4.1)
Objection countered by a series of signs (4.2–9)
　　Moses' fourth objection (4.10)
Objection countered by a word of assurance (4.11–12)
　　Moses' fifth objection (4.13)
Objection angrily dismissed, but assurance repeated (4.14–18).

This pattern, with its reiterated objection theme, does not stand alone in the Old Testament. It finds a close parallel in the narrative of the call of Gideon in Judges 6. It also contains, as has been frequently pointed out, marked points of contact with prophetic experience, for example the call of Jeremiah (Jer. 1.4–10). 'Particularly in the expanded form of the present text the series of questions raised by Moses in objection to being sent echo the inner and outer struggle of the prophets of Israel.'[7] It is problematic, however, which way the influence lies, whether from prophetic experience to the present form of the Mosaic narratives, or whether the Mosaic narratives, handed down in cultic circles, have influenced the shape of the prophetic vision of the calling. In the complex interplay of traditions behind the Old Testament there may have been influence in both directions. Granted the broad similarities, however, the Mosaic narratives are by no means identical with the prophetic visions of calling. They cannot be. In spite of the Deuteronomic verdict, the role of Moses in the narratives is not merely that of being a prophet. Common to both is the sense of being called and sent by God, but the purpose of the sending is different. The prophet is commissioned to be God's spokesman, the bearer of a God-given word, whether of judgment or salvation or both; Moses is commissioned to a role of political leadership: 'Come now, I will send you to Pharaoh and you shall bring my people Israel out of Egypt' (3.10). The prophet will speak to the politician, reminding him, *inter alia*, of the implications of the decisions he takes and the nature of the responsibility he shoulders; Moses is called to be the politician, taking the decisions, assuming the burden of leadership in a crisis situation to the people's experience. It is in the light of this leadership role that we must analyse the objections which feature in the narrative.

The *first* objection contains what seems to be an immediate and natural response to the particular call to service which came to Moses: 'But who am I', Moses said to God, 'that I should go to Pharaoh, and that I should bring the Israelites out of Egypt?' (3.11). This response, however, has been subject to a variety of interpretations. The Midrash on Exodus offers three:

(*a*) Moses was gently reminding God that he himself had in the past promised to do just that, bring his people out of Egypt (e.g. Gen. 46.4).

(*b*) How was it going to be possible for a mere man like Moses to cope with all the practical and political problems involved in providing food and essential community services for the people once they had achieved freedom?

(*c*) Moses did not want to compromise himself by going to 'a place of robbers and murderers' i.e. by having any further direct contact with the Egyptians.[8]

These explanations have this much in common that they tend to place as favourable an interpretation as possible on Moses' response. They soften any suggestion that there may be a personally negative element built into it. Modern commentators, *per contra*, usually see in Moses' words an expression of 'the gaping discrepancy between his own ability and the enormity of the task'[9] and find here a parallel with prophetic experience as

evidenced in Jeremiah 1.6. A comparison with other Old Testament passages which use a similar construction 'Who am I
that. . . ?' suggests another approach; that Moses' initial response
was basically one of surprise.[10] The commission that had come to
him was totally unexpected; the response 'But why me?'. This
does not necessarily imply any sense of his own lack of ability to
face a task of such magnitude – that will come later. The immediate
response is simply one of stunned surprise.

The word of assurance 'I am (or will be) with you' (3.12) is
intended to take the sting out of the surprise by stressing the one
constant element in Moses' experience; the God who has confronted him and commissioned him, is and always will be with
him. Most English versions assume that the sign (Heb. *'ôth*)
attached to the assurance points to the future. Thus New English
Bible, 'This shall be the proof (or sign) that it is I who have sent
you: when you have brought the people out of Egypt, you shall
all worship God here on this mountain' (3.12, cf. Good News
Bible). But it is equally possible that we should translate 'this is
the sign that I have sent you', this sign being the prior theophany
at the burning bush.[11] Worshipping God on the mountain would
then be not the sign that Moses is sent by God, but the consequence
of coming deliverance from enslavement. Either way the sign
does not immediately answer or counter the surprise which Moses
expressed at God's call. If it refers back to the theophany, it merely
recalls the experience of being commissioned, and therefore the
occasion of the surprise; Moses must learn to live with this
surprise. If it points forward to a day on the other side of
deliverance, it can only be taken as a challenge to Moses to
come to terms with his surprise, to accept the burden of leadership, relying on nothing other than a promise that he will find
the meaning of God's call to him in the future life of a free
and worshipping community. But this future is not yet; and
Moses, according to the narrative, has pressing and present
problems.

This becomes clear in the *second* objection: 'If I go to the Israelites
and tell them that the God of their forefathers has sent me to
them, and they ask me his name, what shall I say?' (3.13). We
have already discussed what is involved in the demand of man to
know the name of God within Old Testament tradition.[12] The
question on Moses' lips implies that the people to whom he goes
will rightly wish not only to know the character of the God who

has sent him, but will demand some insight into this God's intentions for them, and how he plans to fulfil these intentions. Are they being offered a relationship, a future on which they can depend? It has been suggested that here Moses 'has cloaked his own doubts as to God's intentions in terms of his people's query'.[13] In support of this it is pointed out that the divine reply is two-fold: first the declaration to Moses 'I am who I am (or I will be who I will be)', and secondly the command to Moses to tell the people that 'I am' has sent him to them (3.14). That we do on occasion cloak our own doubts and uncertainties in the questions we attribute to other people is not to be denied, but this seems an over-subtle interpretation of this second objection. If the objection expresses a reluctance on the part of Moses to obey God's commission, the reluctance is rooted not in Moses' doubts as to God's nature and intentions, but in what he anticipates the response of the people is likely to be. They will demand compelling credentials to authenticate his claim to leadership based upon an appeal to religions authority. How can he communicate to them the theological content of what was symbolized by the theophany he has experienced? Here we are dealing with an issue which was to become central to, and virtually insoluble in, prophetic tradition, the question of the authenticity and the authority of the prophet and his message.[14]

The response to this second objection is contained in a statement 'I am who I am' or 'I will be who I will be' (3.14), a statement which has provoked more inconclusive discussion than almost any other in the Old Testament. Since this statement has, I believe, important implications for the presence within the Old Testament of the general theme we are exploring, we shall leave discussion of it till a later context.[15] Suffice at the moment to indicate that within the context of this second objection this response to the question about God's name 'carries the connotation of divine presence, but it also confers upon that presence a quality of elusiveness. The God of biblical faith even in the midst of a theophany is at once *Deus revelatus atque absconditus*. He is known as the unknown'.[16]

The *third* objection 'But they will never believe me or listen to me: they will say "the Lord did not appear to you" ' (4.1) is a further development of the second. In its present context it is preceded by a lengthy passage in which God declares his identity, reiterates his concern for the oppressed people, assures Moses that the people will listen to him, and that in spite of opposition from Pharaoh his mission will succeed (3.15–22).[17] The third objection takes as its starting point one element in this speech 'They will listen to you . . .' (3.18). 'No they won't' retorts Moses. In spite of attempts by over-pious commentators to soften the impact of this retort,[18] the Midrash is surely more honest in recognizing that 'Moses then spoke not befittingly; for God had said to him "And they shall hearken to thy voice" . . .'. It then proceeds to interpret the signs which follow (4.2–9) as forms of punishment sent upon Moses for his sin of disbelief. This interpretation of the signs is erroneous, but it does witness to the extent to which once the presence of protest and disbelief are recognized in biblical narratives there is a marked tendency to pass the verdict 'sinful'. The narrative itself passes no such verdict. It leaves us with a direct clash between a divine promise and a man who voices his doubt as to whether this promise can or will be fulfilled.

The *fourth* objection moves from the feared response of the people to the personal inadequacy of the messenger. 'But Moses said, "O Lord, I have never been a man of ready speech, never in my life, not even now that thou hast spoken to me: I am slow and hesitant of speech" (4.10). Moses thus sees between himself and the people a communication problem. He has no persuasiveness fluency, no oratorial charisma. In characteristic wisdom style this objection is met by a series of rhetorical questions (4.11, cf. Psalm 96.9–11 and the repeated use of this motif in Second Isaiah, e.g. Isa. 40.12ff.; 41.1–3). The questions stress God's total control over man, whatever his human condition may be. They are tantamount to God saying to Moses, 'Are you accusing me of making a mistake in choosing you? Do you think I am not aware of your personal limitations?' The questions then turn into a promise 'I will help your speech and tell you what to say' (4.12).[19] Here again the Midrash preserves an attempt to blunt the force of Moses' objections by attributing to R. Phinehas the interpretation 'Moses argues, "I am not a man of words, and moreover I see no place for words here. For the man to whom I go is a slave" (i.e. following the tradition in Gen. 9.25 where the line of Ham, which includes Egypt, is destined to be "slave of slaves") and will not accept reproof; as it says, A servant will not be corrected by words (i.e. Prov. 25.19). I will go only if I can chasten him with suffering'.

Again however, in this fourth objection the narrative itself merely sets over against each other human objection and divine promise.

That the human objection is not believed to be immediately resolved by the divine promise is apparent in the *fifth* objection; 'But Moses still protested, "No, Lord, send whom thou wilt" ' (4.13); literally 'send by the hand you will send'. The meaning of this circuitous phrase has been vigorously discussed in both Jewish and Christian sources. The Midrash preserves several different interpretations. Moses reminds God that he had employed angels to rescue both Lot and Hagar, so how could he reasonably expect one mere man to deliver six hundred thousand Hebrew slaves? It was further argued that it was wrong to infer from the words that Moses was refusing to go; he only wished to pay proper respect to Aaron his elder brother, with various texts being cited to prove that it was the responsibility of Aaron as the elder brother to take the lead. Christian exegetes early tended to see in the words 'by the hand you will send' a reference to the coming Messiah, and therefore gave a christological interpretation, a view which Calvin trenchently repudiates.[20] It has long been recognized by both Jewish and Christian exegetes, however, that the correct rendering is 'make someone else your agent', 'send anyone you like except me'.[21] The fifth objection, therefore, takes the form of a point blank refusal to accept God's commission; a refusal which is met by God's anger (4.14) and a warning that the time for argument is over. The only objection which has appealed to Moses' own lack of ability, the fourth, is then countered by the provision of Aaron as the spokesman, Aaron fulfilling the later prophetic role of being the 'mouthpiece', with Moses functioning vis à vis Aaron in the role of God, telling him what to say, putting the words in his mouth (4.14–16).

These early chapters in Exodus are closely paralleled in the account of the renewed call to Moses in Exodus 6.2–7.7. This section is in all probability the priestly P variant of the Mosaic call tradition.[22] Instead of the theophany in the mysterious burning bush, there is the repeated phrase of divine self-identification 'I am the Lord . . .' (6.2, 6, 8, 28, cf. 6.7). On the human side objections three and four appear in variant form. When Moses declared to the Israelites God's concern for them and his promise to deliver them, 'they did not listen to him: they had become impatient because of their cruel slavery' (6.9). The Palestinian Targum expands this verse by adding at the end the words 'and because of the idolatry which they practised',[23] understanding the Hebrew *'abhōdhāh'*, work (slavery) to mean the cult, the service of the deity. Again we note the tendency to assume that any failure to respond positively to God's messenger must be sinful, spelled out, in this case, in terms of idolatry. This failure to convince the people leads Moses to protest when the Lord tells him to go to Pharaoh. 'If the Israelites do not listen to me, how will Pharaoh listen to me, seeing that I am uncircumcised of lips' (6.12). Here 'uncircumcised of lips' (6.12, 30) replaces 'I have never been a man of ready speech' in 4.10, but the meaning is the same. The respective roles of Moses and Aaron are then delineated, this time without any expression of divine anger. Moses is to be 'like a god for Pharaoh, with your brother Aaron as your prophet' (7.1); the word 'prophet' here functioning as a synonym for the mouthpiece or spokesman of 4.16.[24]

What is remarkable about these Mosaic call traditions is that in their present form they preserve no less than five different objections, ranging from stunned surprise, through the conviction that failure is inevitable because of the obduracy of the people, disbelief in the promises of God, and a sense of personal inadequacy, all the way to a point blank refusal to go.[25] It is true that the objections are each in turn countered; that Moses in the end does go, but not without a struggle. Only the final defiant refusal to go is condemned in the narrative. In face of the other objections, the narrative depicts God as remaining patient, careful to provide counters to the objections in the form of assurances and signs which are not accepted as immediately convincing because they point forward to a reality of faith which only the future can verify. And the immediate future brings its own perplexity.

His objections stymied, if not resolved, Moses sets out for Egypt to take up his God-given burden of leading his people out of enslavement. On the way there takes place a nocturnal incident described in three of the most puzzling verses in the Old Testament, Exodus 4.24–26, an incident in which 'the Lord met Moses, meaning to kill him' (4.24). Whereupon Zipporah, Moses' wife circumcises her son, touches someone's feet – 'feet' probably here as elsewhere in the Old Testament a euphemism for the sexual organs – with the bloody foreskin, and refers to someone as 'a bridegroom of blood'. Ambiguities abound, some of them indicated in the vagueness of our description of the incident. Certain well-defined lines of interpretation of this incident developed within Jewish tradition.[26] Modern scholars have spun numerous theories in attempts to explain the pre-history of these verses.[27] No hypothesis has satisfactorily explained all the puzzling features in the story. What is even more problematic, and often studiously ignored, are questions concerning the possible meaning of these verses in their present context in the Exodus narratives. U. Cassuto, who does try to find a contextual meaning, claims that on the journey to Egypt Moses contracted a serious illness. This illness was taken to be a warning that, even though the family were wayfarers, their child ought to have been circumcised. The shedding of the child's blood in circumcision is taken as 'an additional and decisive consecration of the father to the Lord's mission'. Once the child had been circumcised, the illness abated. Cassuto admits that this interpretation leaves some of the detail of the story obscure, the inevitable result, he believes, of these verses being an abridgement of a once more detailed epic tradition.[28] Cassuto's interpretation is far from convincing, but he is right in two respects: (*a*) the verses must be capable of being given a meaning which makes sense of their present context, and (*b*) the verses are the residual fragment of a piece of ancient tradition which long predates the present form of the book of Exodus. It is reasonably easy to see why, on purely formal grounds, the verses were inserted here. Motifs prominent in the surrounding verses are echoed – the motif of killing, 'all those who wish to kill you are dead' (4.19); 'I will kill your first born son' (4.23); now another seeks to kill Moses: the motif of the son, 'Israel my first born son . . . my son . . . Pharaoh's first born son' (4.23); now another son: the motif of meeting, 'the Lord met Moses . . .' (4.24), anticipating the order to Aaron to go and meet Moses (4.27). But the purely formal links do not in themselves explain the significance or the impact of these verses in their present context. 'The Lord spoke to Moses in Midian and said to him, "Go back to Egypt for all those who wished to kill you are dead"' (4.19) – all apparently except the Lord, for on the way 'the Lord met Moses meaning [or "wishing", the same Hebrew verb being used here as in verse 19] to kill him'. Thematically we seem to be moving here into the same mysterious world we entered when 'a man' met and wrestled with Jacob at the ford Jabbok.[29] After initial protest and struggle Moses had accepted the inevitable. He had set out on his God-given mission. But that did not mean that he had moved from a world of uncertainty to one of certainty, nor that having, albeit reluctantly, said 'yes' to God, his relationship with God was now untroubled. As M. Buber comments: 'We know from the life of the founders of religion and also from that of other souls who live in the deeps of faith that there is such "an event of the night", the sudden collapse of the newly-won certainty, "the deadly factual" moment when the demon, working with apparent unbounded authority, appears in the world where God alone had been in control but the moment before. The early stage of Israelite religion knows no Satan: if a power attacks a man and threatens him it is proper to recognise YHVH in it or behind it, no matter how nocturnally cruel or dread it may be . . .'.[30] Even before he begins his mission in Egypt, Moses has to face a threatening encounter with God, and that encounter symbolized much that lay ahead. Moses was to live dangerously, not least in terms of some of the certainties which delineated his relationship with God.

Moses' mission soon ran into difficulties. The initial request to let the slaves go into the desert to keep a pilgrim feast is met by Pharaoh demanding from the slaves increased productivity with fewer resources (Exod. 5.1–19). A testy interview takes place between the Hebrew shop stewards and Moses and Aaron. Moses and Aaron are accused of adding to the people's difficulties by hardening the attitude of the Egyptian authorities towards them. In the face of this protest Moses turns to God with two questions: 'Why, O Lord, hast thou brought misfortune on this people? And why didst thou ever send me?' (5.22). The questions are the preface to a complaint: 'Since I first went to Pharaoh to speak in thy name he has heaped misfortune on thy people, and thou hast done nothing at all to rescue them' (5.23). This complaint is tantamount to accusing God of failing to keep promises he has solemnly made. The uncompromising frankness of Moses' words has long been recognized and variously explained. The Midrash, playing on the Hebrew word '*yāshûbh*', 'went back' in verse 22, acknowledges that Moses 'exchanged' (Heb. *hēshîbh* from the same root) words with God, i.e. he was prepared to question the way in which God was acting, or failing to act. It claims, however, that Moses' problem stemmed from his reading of Genesis. There it is clear that both in the flood story and in the Sodom incident the people were justly punished for their sins; but what had the present generation done to justify such severe affliction? If they are being punished for the lack of faith implied in Abraham's question 'Wherefore shall I know that I shall inherit the land?' (Gen. 15.18), why had equally severe punishment not been meted out to Esau and Jacob, Abraham's earlier descendants? The heavenly attribute of justice demands that Moses should be struck down for his presumption. The demand is refused because God claims that Moses is arguing, not on his own behalf, but on behalf of Israel. Yet Moses' attitude is not allowed to go unpunished. The emphatic 'now' at the beginning of 6.1 'Now you shall see what I shall do to the Pharaoh . . .' is taken to mean that although Moses will be permitted to witness God's present decisive action against Pharaoh, he will not be allowed to experience God's future acts of deliverance under Joshua. 'From this we divine that it was at this point that Moses received the sentence that he should not enter the land.'[31] It became commonplace to see in Moses' questions and complaint lack of faith, a lack of faith for which he was justly censured. So Calvin can say of Moses' complaint: 'it is apparent how deep is the darkness which has taken possession of his mind'.[32] More recently it has been urged that 'Such daring questions only a man like Moses, after he had overcome his doubts and completely dedicated his life to the fulfilment of his exalted mission, could permit himself to ask'.[33] But such questions and complaint do not speak of doubt overcome, they witness to continuing doubt. They are not the kind of questions you permit yourself to ask, they are questions that spring unasked from the apparent meaninglessness of a crisis situation. They are born out of the tension created by a belief in God-given promises which still lie unfulfilled. They are the unsought consequences of continuing dedication to a God-given task, the product of tenacious obedience. The alternative is to renounce such obedience and assume that what has hitherto been believed is meaningless or wholly irrational.

This picture of a Moses who questions, complains, and objects runs right through the book of Exodus (cf. 17.41; 19.12, 21). Confirmation of this is to be found in one of the other major blocks of material within the present book. Exodus 32–34, although built up from different sources or units of tradition, possess within the framework of the overall composition of the book, a unity which, in terms of their covenant orientation, links them with Exodus 19–24. These chapters have been placed within 'an obvious theological framework of sin and forgiveness. Chapter 32 recounts

the breaking of the covenant; ch. 34 relates its restoration. Moreover these chapters are held together by a series of motifs which
are skilfully woven into the unifying pattern. The tablets are
received, smashed in ch. 32, recast and restored in ch. 34. Moses'
intercession begins in ch. 32, continues in ch. 33 and comes to its
climax in ch. 34.'[34] It is on the portrayal of Moses in these chapters
as intercessor and mediator that we wish to focus attention. The
words 'intercessor' and 'mediator', frequently used to summarize
Moses' role in these chapters, can be dangerously religious jargon
words, which too easily convey the impression of one who in
faithfulness prays on behalf of the faithless, and who in obedience
acts as a go-between on behalf of the disobedient. But neither
unquestioning faithfulness nor eager obedience are characteristic
of the intercessor in these chapters.

The pattern is set by the first dialogue between the Lord and
Moses on the mountain top. Reacting in anger against the apostate
junketing around the golden image of the bull calf at the foot of
the mountain, the Lord says to Moses, 'I have considered this
people and I see that they are a stubborn people. Now let me
alone to vent my anger upon them, so that I may put an end to
them and make a great nation spring from you' (32.9–10). The
phrase 'Now let me alone' (Heb. *we'attāh hannîhah lî*) has been
the subject of much exegetical speculation. The Midrash reflects
a psychological approach which has found wide acceptance
among both Jewish and Christian commentators down to the
present day.[35] 'Why does God say, "Now therefore let me alone?"
Was Moses holding him? To what can the thing be compared? To
a king who was angry with his son, and when the son was brought
into the chamber and about to be beaten, the king cried from the
chamber "Let me alone that I may smite him". Now the instructor
(of the son) happened to be standing without and he thought to
himself, If both the king and the son are within the chamber, why
then does he say "Let me alone". It must be that the king is
desirous that I should entreat him on his son's, behalf, and for
that reason does he say "Let me alone". Similarly God said to
Moses "Now therefore let me alone"; from this Moses inferred;
God is desirous that I should intercede with him on Israel's behalf,
and hence he is saying "Now therefore let me alone". Forthwith
Moses began to plead for mercy on Israel's behalf . . . '.[36] This
ingenious attempt to make the divine statement 'Now leave me
alone' more theologically palatable is far from convincing. This is

the only passage in the Old Testament where this particular expression is attributed to God. It occurs three times (II Sam. 6.11; II Kings 23.18; Hosea 4.7), with reference to a human situation, in each case strongly indicating that there must be no interference of any kind. By analogy we would therefore expect the expression in Exodus 32.10 to indicate God's determination to vent his anger upon the people, and to underline that this decision is final and irreversible. Not only so, but it is a decision which from Moses' point of view has a certain attractiveness. The people are to perish, but God's promise of a great nation is not cancelled; it is simply to be rechannelled through Moses. Moses refuses to accept. He demands the right to interfere, to argue God into changing his mind. This daring response is indicated in the words which introduce Moses' response 'But Moses set himself to placate the Lord his God' (32.11). The Hebrew expression for 'set himself to placate' (*wayehal . . . 'eth penê . . .*) is widely used in the Old Testament in contexts which imply a background of God's anger or displeasure, and look for a change in God's attitude.[37] Midrashic discussion of the phrase is extensive, fastening upon different possible nuances in the verb or different possible verbal roots. The discussion is introduced by a statement attributed to R. Ḥama b.Ḥanina: 'The good advocate knows how to present his case clearly before the tribunal. Moses was one of two advocates that arose to defend Israel, and set themselves as it were against the Holy One, blessed be He'.[38] The other such advocate was believed to be Daniel on the strength of Daniel 9.3. It is as an advocate seeking to have a divine decision reversed that Moses proceeds to ask two questions:

1. 'O Lord, why shouldst thou vent thy anger upon thy people whom thou didst bring out of Egypt with great power and with a strong hand?' (32.11) i.e., why do something which will negate purposes which you have already initiated and upon which you have expended energy?

2. 'Why let the Egyptians say "So he meant evil when he took them out, to kill them in the mountains and wipe them off the face of the earth"?' (32.12) i.e. why give comfort to those who seek to thwart your purposes, why allow them to mock you? (cf. Ps. 79.9–10).

Both questions seek to point out that God seems set on a course of action which runs contrary to his nature and purposes, and which can only be detrimental to his own best interests, as they have already been made known. The questions become the basis of an appeal to God 'to turn from his anger', to change his mind, 'to think better of the evil' he intended against his own people. This appeal is strengthened by calling upon God to remember, to remember the promises he had already made to his people, the promises of countless descendants and a homeland. 'So the Lord changed his mind, and spared the people the evil with which he had threatened them' (32.14). Commentators have been quick to point to what this dialogue tells us about the doctrine of God in ancient Israel. He is not conceived of as a static being 'but rather a dynamic and living Person in a vital relationship with earthly persons, responding to their needs and their attitudes and their actions'.[39] Far less attention has, however, been paid to the attitude of the human partner in the dialogue. It is the human protest, the intercessor's refusal to accept what is presented to him as a divine decree, brooking no human interference, which calls forth the divine response. This human protest is rooted in the ambiguous nature of the experience of God, in the struggle to comprehend the relationship between God's anger and his saving purposes, between promises made and decisions which seem to threaten to annul these promises.

A parallel version of this dialogue is to be found in Deuteronomy 9.13, 14, 25–29. The setting is different. Moses' appeal to God takes place after he has come down the mountain, viewed with horror the image of the bull calf, smashed the tablets of the law, and prostrated himself for forty days and nights. The parallelism is no reason for assuming that the Exodus passage is Deuteronomic. Indeed, in certain respects Deut. 9.12ff. reads like an early attempt to make the Exodus tradition more theologically acceptable. The sharp 'Leave me alone' is replaced by the expression 'Let me be' (Heb. *hereph mimmenî*)[40] which does not convey the same sense of brooking no interference. Moses' intention to 'placate the Lord' is replaced by the more general and neutral expression 'I prayed to the Lord'. The first direct question 'why' is replaced by the negative 'don't destroy'; the second 'why' by a clause introduced by 'lest'. There is no parallel in Deuteronomy to the requests to God 'to turn from his anger' and 'to change his mind'; nor is there any statement that the Lord did so change his mind. The disturbing urgency of the Exodus tradition has disappeared; protest has been transformed into respectful plea. By the time we come to the account of the incident in Philo *De Vita Mosis* the transformation is complete. Informed of the dire happenings at the foot of the mountain Moses 'yet took the part of mediator and reconciler and did not hurry away at once, but first made prayers and supplications begging that their sins might be forgiven. Then when the protector and intercessor had softened the wrath of the Ruler, he wended his way back in mingled joy and dejection. He rejoiced that God accepted his prayers, yet was ready to burst with the dejection and heaviness which filled him at the transgression of the multitude.'[41] Whether such a transformation should be regarded as theological gain depends on the spiritual presuppositions we bring to the text.

Exodus 32 concludes (verses 30ff.) with a further dialogue between the Lord and Moses on the theme of God's attitude towards his sinful people. It is generally held that this passage is independent of, and probably earlier, than verses 7–14. The various stages in this incident are marked by the three-fold occurrence of 'And now' (Heb. *we'attāh*): 'And now I will go up to the Lord', v. 30, Moses speaking to the people: 'And now if you will forgive', v. 32, Moses speaking to the Lord: 'And now go . . .', v. 34, the Lord speaking to Moses. At first sight there seems to be no argument designed to make God change his mind. Punishment is not revoked, only postponed: 'a day will come when I will punish them for their sins' (v. 34). The nature of Moses' intercession, however, witnesses to the element of protest, and implicit in the protest there is argument about the way in which God intends to fulfil his purposes. Granted the fact that the people have sinned, two courses of action are placed before God by Moses: 'If thou wilt forgive them . . .'[42] but if not, blot out my name from thy book which thou hast written' (32.31). Traditionally, Jewish and Christian exegesis has tended to see in these words Moses' willingness to sacrifice himself for the sake of Israel.[43] It is questionable, however, whether this idea is present in the text. Within the present context of Exodus 32, Moses' words most probably refer back to verse 10 where God decreed the destruction of the people but transferred the promise of a great nation to Moses. This suggestion is here firmly rejected. If the people are not to be forgiven, then Moses wants no future for himself. He will share the fate of the people; his name too must be eradicated from the census list of God's people. In effect, Moses is saying to God; 'If you are looking for a substitute to take the place of the people in your purposes, count me out: either you forgive them or you must think again about the future.' Calvin, while seeking to emphasize the providential framework within which the narrative must be interpreted, recognizes that it contains things which in certain respects seem to be absurd, 'for Moses imperiously lays down the law to God, and in his eager impetuosity seeks to overthrow as far as he can His eternal counsel and inconveniently robs Him of His justice'. He further notes that this corresponds to a continuing spirituality: 'That when believers unburden their care into God's bosom, they do not always do so discreetly, nor with well-ordered language, but sometimes stammer, sometimes pour forth "groans that cannot be uttered", and sometimes pass by everything else and lay hold on and press some particular petition.'[44] It is Moses' persistence in pressing his petition, in the face of what God has already decreed, which is the most striking feature of the concluding section of Exodus 32.

We turn now to Exodus 33. Whatever the problems of source division or of the pre-history of some of the material in this chapter, in its final form it contains a series of variations on the theme of the presence (Heb. *pānîm*) of the Lord. Verses 1–6 stress the dangerous nature of this presence in the midst of a stubborn people; verses 7–11 describe the Tent of Meeting, pitched outside the camp, where the Lord used to speak to Moses 'face to face' (Heb. *pānîm'el pānîm*); in verses 12–17 Moses' plea to know the way of the Lord is answered by the promise 'my presence (Heb. *pānāi*) will go with you'; and verses 18–23 discuss to what extent it is permissible for Moses to experience the nature of this presence. In his analysis of the central section (vv. 12–17) in terms of language and structure J. Muilenburg described it as 'shrouded in holy awe, freighted with urgency and passion, and burdened with a sense of destiny',[45] the kind of language which has its natural setting in the worship of the covenant community. Not only did the emphasis on the presence of God lead to the inclusion of this passage in its present context in the Sinai covenant complex, but 'it was preserved because its content focused upon the motif that is central to all worship, namely, the presence of God, for worship is only possible when and where God is believed to be present'.[46] But there always are two presences in worship, God and the worshipper. In the attitude and spirit of Moses, the covenant mediator, we may expect to see reflected elements which were central to the continuing experience of worship as it was known in Israel. The passage falls into two major sections.

1. Moses' first plea (vv. 12–13) is characterized by the reiterated and emphatic 'thou' (Heb. *'attāh*) addressed to God, and echoed in the similar sounding 'and now' (Heb. *we'attāh*):

> Thou didst tell me to bring this people up . . .
>   but thou hast not let me know. . . .
> Thou hast said, 'I know you by name and you have found favour in my sight,
>   but now. . . .'

In his relationship with God Moses seems to be standing trembling between a past built upon a given experience of God – he is under orders, he has been chosen by God,[47] he has been conscious of God's gracious attitude towards him – and a future in which he fears that this past experience of God will not be adequate. '. . . Thou hast not told me whom thou wilt send with me . . . teach me to know thy way, so that I can know thee and continue in favour with thee.' Thus is expressed the search for a deeper knowledge of God's way, a richer experience of his graciousness. Moses knows that he cannot live in the past or solely on the spiritual capital of the past. Only such a continuing and deepening knowledge of God is consistent with the ongoing experience of the people as the covenant community 'for this nation is thy own people'.

God's reply is brief: 'My presence will go with you and I will give you rest' (33.14). Behind the phrase 'my presence will go with you', there may be the lurking fear that God's presence could only be fully known at Mount Sinai where he had come to enter into covenant with his people. Perhaps he would not journey with them into the wilderness and on to the promised land. Localized deities were well known in the ancient world. The more hallowed the site the greater the temptation to identify the deity with it. To this temptation Israel was not immune, especially in terms of the ideology which grew up around the Jerusalem temple.[48] The phrase 'And I will give you rest' has been variously interpreted. It has been connected with the entry and the possession of the land of Canaan (cf. Deut. 3.20), or taken to indicate the comfort of God-given protection from annihilation or the transformation from a fretful to a secure person.[49] Too little attention has, however, been paid to the precise language used here, and in particular to the close association of presence (Heb. *pānîm*) and the verb translated 'give you rest'. There is one other place where these words occur in close proximity in this section; at the beginning of the dialogue between the Lord and Moses in Exodus 32.10, 11. The Lord says to Moses 'Leave me alone' (using the same verb as is translated 'give you rest' in 33.14); and Moses' response is to seek to 'placate the Lord' (literally the face – or presence – of the Lord). Cassuto notes the two-fold occurrence of the verb to rest and claims that this points to the fact that Moses' prayer and the Lord's compassion have now affected a radical change in the situation.[50] But can we not go further? Is it not the *nature* of Moses' plea and prayer which is an all-important factor in effecting the change? Precisely because, faced with the decree of destructive divine anger, he refused to give the Lord 'rest', but strove instead to change the Lord's attitude from anger to compassion, so now Moses is given the assurance of the Lord's presence and is himself given 'rest'. It is his wrestling with God which is the prior condition of this 'rest', the new assurance and peace which comes to him.

2. Moses' second plea (vv. 15–16) takes as its starting point the divine promise which answers his first plea: 'if thy presence does not go with us, do not send us up from here' (v. 15). It is only this continuing presence which will mark out Israel as being the recipients of God's favour, and thus a nation with a distinctive destiny. Just as previously Moses had refused to contemplate any future for himself, if there were to be no future for the community, so now he insists that God's gracious presence must be shared with the people. Twice, and emphatically, the words occur in verse 16 'I and thy people'. The divine reply in verse 17 looks back to and echoes the words of Moses' first please in verse 13, 'I will do this thing that you have asked, because you have found favour with me, and I know you by name'.

Exodus 33.12–17 touches upon themes which were to be of recurring interest for the Old Testament. Moses symbolizes the vulnerability of faith, the fear that what the past has known may not be adequate to meet the stress of the present or to sustain the problems of the unknowable future. What guarantee can there be that the future will be characterized by the presence of God? It may be going too far to claim that 'Such a story is told by someone who has personally experienced the horror and fear of sensing divine separation, the drought of spiritual loneliness and the anxiety of Godless living',[51] but it is certainly capable of speaking to such a situation. The climax to the divine reply is, in this context, equally instructive. The plea 'teach me to know thy way, so that I can know thee' (v. 13) is answered not by 'you shall know me', but by the repeated 'I know you by name' (v. 17). In his search for security, Moses is driven back to accept that he has been chosen by God, that the only lasting certainty is not his grasp of God, but God's grasp of him. It is, I believe, dangerous and misleading to transfer this as S. Terrien does into the generalized statement that 'Theology is not the science of a divine object, but the knowledge of self-transcendence by a divine subject. Moses discovers unwittingly that theology is not to know God, but to be aware of being grasped and called to do the will of God in history.'[52] Theology and religious experience cannot be so easily identified. But we are being pointed to an aspect of Israel's religious experience which any biblical theology must take into account.

The limitations surrounding man's knowledge of God – even the knowledge of the chosen leader of God's people – are dramatically underlined in the concluding section, Exodus 33.18–23. Moses' request to see 'the glory' (Heb. *kābhôdh*) of the Lord (v. 18) is rejected (vv. 19–20); but he is granted a concession, daringly described in highly anthropomorphic terms in verse 23, he is to see the Lord's back but not his face. Both in structure and content this section raises difficult issues. Whereas in other sections in Exodus 32 and 33, when Moses makes a plea to the Lord, the Lord replies once and briefly, with Moses' contribution to the dialogue usually exceeding that of the Lord's in length, in this section we find one brief request from Moses 'Show me thy glory' (v. 18), followed by three different statements each introduced by 'And the Lord (or 'he') said' (v. 19.20.21), any one of which could by itself be an answer or part answer to Moses' plea. This probably points to the fact that behind the present form of the text there lies a complex history of traditions. Attempts, however, to reconstruct that history are highly subjective.[53] Given that there are rough edges in this section, what does it mean in context? The passage seems to serve as a bridge between Moses' intercession for Israel in chapters 32 and 33 and the account of the renewal of the covenant in chapter 34. It is the nature of the bridge, however, that is interesting. It describes a theophany; but a theophany which occurs not unexpectedly, as in the case of the burning bush of Exodus 3, but in response to a request from Moses. It marks not the call of Moses to God's service, but the frontier beyond which not even Moses can venture in his knowledge of God. 'Show me thy glory' is the request to be given access to the ultimate wonder and splendour of God's own nature. This request is countered by the statement that Moses may receive a passing glimpse of God's goodness' (Heb. *ṭûbh*). Since God's goodness is usually in the Old Testament the expression for what God does on behalf of his people, his mighty deeds for them, his bounty to them, this is equivalent to saying, 'You may know something of the way in which I act graciously in the world, but the ultimate mystery of my nature remains hidden'. To this experience of God's goodness there is added the privilege of hearing the 'name, the Lord' (Heb. *YHWH*); but just as in Exodus 3 this name is immediately qualified by the apparently tautologous statement 'I will be who I will be', so here a similar kind of statement stresses the divine freedom to which even Moses dare not dictate: 'I will be gracious to whom I will be gracious, and I will have compassion on whom I will have compassion' (v. 19). Corresponding to the distinction between 'glory', which remains inaccessible, and the 'name' which is knowable, there comes in verses 20–21 the distinction between God's face, which Moses may not see, and God's back which, after elaborate safeguards, he may be permitted to see.

Thus the Exodus narratives leave us with an unresolved – and possibly unresolvable – dilemma. They describe a leader who, standing in a special relationship with God, is not afraid to voice objections to God's purposes, and who is prepared on behalf of his people to question the validity of God's intentions. He will argue with God, till God changes his mind. Yet there is a frontier beyond which even Moses may not go, a mystery in God's nature, which he is not allowed to penetrate, and to which he dare not dictate. The location of this frontier was to be one of the major issues raised, in different ways, in Job and Ecclesiastes.

In his essay on 'Moses in Old Testament Tradition' A. C. Welsh[54] draws a dual portrait of Moses. There is the Moses of late Judaism and later art, Moses the almost inhuman law-giver, who gazes blankly out into the void, little more than 'a pedestal which supports on knee or arm the tablets of the Decalogue':[55] and there is the very human Moses of the earlier narratives, the deliverer of his people, the man who intercedes on behalf of the people before God. There is, however, a richness in the humanity of this Moses to which even A. C. Welsh did not direct attention, a richness bound up with those elements of objection, protest, questioning and doubt, with which we have been concerned.

5

THE CHANGING WORD –
PROPHETIC NARRATIVES

We have already had occasion to note in our discussion of the
patriarchal and Mosaic narratives certain links with prophetic
tradition.[1] Broadly speaking, the Old Testament contains two
main sources of information concerning the prophets:

1. There are narratives, found mainly in the Deuteronomic
history of the rise and fall of the Hebrew monarchy (I Samuel–II
Kings), which purport to preserve traditions concerning the
activity of certain major prophetic personalities, notably Elijah
and Elisha.

2. There are collections of logia or oracles attributed to certain
prophets, material handed down and collated by followers of the
prophets, and often in its present form reshaped, edited and
expanded to meet the changing religious situation of later ages.[2]

The relationship between these two sources of information is
far from clear. While the narrative material contains oracles
attributed to the prophets and the collected oracles sometimes
contain biographical and autobiographical information, the narrative traditions and the collected oracles seem to have been
handed down more or less independently. At least they reflect
different theological interests. A major prophet like Jeremiah,
who, according to the book of Jeremiah, was deeply involved in
the religious and political issues of the day, receives no mention
in the Deuteronomic history of the period, while the stance taken
by the prophet Isaiah in the narrative material in II Kings 19–20
conveys a somewhat different impression from that of the parallel
and related material embedded in Isaiah 36–39.[3] Whatever the

explanation of this ambiguous relationship, there is little doubt that the prophetic narratives incorporated into the Deuteronomic history serve to illustrate one of the major themes of that history, 'the operation of the word of God in history'.[4]

The operation of that word may be depicted as inexorable and swift. Thus when Ahaziah king of Israel attempts from his sickbed to consult a non-Israelite deity, the prophet Elijah intercepts his messengers and confronts the king himself with these trenchant words: 'This is the word of the Lord: "You have sent to inquire of Baal-zebub the god of Ekron, and therefore you shall not rise from the bed where you are lying: you will die" ' (II Kings 1.16, cf. vv. 3b–4). The narrative continues: 'The word of the Lord which Elijah had spoken was fulfilled, and Ahaziah died' (II Kings 1.17; for similar instances of swift fulfilment see, for example, I Samuel 3– 4; 10–11; I Kings 2–4; 16.7, 12–13). Sometimes the fulfilment of the prophetic word comes after a considerable lapse of time. Thus II Kings 23.15–16 claims to describe the fulfilment of a word which had been spoken some three centuries earlier (see I Kings 13). Whether swift or delayed, however, the certainty of the fulfilment of the word is matched by the apparently untroubled assurance with which it is spoken. Such prophetic certainty has often been underlined by contrasting it with the more rational, critical and reflective attitude characteristic of the wisdom tradition in Israel, particularly in books such as Job and Ecclesiastes. A study of *The Hebrew Philosophical Genius*[5] justified its neglect of prophetic material by arguing that prophetic experience and thinking are grounded in 'the mystical revelation and the religious attitudes produced by dependence upon it. . . . They (i.e. the prophets) were perfectly sure: and on their perfect sureness they built up their system.'[6] The typical introduction to prophetic speech, 'This is the word of the Lord' seems to leave little room for argument and even less room for doubt. Such a judgment, however, fails to take cognizance of the problems raised by the failure of prophecy in many cases to find specific fulfilment, and it ignores certain elements which are present even in the narratives placed in a document which seeks to illustrate 'the operation of the word of God in history'.[7] The given certainty of the word must not blind us to its flexibility. The apparent sureness with which it is spoken may often mask tensions and questions present both in the mind of him who speaks and in the mind of those to whom he speaks.

The prophetic narratives introduce us to certain broad issues which surface in varied shape and form in prophetic experience.

1. *The word for yesterday may not be the word for today*

I Samuel 2.27ff. contains an account of a word of judgment delivered against the priestly family of Eli by an unidentified 'man of God', a common synonym for a prophet in such narratives. The passage has undergone extensive theological reshaping probably at the hands of Deuteronomic editors; its word of judgment anticipates the word given to Samuel in I Samuel 3.11–14, and it seems explicitly to envisage the replacement of the family of Eli by the family of Zadok as a royal priesthood (cf. I Sam. 2.35). There is no reason, however, for assuming that the incident is purely a propagandist invention. The message of the man of God hinges upon two statements each introduced by 'the Lord's word' or 'oracle of the Lord' (Heb. *neûm'adōnāi*):

(a) 'The Lord's word was, "I promise that your house and your father's house shall serve before me for all time";

(b) 'but now the Lord's word is "I will have no such thing: I will honour those who honour me, and those who despise me shall meet with contempt. The time is coming when I will lop off every limb of your own and of your father's family so that no man in your house shall come to old age. . . ." ' (I Sam. 2.30–31). We find here: (i) a sharp antithesis between the word that was and the word that is. This cannot be explained in terms of a minor modification of an earlier word to suit changed circumstances. The modification takes the form of a direct *volte face*. The earlier word contained an unconditional promise to the house of Eli, a promise that is to last *for all time*; the subsequent word destroys that promise.

(ii) This antithesis springs from what is believed about the character of God in his relationship with men. The words translated, 'I will have no such thing' are in Hebrew a strong form of protestation (*halîlāh lî*), usually found on the lips of men and conventionally translated, 'Far be it from me' or 'the Lord forbid' (e.g. Gen. 44.7, 17; I Sam. 1.20; 20.9; 22.15; 24.6; 26.11). This is the only passage in the Old Testament where the expression is directly attributed to God. The closest analogy is Genesis 18.25, where Abraham points out to the Lord that it would be wholly inconsistent with his character if he were to condemn indiscriminately innocent and guilty alike.[8] This passage affirms that given changed circumstances – in this case the scandalous conduct and reprobate character of Eli's family – God could not remain true to himself and leave an already given word unchanged. Because of what God is, and how men act or react towards him, the word may and indeed must change.

A similar situation is described in I Samuel 15. In response to a word from the Lord, Samuel, according to I Samuel 9.15ff. had taken the initiative in anointing Saul to a position of leadership over the people. Now, in consequence of Saul's failure to follow accepted practice to place the entire Amalekite community and its possessions under the ban (I Sam. 15.9), the word of the Lord comes again to Samuel: 'I repent of having made Saul king, for he has turned his back on me and has not obeyed my commands' (I Sam. 15.10). Although Saul confesses his guilt and pleads for forgiveness (I Sam. 15.24), he is brusquely dismissed with the words 'You have rejected the word of the Lord and therefore the Lord has rejected you as king over Israel' (I Sam. 15.26). Just as the house of Eli has to make way for the royal Zadokite priesthood, so the family of Saul, according to the narrative, has to make way for the Davidic dynasty. The chapter ends by reverting to the theme that 'the Lord had repented of having made him (i.e. Saul) king over Israel' (v. 35). The antithesis in this case is not so sharp. There is no suggestion that the original word to Saul contained any unconditional promise valid for all time. The narrator, or the later editor, however, seems to be aware that there are difficult theological problems involved in speaking about God 'repenting' or 'changing his mind'. In what circumstances is it legitimate to speak of God 'repenting'? If he changes his mind in face of Saul's disobedience why does he not change it again when Saul confesses his guilt and pleads for forgiveness? Is not this language of 'changing ones mind' and 'repenting' dangerously anthropomorphic? The narrator, therefore, declares 'God who is the Splendour of Israel does not deceive or change his mind; he is not a man that he should change his mind' (I Sam. 15.29). Modern English translations tend to suggest a distinction between 'changing his mind' in verse 29 and 'repenting' (NEB) or 'being sorry' (Good News Bible) in verses 11 and 35, and English usage may justify the differing rendering contextually, but in Hebrew the same verb is used in each case, the verb used of God changing his mind in Exodus 32.[9]

As a generalized, theoretical statement of religious principle this assertion in I Samuel 15.29 is unexceptional. It has close links with a similar statement in the second oracle of Balaam in Numbers, 23.19. The context of the Numbers passage which insists that 'God is not mortal that he should lie, (Heb. *kzb*), not a man that he should change his mind' makes it clear that what is intended is that no human pressure or cajolery can make God depart from a decision he has already taken. God's change of mind cannot be equated with that human fickleness and inconstancy with which we are all only too familiar. Merely to assert this principle, however, leaves many difficult questions unasked and unanswered. In both I Samuel 2 and I Samuel 15 a significant time lapse intervenes between the contradictory words, a time lapse in which events occur which, it may be claimed, justify the changed word. But suppose that two contradictory words, each claiming to be the word of the Lord, are spoken without any such significant time lapse intervening or any obvious change taking place in the human situation. Can this be explained in terms of some swift, and perhaps inscrutable, change of mind on the part of God, or is it possible that the first word was deceiving . . . or is it the second . . . or is it both?

Such questions are inherent in the narrative in I Kings 13.[10] The popular midrashic character of the chapter is evident. It may have been used to explain why an otherwise unidentified 'man of God' from Judah in the south was buried in the vicinity of the northern town of Bethel (cf. vv. 30ff.). In its present context it serves to illustrate another of the major themes of the Deuteronomic historians, the rejection by God of the northern kingdom of Israel and its religious establishment. Coming immediately after the story of Jeroboam's secession from the Jerusalem centred Davidic dynasty (I Kings 12), it depicts 'a man of God from Judah' declaring a word of judgment and doom upon the altar at Bethel as Jeroboam prepares to offer sacrifice (vv. 1–2).[11] Although this word of judgment seems to have been edited in the light of Josiah's reformation centuries later – note the introduction of Josiah's name in verse 2, and the narrative in II Kings 23.15–20 – it would be wrong to dismiss the story as merely a fabrication by the Jerusalemite religious establishment in pursuit of its vendetta against what it regarded as the schismatic and heretical north. The story, which is probably rooted in authentic, early narrative traditions, hinges upon the curiously ambivalent relationship between this 'man of God from Judah', who declares what the story regards as a true word of divine judgment against the altar at Bethel only to fall himself under divine judgment as 'the man of God who defied the word of the Lord' (v. 26, cf. v. 21); and 'an aged prophet living in Bethel', who first proclaims a word which the narrator describes as a lie (v. 19) and then becomes the messenger of a true word of judgment against the man of God. Both 'the man of God from Judah' and 'the aged prophet living in Bethel' point to certain dilemmas inherent in prophecy in the Old Testament.

Let us consider first the dilemma facing the man of God. In the presence of the king he pronounces doom upon the altar at Bethel, symbol of the rival religious establishment by means of which Jeroboam hoped to wean the north from any lingering religious attachment to Jerusalem. The word of doom is to be confirmed by a portent (Heb. *môphēt*) or sign: 'This altar will be rent in pieces and the ashes upon it will be spilt' (v. 3). Jeroboam reacts by pointing to this dangerous subversive, and ordering his immediate arrest. The king's outstretched arm is immediately paralysed, a feature in the narrative which, whatever its basis, is probably best regarded as an extension of the word and portent of judgment which are immediately fulfilled, the altar rent in pieces, the ashes spilt. Through the man of God Jeroboam now seeks 'to pacify the Lord'.[12] The prayer of the man of God is effective; the king's 'hand was restored and became as it had been before' (v. 6). To this extent the narrative assumes an element of flexibility in God's attitude; what God is believed to have done is undone in response to the prayer of the man of God. But how far does such flexibility go? In spite of a royal invitation, the man of God adamantly refuses to accept any hospitality 'for the Lord's command to me was to eat and drink nothing, and not to go back by the way I came' (v. 9). The north is doomed; the man of God from the south in whom resides God's power and potentially God's blessing must shun all friendly contact with it, and leave it without delay. Thus the word of the Lord (vv. 9, 17). Then he hears another word from the prophet, a word claiming equal authority and equal status: 'I also am a prophet as you are; and an angel commanded me by the word of the Lord to bring you home with me to eat and to drink' (v. 18). As Karl Barth has put it, 'The whole issue now rests on a razor's edge. One word of the Lord, asseverated by its recipient, is balanced against the other, a later against an earlier.

The man from Judah has to decide whether what he has received
has to be revised and corrected by what the prophet asserts he
has received.'[13] And it is precisely because, as we have seen, a
later word may modify or cancel an earlier word that the dilemma
is acute. A paralysed hand is restored; why may not an isolating
word be rescinded by another word claiming divine authority? If,
as the narrator claims, this other word was a lie, how was the man
of God to know this? The dark abyss into which he gazes is not
merely the possibility that a genuine prophet may become a traitor
to the word he is called to bear,[14] it is the darkness of conflicting
certainties challenging him and mocking him. He must be a traitor
to the one word of the Lord or to the other. Perhaps God has
changed his mind.

The aged prophet living in Bethel highlights another problem.
The word he first proclaims to the man of God in the name of the
Lord is bluntly described by the narrator as false, 'He was lying'
(v. 19). But was he consciously and deliberately lying, or is this no
more than a later, theologically prejudiced verdict? It is true that
his initial word may be interpreted as an attempt to modify the
man of God's total rejection of the northern kingdom, and thus as
a reflection of the self-interest of the northern religio-political
establishment of which he was probably a representative. But this
in itself does not guarantee that his word must be false. With
equal cogency it may be argued that the word on the lips of the
man of God represented the religio-political interests of a
Jerusalem-based establishment in the south, and for that reason
ought to be regarded with suspicion. There is no reason to believe
that the prophet from Bethel was proclaiming anything other
than a word which was to him self-authenticatingly true and
which he believed to be of divine origin. Yet, according to the
narrator, it was false, a decoy luring the man of God into the net
of God's judgment. This seering word of condemnation against
the man of God is then truly declared by the same prophet, and
swiftly vindicated by events (vv. 23–32). The fact that this later
word of judgment assumes that the prophet's prior word was
misleadingly false, does not guarantee that the prophet himself
knew this from the beginning since, as we have seen, prophetic
tradition allows for the possibility of a changing word.

The issue as to whether from this, or from any other Old
Testament prophetic narratives, there emerge clear criteria for
distinguishing between true and false prophecy is not our con-

cern. This narrative, however, highlights the vulnerability of both the man of God and the aged prophet living in Bethel. Both speak from within certain religio-political assumptions which they do not seem to question. The one is destroyed by listening to a later word cancelling an earlier word, a later word whose authenticity he has no good grounds for doubting; the other first proclaims this later false word in good faith and then becomes the bearer of a true word of judgment. Both seem to accept without hesitation that a word proclaimed as 'the word of the Lord' must be the word of the Lord for the moment in which it is proclaimed. To this extent they are like puppets dancing to the varied melodies of a changing word.

2. *The word for today may be self-contradictory*

When we turn to I Kings 22 we find a scenario which, according to some of the prophetic books, was to be a commonplace in Israel's experience,[15] the listener, be he the community or an individual, confronted by two diametrically opposed words each prefaced by 'This is the word of the Lord'. The four hundred court prophets at Samaria and their spokesman Zedekiah, son of Kenaanah, give the imprimatur of the national religion to the territorially expansionist policies of King Ahab of Israel and his somewhat reluctant junior partner in aggression, King Jehoshaphat of Judah. To Ahab's question, 'Shall I attack Ramoth-gilead or shall I refrain?' 'Attack', they answered; 'the Lord will deliver it into your hands' (I Kings 22.6, cf. v. 12). Micaiah, son of Imlah, already something of a *persona non grata* in Ahab's eyes for previous undiplomatic utterances – 'I hate the man, because he prophesies no good for me, never anything but evil' (v. 8) – has a different word. After a preliminary skirmish in which he mockingly echoes the victory chant of the four hundred (v. 15), he declares in visionary form a word of impending disaster: 'I saw all Israel scattered on the mountains like sheep without a shepherd: and I heard the Lord say, "They have no master, let them go home in peace" ' (v. 17). Which is the authentic word of the Lord? This is the dilemma which confronts Ahab and Jehoshaphat, and potentially the issue is one of life and death.

Formally there seem to be no simple criteria or credibility tests which may be applied. Both Zedekiah and Micaiah speak the same religious language; they introduce their statements by 'This

is the word of the Lord'. Both resort to well-known prophetic
techniques. Micaiah claims to have seen visions (vv. 17, 19ff.).
Zedekiah backs up his prophetic word by a symbolic act; he

> made himself horns of iron and said, 'This is the word of the
> Lord: "With horns like these you will gore the Aramaeans and
> make an end of them" ' (v. 11).

In like fashion Jeremiah, for example, will later walk through the
streets of Jerusalem with an ox yoke across his shoulders to warn
Judah and her allies that they are doomed to come under the yoke
of Babylon (Jer. 27.1–5). Nor is there any sincerity test that can be
applied. There is not the slightest reason to assume that Zedekiah
is merely a hired religious charlatan. He is probably as totally
convinced as Micaiah is, that the word he proclaims is the
authentic word of the Lord for the contemporary situation. He
could have appealed for support to the religious traditions of the
people: after all, the Lord had given them the land of Canaan and
driven out their enemies, why would he not now help them to
recover disputed border territory? With comforting hindsight
later writers will resolve the dilemma by attaching to the four
hundred the label 'false' – thus Josephus in his retelling of the
story in the *Jewish Antiquities*.[16] Modern theological rationaliza-
tions abound. The part Jehoshaphat plays in verses 4–18 is
claimed, with some justification, to be an indicator of the way in
which the story has been elaborated by the Deuteronomic school
with its inbuilt anti-northern and pro-southern Judaean bias. The
contrast between Ahab and Jehoshaphat can then be drawn in
the following terms: 'The former (i.e. Ahab) employed the
prophets as agents of imitative magic in word, and in the case of
Zedekiah, in symbolic action, and there was a whole corps of
prophets willing to give him the moral support he required.
Jehoshaphat, at least by implication, regarded the prophet not as
an agent of the community in its effort to influence God by
autosuggestion, but as an instrument of the will of God to the
community.'[17] The distinctions here are too sharply drawn and
assume unquestionably the theological stance of the editors of
the narrative. If Zedekiah and the four hundred are to be dismissed
as politically motivated, using God at Ahab's instigation, can it be
claimed that Jehoshaphat is innocent of all political motivation?
He is very much the junior partner in the coalition. It may be
inferred, at least by implication, that he may have had a vested

interest in finding another prophetic voice to keep in check the political ambitions of his more powerful northern neighbour. The message of coming military disaster for Israel was no doubt as agreeable to Jehoshaphat, as the message of success and victory was to Ahab. If Zedekiah and the four hundred provided Ahab with the moral and political support he required, Micaiah may well have fulfilled a similar function for Jehoshaphat.

To attribute different motivation to Ahab and Jehoshaphat, different skills and professional techniques to Zedekiah and the four hundred on the one hand and to Micaiah on the other is hardly the purpose of the narrative. It does, however, have a strong interest in the question: 'Why is it that two such diametrically opposed words of the Lord may be heard at one and the same time on the lips of prophets?' The answer it gives is contained within the vision which Micaiah recounts in verses 19–22.[18]

> Listen now to the word of the Lord. I saw the Lord seated on his throne, with all the host of heaven in attendance on his right and on his left. The Lord said, 'Who will entice Ahab to attack and fall on Ramoth-gilead?' One said one thing and one said another; then a spirit came forward and stood before the Lord and said 'I will entice him'. 'How?' said the Lord. 'I will go out,' he said, 'and be a lying spirit in the mouth of all his prophets.' 'You shall entice him', said the Lord, 'and you shall succeed; go and do it.'

The Lord tables a proposal for discussion by the members of the heavenly council, 'the host of heaven', the Old Testament equivalent of the council of the gods in other polytheistic Ancient Near Eastern cultures. 'Who will entice Ahab to attack and fall on Ramoth-gilead?' (v. 20) There is an element of ambiguity in the proposal since the phrase translated 'fall on', equivalent to attack, may equally be translated 'fall at', that is be killed at Ramoth-gilead (cf. NEB footnote). The proposal provokes a lively discussion as the result of which 'a spirit' volunteers to go and become 'a lying spirit in the mouth of all his (i.e. Ahab's) prophets' (v. 22). The word on the lips of these prophets is thus described as a lie, falsehood (Heb. *sheqer*),[19] yet this word is attributed directly to the Lord. Martin Buber tries to limit God's responsibility at this point by arguing that in verses 21 and 22 *haruah* should be translated not as 'a spirit', but as 'the wind'. The court prophets of Ahab are thus being filled with wind instead of prophetic spirit. It is difficult to accept that the ambiguity in the word *ruah* has any relevance to this scene in the heavenly council. He further claims that the Lord 'entices' (v. 20) but he does not deceive; 'the one enticed hears from him that it is enticement, that the Spirit sent to him and in which he trusts in a false spirit; so the decision lies after all with the man. This is the true prophetic situation'.[20] Although this fits in well with Buber's emphasis upon the freedom to decide as being central to the Old Testament prophetic faith, the distinction he draws between 'entice' and 'deceive' is hardly substantiated by the general usage of the verb *pth* in the Old Testament. While in certain overtly sexual contexts it means to entice (e.g. Judges 14.1; 16.5; Hos. 2.16) or in terms of a legal offence 'to seduce' (Exod. 22.15), in other instances it means no more than to deceive, often with deliberate intent (e.g. II Sam. 3.25; Prov. 24.28). In Psalm 78.36 the verb is used in parallelism with the verb meaning 'to lie' (Heb. *kzb*). Since the narrative in I Kings 22 lacks any sexual context, it is hard to avoid the conclusion that the narrative is stating baldly that the Lord sends the lying spirit deliberately to deceive or mislead Ahab, and thus lure him on to his predetermined doom. An analogous situation is discussed in Ezekiel 14.1–11, with the same explanation being offered for what can only be regarded as the false or misleading prophetic word. As part of his attack upon the evil which must be eliminated from the life of the community before it can become truly God's people, Ezekiel depicts a scene where certain elders of the community, personally involved in idolatry, may yet come to consult the Lord through a prophet. In such a situation, claims Ezekiel, God will use such a prophet to ensure the destruction of his faithless people and to seal the prophet's own fate. In this context the New English Bible translated the verb *pth* by seduce: 'If a prophet is seduced into making a prophecy, it is I the Lord who have seduced him' (Ezek. 14.9).[21] It would be equally, if not more, appropriate to translate 'deceived' (cf. RSV and Good News Bible). Thus God is depicted as personally deceiving the prophet, giving him a false word, so that through that false word both the prophet and the one who consults him may be punished.[22]

It is tempting here to speak about 'primitive theology'[23] or to try to lessen the impact of the language of God 'deceiving', by stressing that the prophets in I Kings 22, for example, were merely being used by God to play their part in ensuring that Ahab kept this rendezvous with a destiny already prophesied by Elijah (see

I Kings 21.20–24). But the problem cuts deeper. Faced with simultaneous and contradictory words on the lips of the prophets, I Kings 22 asserts that all prophets, even those with conflicting messages, are inspired by God: but some of them are lyingly inspired, deliberately sent by God with a false message. This safeguards a somewhat naive doctrine of inspiration, but it may also claim to be a logical corollary of a movement within Israel's religious traditions to exhibit a strongly monotheistic tendency; in its early stages in purely practical terms – Yahweh to be the sole deity as far as Israel was concerned (cf. the first injunction in the decalogue – Exod. 20.3; Deut. 5.7) – but later in more reflectively theological terms, which may be said to reach their climax in Isaiah 40–55

> I am the Lord, there is no other;
>   there is no god beside me.

. . .

> I am the Lord, there is no other;
> I am the light, I create darkness,
>   author alike of prosperity and trouble (literally 'good and
>   evil')
> I the Lord do all these things (Isa. 45.5, 7–8 cf. 45.18–25; 18–25;
>   46.9–10).

The daring catholicity of this vision should not blind us to the fact that such a monotheistic stance, whatever its advantages or necessity, suffers from certain disadvantages over against a poly-theistic creed. In a polytheistic system the polarities of life may be shared out among many deities – a god of order and a god of chaos, a god of the life-giving rain, a goddess of fertility and a god of drought and death, a craftsman's god and a farmer's god, a god of good luck and a god of misfortune, a god and goddess of love, a god and goddess of war. Psalm 82 uses the traditional mythology of the assembly of the gods to assert the total supremacy and uniqueness of the God of Israel. As supreme judge he condemns all other gods to a most ungodlike fate 'you shall die as men die' (Ps. 82.7). The basis for such a death sentence is declared to be the evil which corrupts the world. Such evil, it is claimed, can be laid at the door of the other gods who '. . . judge unjustly and show favour to the wicked' (Ps. 82.2). But if there be no such other gods, if the Lord, the God of Israel, is the one who makes the light and creates the darkness, author alike of prosperity and trouble, what then? In certain respects the problem is intensified. The omnipotence of God may be uncompromisingly affirmed – in terms of I Kings 22 he is directly responsible for sending a lying spirit to lure Ahab to his doom – but awkward theological questions are left unanswered, questions which were to lead at a later age to the acceptance of at least a modified form of dualism.[24] But it also faces the prophet and his audience with acute personal problems. If every word on the lips of prophets is assumed to be a word from the Lord, how do the listeners respond to contradictory words? They can but choose, as Ahab chose to listen to the victory chant of the four hundred led by Zedekiah, and turned a deaf ear to Micaiah's word. He chose wrongly, deceived by a lying word, and from the dire consequences of his choice there was no escape (cf. I Kings 22.29ff.). What of the prophet himself? If it be held that the Lord uses a lying spirit to put into the mouths of prophets a deceiving word, what certainty can any prophet have that he is speaking the true word of the Lord? Must he not always wonder whether God may not merely be toying with him, using him as the agent of a deceiving word?

It was Jeremiah, more than any other prophet in Israel, who seems to have been caught up in the tensions produced by conflicting prophetic words. The Micaiah versus Zedekiah and the four hundred in I Kings 11 has its parallel in the clash between Jeremiah and Hananiah (Jer. 28). Scattered throughout the book of Jeremiah there are many scathing references to prophets, often in conjunction with priests, who have lulled the people into a false sense of security (e.g. 5.31; 6.13–15; 8.10–12). One section in the book, entitled 'concerning the prophets' (23.9–40) gathers together varied material on this theme. Of the many questions which this material raises concerning possible criteria for distinguishing between true and false prophecy, two have relevance for our discussion.

1. There is little evidence in this material that Jeremiah, or the editors of the Jeremianic traditions, were prepared to hold God directly responsible for what was considered to be false, misleading prophecy. In 28.15 Jeremiah bluntly says to Hananiah: 'Listen Hananiah. The Lord has not sent you, and you have led this nation to trust in false prophecies.' Repeatedly in the section 'concerning the prophets' the same point is made:

These are the words of the Lord of Hosts:
Do not listen to what the prophets say,
  who buoy you up with false hopes;
the vision they report springs from their own imagination,
  it is not from the mouth of the Lord (23.16).

Jeremiah denies categorically that such prophets could ever have stood in the council of the Lord or heard the word of the Lord (cf. 23.18, 22b).

I did not send these prophets, yet they went in haste;
  I did not speak to them yet they prophesied (23.22a).

He attacks 'these prophets who prophesy lies and give voice to their own inventions' (23.26). How far this takes us along the road towards identifying the false prophet may be questioned; what it does provide is positive evidence for a different response to the phenomenon of conflicting prophetic voices from that contained in the Micaiah story. Such a response only makes sense when someone is prepared to doubt the adequacy of a theology which attributes everything, including false prophecy, directly to God. A move in this direction does not of itself solve the problem of how to identify the false prophet – witness Deuteronomy which assumes that such prophets are not sent by the Lord, yet in 13.1– 5 and 18.18–25, suggests general guidelines which are of very limited value, and are as likely to damn the true prophet as the false[25] – nevertheless without this move there is no possibility of further understanding.

2. If such prophecies are to be attributed to the imagination of the prophets and their lies are nothing other than their own inventions, why is it that they so confidently proclaim them as the word of the Lord? Some light may be thrown on this question by a verse which at first sight seems both puzzling as to its meaning and of dubious relevance in its present context–Jeremiah 23.23. The RSV translates literally; 'Am I a God at hand, says the Lord, and not a God afar off?' (cf. NEB). The significance of this statement with its double question, positive and negative, seems to have been early in doubt. The Septuagint, assuming that it was reading something very close to our present Hebrew text, converts the question into a positive statement of unimpeachable theological orthodoxy: 'I am a God at hand, and not very far away'. The Good News Bible likewise endeavours to eliminate any uncertainty by paraphrasing 'I am a God who is everywhere and not in

one place only'. Such renderings no doubt satisfy the theology of
the translators, but at the expense of ignoring the form of the
Hebrew text. The effect of the double rhetorical question in
Hebrew is strongly to emphasize the positive assertion implicit in
the second negative question. To convey the meaning in English
we need a more expansive paraphrase, such as 'do you really
think that I am merely a God near at hand; never forget that I am
also a distant God'. This may be taken as a general theological
truism pointing to the fact 'that God is no small local deity from
whom one might conceivably hide, but a God who is in heaven
and sees all'[26] or as affirming both the transcendence and the
immanence of God, the one who knows and sees all, yet who is
also always close at hand to find men wherever they are.[27] Such
an approach does not, however, adequately explain the present
context of the verse in a section 'concerning the prophets'. Does
it have anything to say about prophecy, and in particular about
the problem of the false prophet? One of the charges that Jeremiah
makes against the prophets is that they dream dreams and out of
their dreams come the lies which express nothing other than what
they themselves have invented (cf. 23.26). The word they proclaim
challenges and hurts no one, least of all themselves. They give
the impression of being on remarkably free and easy terms with
God as if God were 'their next-door neighbour, whose door
always stands open'.[28] They seem to be totally unaware of the
transcendence of God, of the awesome distance between themselves and a God who knows them through and through, yet
cannot be easily known by them since he fills heaven and earth
(23.24). Elsewhere Jeremiah accuses 'the wicked', his opponents
of having God 'ever on their lips yet far from their hearts' (12.2).
The particular wickedness of the prophets is to spread among the
people a false sense of security, and the roots of this lie in the fact
that they themselves suffer from a false sense of security in their
relationship with God.[29] They speak too easily, too glibly, their
God is too close, an honoured member of their dreamers' circle.
It may be that we have here another example of a deliberate
prophetic inversion of an element in Israel's faith which Deuteronomy claims to be distinctive: 'What great nation has a god close
at hand as the Lord our God is close to us whenever we call' (Deut.
4.7). Against the background of the belief that God will guarantee
the continuing prosperity and security of his people, such 'clo-
seness' could be dangerously misleading. The god these prophets

knew was a god they knew too well, and the word of this god was a word that came too easily into their minds and on to their lips.

We are so accustomed to tune into the apparent certainty with which the Old Testament prophet declares, 'This is the word of the Lord', that we often fail to recognize the tensions which these words mask. What the authentic prophet had to say was seldom an easy word; often he had to be driven to say it. His sense of the transcendence of God, God's distance, often forced him to tear apart the neat packaging in which the community had wrapped God. There is an arrogance of certainty, rooted in a belief in God's comforting nearness, which eliminates the uncertainties and the questioning which a realistic faith may compel. The true word was often given to those who claimed the freedom to dissent from such easy certainties.

3. *The presence in the unexpected*

In the Elijah narratives in I Kings we find distilled the essence of a central strand in Israel's prophetic heritage. It focusses on a twofold emphasis: the maintenance of the nation's sole loyalty to Yahweh, the God of Israel – hence the Mount Carmel conflict narrative in I Kings 18 – and the insistence that such loyalty is meaningless unless it finds expression in the life of a community characterized by justice and equity; and that from the demands of such justice and equity, no one, not even the most powerful member of the community is exempt – hence the *cause célèbre* of Elijah's confrontation with King Ahab over the judicial murder of Naboth, whose vineyard stood in the way of the expansion of the royal gardens (I Kings 21). The Elijah narratives are characterized by dramatic contrasts; Elijah the solitary prophet of the Lord challenging the four hundred and fifty prophets of Baal (I Kings 18); Ahab the hesitant Israelite king, caught between the sanctions of his people's traditions and the power he fain would wield as king, Jezebel his foreign royal consort, untroubled by any such sanctions, decisive and ruthless in wielding royal power (I Kings 21). No contrast, however, is more dramatic than that between the portrait of Elijah triumphant on Mount Carmel in I Kings 18, and Elijah in despair, fleeing south into the desert in I Kings 19. Questions concerning the original connection between these two chapters, if any, and the historical kernel, if any, which lies behind each of them have been vigorously debated.[30] As in the case of the patriarchal and Mosaic narratives, however, our concern is with the present form of the text, and in particular with what it has to say about prophetic activity and experience.

I Kings 18 describes Elijah, prophet of the Lord, locked in lonely conflict with the prophetic devotees of a rival faith, the four hundred and fifty prophets of Baal. While an important theological motif in the narrative centres upon which god has the power to break the drought and send the life-giving rain, Elijah is depicted as confronting the people with a clear-cut choice:

> Elijah stepped forward and said to the people, 'How long will you sit on the fence? If the Lord is God, follow him: but if Baal follow him' (I Kings 18.21).

Throughout the incident Elijah is depicted as acting with calm assurance, openly mocking the prophets of Baal as they whip themselves up into an orgiastic frenzy, in an attempt to channelize the power of their god. 'Call louder', mocked Elijah, 'for he is a god; it may be he is deep in thought, or engaged, or on a journey; or he may have gone to sleep and must be woken up' (v. 27) – words which have been described as 'one of the raciest comments on paganism ever penned'.[31] In contrast to this frenzied paganism, Elijah quietly repairs the broken altar of the Lord, prepared the sacrifice, and prays:

> O Lord, the God of Abraham, Isaac and Jacob, let it be known today that thou art God in Israel and that I am thy servant and have done all these things at thy command. Answer me, O Lord, answer me. . . . (vv. 36, 37).

And the Lord answered, vindicating Elijah's stance through the fire which fell from heaven to consume altar and sacrifice. For good measure, the prophets of Baal, a cancerous growth in the body politic, are liquidated at Elijah's command (v. 40). Confident, decisive, dominating, such is the Elijah of I Kings 18. Enter Queen Jezebel, royal devotee of the cult Elijah had tried to eradicate, a resolute woman, apparently singularly unimpressed by any reports of Yahwistic pyrotechnics on Mount Carmel. Faced with this angry Queen, threatening to cut short his life – and with ample power to make her threat effective – Elijah flees despairingly south into the safety of the distant desert, and on to Horeb the traditional mountain birthplace of Israel's covenant faith:

> he went on for forty days and forty nights to Horeb, the

mountain of God. He entered a cave and there he spent the night (I Kings 19.2).

The parallelism with Mosaic tradition is explicit and intentional – Moses who spent forty days and forty nights on the mountain (Exod. 24.18), Moses who experienced his strange theophany as he sheltered in the crevice of a rock (Exod. 33.22). But if the parallelism is intentional, its effect is to heighten the contrast between Moses and Elijah. In response to Elijah's self-pitying explanation as to why he had fled far from the scene of action to this southern mountain of God, The answer came:

> Go and stand on the mount before the Lord. For the Lord was passing by: a great and strong wind came, rending mountains and shattering the rocks before him, but the Lord was not in the wind; and after the wind there was an earthquake, but the Lord was not in the earthquake; and after the earthquake fire, but the Lord was not in the fire (I Kings 19.11–12).

The Lord was not in the wind . . . not in the earthquake . . . not in the fire . . . *but he ought to have been*. Wind, earthquake and fire are recurring symbols of God's mysterious presence in many early narrative and poetic traditions in the Old Testament, not least in the Exodus traditions. The Lord had been in the wind, 'the strong east wind' that turned the sea-bed into dry land to enable the Hebrew slaves to escape from the pursuing Egyptian forces (cf. Exod. 14.21–23 and its poetic parallel in 15.8). The Lord had been in the earthquake. The Song of Deborah, one of the earliest poems in the Old Testament, describes the Lord coming to the aid of his people:

> O Lord, at thy setting forth from Seir,
> when thou camest marching out of the plains of Edom,
> earth trembled; the heavens quaked:
> Mountains shook in fear before the Lord, the lord of Sinai,
> before the Lord, the God of Israel (Judg. 5.4–5).

The Lord had been in the fire: in that bush, strangely on fire, yet not burned up, when Moses received his call (Exod. 3.2–3, cf. the symbolism of the 'smoking brazier and the flaming torch' in the narrative of the covenant with Abraham in Genesis 15.17). All accounts of what happened at Mount Sinai/Horeb speak in terms of fire: 'Mount Sinai was all smoking because the Lord had come down upon it in fire' (Exod. 19.18, cf. 24.17).

The mountain was ablaze with fire to the very skies: there was darkness, cloud and thick mist. When the Lord spoke to you from the fire you heard a voice speaking, but you saw no form: there was only a voice (Deut. 4.11–12, cf. 5.24).

And who better than Elijah to know from personal experience that the Lord was powerfully present in fire. In response to his prayer on Mount Carmel,

> . . . the fire of the Lord fell. It consumed the whole-offering, the wood, the stones and the earth, and licked up the water in the trench. When all the people saw it they fell prostrate and cried, 'The Lord is God, the Lord is God' (I Kings 18.38–39).

But now the Lord was *not* in the wind . . . *not* in the earthquake . . . *not* in the fire. If a voice had once spoken to the people from the fire, the fire was now dumb. It was as if the traditional symbols, which had once conveyed the reality of God's presence, had been emptied, left meaningless, no longer able to bear the burden of the reality of God's presence, no longer able to speak. But the Lord was not absent: He was there, his presence indicted by a phrase which most traditional English translations, including the RSV render 'a still small voice': the NEB has 'a low murmuring sound', the Good News Bible 'the soft whisper of a voice'. Behind these different renderings lies a strange Hebrew expression. The adjective differently rendered 'still', 'low', 'soft' (Heb. *dqh*) is nowhere else in the Old Testament used of sound. Usually it refers to a very fine material or cloth. The other key word in the phrase, the noun which it qualifies, (Heb. *dmmh*) is related to verbal forms which can either mean to be silent or to whisper. In Psalm 107.29 the word is used in the context of the stilling of a storm; in Job 4.16 it occurs as part of the description of a night vision which strikes dread into Job; an apparition looms before him and he hears 'the sound of a low voice' (NEB) or 'a voice out of the silence' (Good News Bible).[32] In I Kings 19.12 the phrase seems to be pointing to a kind of silence so intense that you can hear it; what S. Terrien has called 'the sound of utmost silence . . . the stillness which, by dramatic antithesis, may indeed be heard'.[33] It is in this intense silence that there comes a voice, the challenging, demanding voice of the Lord. We are not dealing here with the inner voice of conscience. This is not the description of a man turning away from the external God of nature to the God of his own inner soul. The intense silence is as much part of nature as wind, earthquake and fire. Nor is this, as has been claimed, the whispered word of the personal and spiritual God of the prophet replacing the nature mythology he has destroyed. Prophetic experience is never so described anywhere else in the Old Testament.[34] Terrien argues that Elijah at Horeb marks a turning point in Israel's spiritual pilgrimage and perception; 'it closed the era of theophany and relegated it to the realm of the unrepeatable past. At the same time it opened the era of prophetic vision when miracles of nature became miracles of character.'[35] This draws far too sharp a contrast between theophany and prophetic vision, nature and character. Rather than seeing the incident as a turning point in Israel's religious history, it is better to keep it firmly within its given context, the prophetic experience of Elijah. Gerhard von Rad has rightly drawn attention to the 'strange and effective contrast' between the silence and what preceded it, but he fails to press the theological significance of this insight.[36] On the one hand there is noise, turbulence, the power of wind, earthquake and fire; on the other what appears to be the exact antithesis, total silence. According to the narrative Elijah had reached a crisis point in his life. He had played his ace against what he believed to be paganism, only to find it trumped by Queen Jezebel. The fire of the Lord had fallen, but on the other side of momentary triumph, Elijah is gripped by despair. 'It is enough', he said 'now, Lord, take my life for I am no better than my fathers before me' (I Kings 19.4). The traditional symbols of the Lord's presence and activity no longer seemed to carry power or conviction. Where he had been taught to believe that the Lord was present, in wind, earthquake and fire, there he found him to be disturbingly absent. Yet the Lord was there in something that appeared to be totally different in character from what had hitherto been comfortingly familiar. The unexpected replaced the expected. The Lord's puzzling absence was the prelude to his surprising presence. Elijah does not stand alone at this point in Old Testament tradition. Some of the most hallowed symbols of God's presence with his people, whether verbal (e.g. a particular interpretation of God's relationship with his people) or visual (e.g. the temple at Jerusalem) had to be broken so that the people might find God anew. But it is hard to live with broken symbols, hard indeed to accept that the breaking of such hallowed symbols may be a necessary element in continuing faith.

6

AUTHORITY AND AUTHENTICITY – A PROPHETIC PROBLEM

From prophetic narratives we turn now to look at certain elements in the collections of logia attributed to the prophets. Rather than attempting a broad general survey of the material let us focus attention upon two sharply contrasting prophets, both of whom are either questioning assumptions built into the religious trad-itions of their day or are wrestling with perplexing problems which the challenge of events has produced:

1. *Amos* – the earliest prophetic voice to which any considerable collection of prophetic oracles is attributed, whose ministry was located in the northern kingdom of Israel in the middle of the eighth century BC.

2. *Habakkuk* – whose words speak to events impinging upon the southern kingdom of Judah in the last decade of the seventh century BC.

1. *Amos*

There are severe limitations surrounding what we may say with any certainty about Amos himself. He was a Judaean, from the hill town of Tekoa, a sheep breeder (Amos 1.1) and a 'dresser of sycamores' (7.14). Whether he was rich or poor, a man of standing in the community or a man who held any official religious function within the community, we do not know. His ministry was located in the northern kingdom of Israel, perhaps in and around Samaria and Bethel. How long it lasted, how or when it ended, are matters of speculation. All this is hardly surprising since as far as prophetic literature is concerned, 'the canonical interest lies in the message, not in the witness to the prophetic personality as such, even though this cannot remain altogether hidden.'[1] Further there is general agreement that the present book of Amos comes to us through a lengthy and varied redactional process, though the extent of such redaction and the conclusions to be drawn from it, are open to dispute.[2]

Certain things, however, can be said with reasonable certainty. Increasingly it is recognized that Amos is indebted to the social and religious traditions of his people; to the wisdom tradition,[3] to clan and family instruction, to liturgical material. The exodus, the wilderness wandering, the settlement in Canaan (2.9–10), the special relationship which exists between Yahweh and his people Israel (3.2), all these and more Amos takes for granted as basic assumptions to which he may appeal. Yet what makes Amos significant is not what he shares, but the extent to which he parts company from and challenges the assumptions built into the religious structures and ideology of his day. This is reflected in the literary form of the book. As H. W. Wolff puts it, 'The characteristic structure of Amos' oracles can be found in no older cultic curse, in no older form of the proclamation of the law, in no sapiential instruction. The new forms of his speech can be explained only by the new content of his message.'[4] In what does Amos' radical newness consist?

Basic to everything else Amos challenges the assumption that Israel the nation is to be identified with or can continue to function as the people of Yahweh. Amos is by no means the first voice in ancient Israel to proclaim a theology of judgment. Such a theology is, for example, expressed in the Song of Deborah in Judges 5 where a curse is called down upon one of the tribes

> because they brought no help to the Lord
> no help to the Lord and the fighting men (Judg. 5.23).

Likewise judgment had been a recurring feature in earlier prophetic preaching, for example in Nathan's seering words against David over his adultery with Bathsheba and his liquidation of Uriah (II Sam. 12.1–15), or in Elijah's confrontation with Ahab (I Kings 21.19–24). But such judgment had always operated hitherto within the framework of the continuing existence of the community. It had fallen on groups or individuals, or had been viewed as a general, but temporary chastisement. Amos goes further: he declares unequivocally 'the end' of the kingdom of Israel. This is the theme of his third and fourth visions in 7.7–8 and 8.1–2, each ending ominously with the common refrain 'never again will I pass them by' (7.8; 8.2). In the third vision, that of the plumb-line, Amos is made aware that Israel, like a wall, is off the straight. There is only one thing left to do, pull it down. In 8.1–2, the vision centres upon the ironic word-play involving the similarity in sound between the Hebrew word *qaîṣ* 'summer fruit' and *qēṣ* 'the end', which the New English Bible attempts to convey in English by the double use of the word ripe:

> This is what the Lord showed me: there was a basket of summer fruit, and he said, 'What are you looking at, Amos?' I answered, 'A basket of ripe summer fruit'. Then the Lord said to me, 'The time is ripe for my people Israel. Never again will I pass them by' (8.1–2).

The vision is then annotated by a verse which speaks of the lament of the keening women and the omnipresent silence of death. There is considerable evidence within the Old Testament for reform movements, which sought to reshape and renew the nation's life, both before and after Amos' time (see e.g. I Kings 15.9–15, the Elijah-Elisha traditions in I Kings 18–II Kings 13, Hezekiah's reform in II Kings 18, Josiah's reform in II Kings 22–23); there must have been in all ages priests, concerned about the misuse of forms of worship, seeking to instruct the people in what the demands of true worship were (cf. Pss. 15; 24; 119), but Amos is neither reformer nor corrective teacher. Central to the book of Amos, and visible through all later redactional attempts to modify it, there is a startling sombre message. The time for tinkering with, or making adjustments to, the social and religious structures is over. It is too late; the end has come. The way of Israel has led to death. All that remains is to sing the funeral dirge:

> Fallen no more to rise
> Is Virgin Israel.
> Forsaken with none to uplift her
> Prostrate she lies (5.2).[5]

Amos does not look at contemporary worship and conclude that it is sadly in need of liturgical renewal. He dismisses it in one damning word, 'rebellion' (Heb. *psh'*).

> Come to Bethel – and rebel.
> Come to Gilgal – and rebel the more (4.4).

Worship at the great cult centres may be deeply satisfying to its misguided devotees, but the Lord has already passed sentence, a sentence which Amos announces with studied irony and with a bitter play on words which no English translation can adequately convey:

> for Gilgal shall taste the gall of exile,
>   and Bethel (house of God) shall become nothing (5.5b),

the first line containing in Hebrew a fourfold repetition of the letters *gl*. Although Israel had not always listened to the prophetic word in the past and had on occasion attempted to silence the prophets (2.11–12), the prophet had, nonetheless, been the evident sign in the community that the Lord had something to say to his people (3.8); but no longer:

> The time is coming, says the Lord God,
>   when I will send famine on the land,
> not hunger for bread or thirst for water,
>   but for hearing the word of the Lord.
> Men shall stagger from north to south,
>   they shall range from east to west,
>   seeking the word of the Lord,
>   but they shall not find it, (8.11–12).[6]

What the people had chosen to ignore when present, they will soon search for in vain. An emphatic 'no' is being spoken against all that Israel had cherished or ought to have cherished.[7]

It is consistent with this theology of the end that Amos takes some of the accepted religious traditions of the people and by a process of prophetic reversal turns them from symbols of security into symbols of judgment. They speak no longer of hope but of coming doom.

(i) The election theme

The theme of the Lord's special relationship with Israel his people is fundamental to Old Testament tradition, whether it is expressed in terms of the patriarchal traditions, the exodus, or the giving of the land. Amos echoes it:

Hear this word which the Lord has spoken against you,
O children of Israel, against the whole family which I
    brought from the land of Egypt.
You alone have I known from among all the families of the
    earth . . . (3.1–2a)[8]

The word 'known' (Heb. *yd'*) in this context denotes the establishment of a relationship and comes very close to the idea of choosing
or selecting (cf. Jer. 1.5). The 'therefore' which immediately
follows this statement would be expected to lead into 'I will be
with you' (cf. 5.16) or 'I will be your God and you will be my
people'. The danger to which this theological insight is exposed
is that it can easily be transposed into an unconditional, reassuring
conviction that the Lord is the private patron deity of Israel, the
guarantor of Israel's continuing prosperity, the one who can be
depended upon to carry Israel safely across the storms of history.
Other communities and nations may perish, but Israel never.
Amos challenges this assumption in two ways:

(*a*) You alone have I known
        from among all the families of the earth,
    therefore I will punish you
        for all your iniquities (3.2).

The assertion of a special relationship between the Lord and Israel
is for Amos two-edged. It cannot be a doctrine of reassuring
comfort without at the same time being one of challenge and
threat. The punishment is not specified: it is enough for Amos to
declare that the God-initiated relationship into which Israel has
entered is no passport to undemanding privilege, but a summons
to responsibility, and responsibility ignored can only lead to
national disaster.

(*b*) The most 'radical and perplexing'[9] comment on the election
theme, however, is to be found in chapter 9.7–8a:

Are not you Israelites like Cushites to me?
    says the Lord.
Did I not bring Israel up from Egypt,
    the Philistines from Caphtor, the Aramaeans from Kir?
Behold I, the Lord God,
    have my eyes on this sinful kingdom,
and I will wipe it off the face of the earth.

This section, which in its attitude to other nations seems to go beyond anything explicitly affirmed in earlier sources, is no denial of the election theme – the Lord did bring Israel up out of Egypt. It is, however, a denial of the negative consequences which it was fatally easy to draw from this theme, namely that the Lord was concerned solely with Israel. Amos tears apart the exclusive, nationalistic wrappings of Israel's faith to affirm God's freedom and sovereignty as the lord of all nations, the controller of all history. Those who regarded themselves as belonging to 'the choicest of nations' (6.1) are compared with the distant Cushites, the negroid peoples who inhabited Nubia and the area south of Egypt, almost on the southern fringes of the universe as far as Israel was concerned (cf. Gen. 10.6; II Sam. 18.21; Isa. 20.3–5). The self-complacent pride of Israel is being deflated. The attack on an exclusivist interpretation of election is further pressed home by the statement that it was the Lord who brought the Philistines from Caphtor, i.e. Crete, and the Aramaeans from Kir in Mesopotamia. Philistines and Aramaeans had long been reckoned high on the list of Israel's enemies, and victories over them attributed to the Lord, and made the occasion for religious celebration (cf. 6.1–2). But the God with whom Israel deals, claims Amos, is not a God who is concerned only with that segment of human history which happens to involve Israel. He directs the movement of all nations, Philistines and Aramaeans as well as Israel. Thus he is spelling out a doctrine of divine sovereignty which must burst the bonds of any purely nationalistic distortion. Israel is being thrown out from the cosy comfort of her small self-built shelter into the more chilly air of a world which in its entirety is God's world. 'Amos thinks the rubrics of Yahweh's dealings with Israel out into the sphere of international history because of his fascination by the dimension of divine sovereignty in Israel's theological tradition. In doing so he is both heir and creator, bound and free. He stands within the theological tradition of Israel but understands it in such a way as to leave no room for the way in which his audience understood it.'[10]

(*ii*) Another clear illustration of Amos' reversal of current theological thinking is his handling of the theme of 'the day of the Lord' in 5.18–20. The origin of this 'day of the Lord' in Israel's tradition is uncertain.[11] By Amos' time, however, it seems to have been firmly established in the thinking of the people as an expression of all their hopes for a bright future under God, hopes which burned all the brighter when outward circumstances were oppressive, and which were probably given a prominent place in the worship of the community. Amos' attitude to this 'day of the Lord' and the expectations associated with it, is stark and uncompromising:

> Fools who long for the day of the Lord,
> what will the day of the Lord mean to you?
> It will be darkness, not light.
> It will be as when a man runs from a lion,
> and a bear meets him,
> or turns into a house and leans on the wall,
> and a snake bites him.
> The day of the Lord is indeed darkness not light,
> a day of gloom with no dawn (5.18–20).

Three times the phrase 'the day of the Lord' occurs in this passage: twice it is described as 'darkness, not light', once, in a parallel expression, as 'gloom with no dawn'. Every joyful expectation surrounding this day is being negated. When the Lord acts, it can only be in judgment, dark, inescapable judgment.

Apart altogether from this prophetic reversal theology, there are other examples in Amos of the prophet taking widely accepted ideas and giving them a new, radical interpretation. To take but two illustrations:

(a) In a recent study of *Amos's Oracles against the Nations*[12] John Barton has argued that what lies behind the judgment on the nations in Amos 1.3–2.5 is an appeal to generally recognized standards of international law, common to Israel and other nations in the Ancient Near East. What Amos does is to face Israel with the need to apply such standards to relationships within the community or face the dire consequences of failing to do so. On any interpretation of this section in Amos the climactic oracle against Israel in 2.6ff. must have come as a surprise and shock to Amos' listeners. To arraign and condemn other peoples at the bar of Yahweh's justice was popular and patriotic, but to include Israel among the condemned was to invite another response.

(b) In slightly different vein, but with similar effect, there are to be found in the book of Amos three brief passages usually referred to as 'doxologies', 4.13; 5.8–9a; 9.5–6. Stylistically these passages have all the marks of hymnic material. Almost all the verbs in them are in participial form – though this is seldom clear in English translation – and there is the echoing refrain 'Yahweh (or Yahweh of Hosts) in his name'. If the three passages are taken out of their present context and placed side by side, a strong case can be made out for regarding them as three stanzas of one hymn, a hymn which seems to build up to a climax in the longer third stanza.[13] The date and provenance of these doxological passages has been the subject of considerable dispute. Although there has been a tendency to attribute them to post-Amos redactional material, whether from the seventh-century Bethel cult or from the exilic or post-exilic period, there are no compelling arguments for assuming a late date. On stylistic grounds Amos' authorship is unlikely, but he may well have been using for his own prophetic purpose contemporary liturgical material well-known both to his listeners and to himself. One thing is clear; whatever the origin of these hymn fragments they have not been scattered haphazardly across the present book of Amos. Their present context, however, has not always been taken with sufficient seriousness as the clue to their interpretation.[14] In each case we are presented with a similar pattern. Chapter 4.4–5 contains a biting attack on the mockery which masquerades as worship at the great cultic centres of Bethel and Gilgal. Whatever men may think they are doing at such centres, they are in fact rebelling against God. There follows in verses 6–11 a series of brief statements each of which describes a warning sent by Yahweh, a warning which the people have ignored. The time for repentance is now over; Israel must prepare to meet her God (v. 12). The hymn fragment then celebrates the character of this God, who ominously controls all the forces in the universe and declares his intentions to man.[15] Chapter 5.5–6 similarly begins with an attack on the northern cultic centres of Bethel and Gilgal and on the southern pilgrim shrine of Beersheba, warning that these are the religious options which the nation must not choose. This leads into a solemn threat of judgment on social irresponsibility. The hymn fragment then celebrates the God of awesome and potentially destructive power. Chapter 9 begins with the vision of the destruction of the shrine, possibly the Bethel shrine. Grimly it then portrays disaster from which no one can escape, and leads into the hymn which speaks of God's power over all the forces in heaven and on earth. On each occasion the passage begins with the cult, questions its functioning within the community or declares judgment upon it, and then caps a judgment section by quoting a hymn which focusses attention upon the character of God, limitless in power and might, and potentially destructive. Liturgical material is here being used to raise critical questions about the way in which worship functions, or does not function, in Israel. It may be questioned whether the present shape of these sections goes back to Amos, or reflects to a greater or lesser extent a redactional process, but the general thrust of the argument is consistent with what we find elsewhere in authentic oracles of Amos – the prophet taking a radically new stance over against his people's traditions; in this case challenging his listeners to draw the correct conclusions from the liturgical material with which they are familiar.

The picture of Amos that has emerged so far is that of a man, undoubtedly familiar with the religious traditions of his people, yet alienated from them at least to the extent of questioning the way in which these traditions are being understood among his contemporaries. His theology of doom implies that he has parted company from many of the assumptions which dominate the religion of Israel in the mid-eighth century BC. He is a prophetic outsider, not simply because he comes to the north from Judah, but because of his radical critique of current theology and religious practice. But how did he come to hold such a theology, and how did he seek to validate its authenticity to himself and to others? It is tempting to respond to the first question by simply saying 'revelation'; this was the word of the Lord which came to him. But this, taken by itself, ignores the social context of Amos's ministry. The very extent to which he consciously seems to part company from contemporary attitudes reveals how deep these attitudes are embedded not only in his people's consciousness, but in his own. It is difficult to believe that his radical theological stance came overnight or without creating tensions in his own life. Any attempt to explore such issues involves taking a closer look at chapters 7.1–8.3. This section contains a series of four visions in parallel pairs. Visions one and two, 7.1–3 and 7.4–6, are similar in structure. Each begins with 'This was what the Lord showed me' and focusses upon an event – introduced by 'and behold' (Heb. $w^e hinn\hat{e}$) – in the first vision 'a swarm of locusts', in the second 'a rain of fire',[16] an event whose meaning is ominously clear to the prophet. The prophet intercedes on behalf of the people. The visions then end with 'The Lord relented and said "This (or 'this too') shall not happen".' Visions three and four, 7.7–9 and 8.1–3, have a different structure. Each begins, 'This is what the Lord showed me' (following the LXX at 7.7), each climaxes in 'never again will I pass them by'. At the heart of visions three and four, however, there is no event whose meaning is clear; instead there is an object which provokes a dialogue between the Lord and Amos. Out of this dialogue comes the significance in vision three of 'the plumb-line', and in vision four of 'the basket of summer fruit'. This neat structure of the two parallel pairs of visions is broken by the insertion between visions three and four of the account of an incident involving a clash between Amos and Amaziah, the priest of Bethel (7.10–17). This conflict narrative can hardly have been inserted at random; nor can its present position be explained purely by the appeal to the catchword principal, 'the house of Jeroboam' in verse 9 providing the link with the references to 'Jeroboam' in verse 10, particularly since verse 9 itself is probably an addition to the third vision. The location of this narrative is so obviously disruptive that there must be a strong reason for its insertion. The visions and the conflict narrative must be intended to be taken together and used to interpret each other, at least in the mind of the redactors of this section. In particular it is worth asking why it is that the conflict narrative is inserted immediately after vision three.[17]

There is little doubt that the four visions, succinct and highly stylized, have been gathered together at some stage in the process of editing the Amos material. Do they provide us with any information about Amos himself? It has been argued that the visions are no more than an imaginative literary creation, designed to underline what was believed to be the basic tenor of Amos' message, namely that although God was patient and ready to forgive, the nation had placed itself in a situation in which it faced the final exhaustion of that patience. Thus the visions form a dialogue leading to one conclusion; they are episodes in the one divine drama. 'Amos' intercessions (7.2, 5) are probably nothing more than devices to support the movement of this drama. They are made solely upon the stage of vision and require no correlation to events in Amos' private life or prophetic career.'[18] But it is hard to see why this drama of God's patience exhausted should be couched in the form of such visions – it is adequately represented elsewhere in the book in a much more natural form (cf. 4.7–12) – unless it has some point of contact with Amos' experience. At the opposite extreme it has been claimed that the visions show us

step by step how Amos, who began life as a cultic prophet,
upholding the religious establishment and interceding on behalf
of God's people, became under God a prophet of doom. Only
when he ceases to function officially within the cult – and this
step is reached in the third vision – is he banned from preaching
at Bethel.[19] There is, however, little evidence elsewhere to support
the view that Amos was ever a cultic prophet, nor is it necessary
to hold that Amos changed from being a cultic prophet, with a
message of salvation, into a prophet of doom, in order to see in
the visions a reflection of Amos' own experience.

Although in the conflict narrative Amos appeals to his commissioning by the Lord, 'the Lord took me as I followed the flock and
said to me, "Go and prophesy to my people Israel" ' (7.15), the
narrative is not *per se* a call narrative, nor is there anything in the
visions which would link them with Amos' call to be a prophet.
The visions make most sense, not in relationship to Amos' call
experience or to anything that may have happened prior to that
experience, but as reflecting issues which arose in the course of
the prophet's ministry.[20] Let us examine the visions more closely
in that light.

In the first vision Amos faced with coming disaster, the sign of
God's judgment upon a rebellious people, intercedes on behalf of
the people, 'O Lord God, forgive' (7.2). Such intercession is
widely recognized within the Old Testament as a normal
prophetic function (cf. Gen. 20.7; I Kings 13.5f.; Jer. 7.16; Ezek.
13.4f.). Had Amos been a cultic prophet it is likely that the grounds
of this appeal for forgiveness would have been the religious
traditions of the community with their emphasis upon the continuing graciousness of the Lord. In this vision, however, the plea is
made solely in the light of the weakness and vulnerability of the
people before God, 'What will Jacob be after this? He is so small'.
In response to this plea 'The Lord relented (or changed his mind)
and said, "This shall not happen" ' (7.3).[21] Does this constitute
forgiveness? Does forgiveness in this context merely mean that
the Lord is prepared to accept Israel's continuing existence even
in the midst of her rebelliousness?

In the second vision the prophet similarly intercedes, and on
the same grounds. But there is a significant change of vocabulary.
No longer is the plea, 'O Lord God, forgive', but 'O Lord God,
cease' (7.5). 'Cease' (Heb. *hdl*) is in no sense a valid synonym for
'forgive' (Heb. *slh*). It says nothing about what the Lord's attitude

to Israel is or ought to be. It merely asks the Lord to stop the terrifying fire from utterly consuming the land. Between visions one and two there may well have come to Amos the realization that the people were determined to close the door on any possibility of a renewed life with God based on divine forgiveness. The divine pleas,

Resort to me, if you would live, not to Bethel (5.5);

If you would live, resort to the Lord (5.6);

Seek good and not evil,
   that you may live,
that the Lord the God of Hosts may be firmly on your side,
   as you say he is (5.14);

had fallen on deaf ears. To continue to plead for forgiveness in such a situation was unrealistic: yet Amos apparently cannot yet bring himself to face the awesome truth that the end is at hand. He must still appeal to God, appeal for a stay of execution.

This reluctance to face that the end is at hand may account for the changed form of the third vision. No longer an event whose meaning is clear and unambiguous, but an object 'a plumb-line', the significance of which Amos has to be talked into seeing through a dialogue with the Lord:

The Lord said to me, 'What do you see Amos?' 'A plumb line', I answered, and the Lord said, 'I am setting a plumb line to the heart of my people Israel; never again will I pass them by' (7.8).

This 'never again will I pass them by', which similarly occurs at the climax of the fourth vision, finally closes the door on any possibility of forgiveness.[22] What H. W. Wolff has called 'the uniquely sombre message of Amos concerning the end of Israel'[23] now dominates the prophet's consciousness, and is dramatically confirmed by the fourth vision:

'What are you looking at, Amos?' I answered 'A basket of ripe summer fruit'. Then the Lord said to me, 'The time is ripe for my people Israel. Never again will I pass them by' (8.2).

It is at this point, immediately after the third vision, that the conflict narrative concerning Amaziah and Amos is inserted. Much, perhaps too much, attention has been focussed upon Amos' words in 7.14, 'no prophet I, nor son of a prophet'.[24] Let us

direct our attention instead to the overall purpose of the narrative
in 7.10–17. It is not merely a random fragment of prophetic
biography; not is it correct to claim that the centre of interest in
the story is on Amaziah rather than Amos, with the historical
episode being recorded solely as a lead into the prophetic oracle
concerning the fate of Amaziah in 7.16–17.[25] The narrative deals
with the issue of the authority with which the prophet speaks and
with his right to utter a particular prophetic message in a given
situation. Amaziah does not deny Amos' right to function as a
prophet. He invites, indeed orders, him to return to his home
territory of Judah and there exercise his prophetic ministry. What
he does deny is Amos' right to proclaim in the northern kingdom
of Israel a word which Amaziah characterizes as 'conspiracy'
(7.10) against the ruling dynasty, a word which declares the end
of the king and the nation. The offence is compounded in that this
word is spoken at the heart of the nations' religious life, the royal
sanctuary at Bethel. In response Amos can but claim the authority
of a divine commission: 'the Lord took me as I followed the flock
and said to me, "Go and prophesy to my people Israel" ' (7.15).
This claim is at once irrefutable and unprovable. But why is it that
the question of the authority with which Amos speaks becomes
an issue at this particular point? Precisely because Amos with his
preaching of the end is now proclaiming a word which runs
counter to all normal expectation of what a prophetic word ought
to be. To intercede on behalf of the people, to criticize certain
aspects of the national life or royal policy, is acceptable and
consistent with prophetic tradition, but to declare 'the end' is not.
T. W. Overholt has drawn attention to the fact that the question
of prophetic authority cannot be divorced from the social setting
in which the prophet functions.[26] Citing examples of prophetic
figures from the Paiuti Indians of Nevada, the Seneca tribe of the
Iriquois, and from New Guinea, he argues that 'it is the decision
of the people and not revelation, that is the crucial factor in their
functioning'.[27] Thus Amos too, in spite of his appeal to an
authority which transcends all human institutions, may well have
been only partially independent, since popular expectations about
the prophetic ministry would control the response he could elicit.
But does the problem not cut deeper? If the visions at all reflect
Amos' religious experience, then Amos in all probability began
his ministry sharing many of the popular expectations. He functions as intercessor in the first vision, and with modified hope in

the second. He himself is then caught between the normal paradigm of what constitutes a valid prophetic ministry and a divine commission which inexorably drives him on into hitherto uncharted water. Popular expectation and divine compulsion struggle within his own consciousness. Taken in conjunction with the visions, the narrative in 7.10–17 points to the inner conflict and personal tensions which grip Amos as he seeks to come to terms with his own identity as a prophet of doom and to communicate such a message to his contemporaries. The questioning which led him radically to reinterpret many of his people's religious traditions cannot be divorced from this inner struggle.

2. *Habakkuk*

The book of Habakkuk contains within itself some very curious contradictions. Twice in the book, in the editorial headings at 1.1 and 3.1, Habakkuk is described as 'the prophet', the only time this description is to be found in any book ascribed to a pre-exilic prophet. Such books are usually introduced by a phrase such as 'The word of the Lord which came to X son of Y' (cf. Hos. 1.1; Micah 1.1) or some other phrase indicating the coming of the prophetic word (cf. Isa. 1.1; Jer. 1.1), but never using the term 'the prophet'. But if Habakkuk is designated 'the prophet', there is much in the book which seems to point in a different direction. The key phrases 'Thus says the Lord' or 'oracle of the Lord' which in other prophetic books point to the prophet as a messenger of the Lord, are conspicuous by their absence in Habakkuk. Instead in chapter 1 we hear the 'How long, O Lord?' (1.2) and the repeated 'Why?' (1.3, 13, 14), the complaint and answer pattern, which is characteristic of the psalms of lament; and in chapter 3.2–15 there is a hymn which would have occasioned no surprise had it appeared among the psalms. One explanation of this 'the prophet' who does not speak like a prophet, but sounds more like a psalmist, is to assume that Habakkuk was a cultic prophet, part of the official religious establishment attached to the Jerusalem temple, exercising a prophetic role in the context of the worship of the community.[28] A great deal has been written about cultic prophets in ancient Israel and the relationship, if any, between them and major prophetic figures such as Amos, Isaiah, Jeremiah etc. The fact that a prophet like Jeremiah repeatedly clashed with 'the prophets' of the Jerusalem establishment and had some harshly critical things to say about them (e.g. Jer. 23.9ff.), does not mean that all cultic prophets were necessarily charlatans or religious sycophants. The book of Habakkuk is in fact all the more interesting if it gives us an insight into how the religious situation looked in Judah through the eyes of someone working from within the religious establishment. It reveals how faith, working from within certain main stream assumptions, tries to come to terms with the crisis situation of the day.

The background to the book is the closing decade of the seventh century BC. The Assyrian Empire had collapsed. To many of the small kingdoms in the Ancient Near East it seemed as if a dark shadow had been removed from their life. The prophet Nahum expressed the universal sense of relief and joy:

> Your wounds cannot be assuaged, your injury is mortal;
> all who have heard of your fate clap their hands in joy.
> Are there any who your ceaseless cruelty has not borne
> down? (Nahum 3.19)

Babylon and Egypt sought to fill the power vacuum, with the odds heavily in favour of Babylon. Although dreams of an Egyptian revival were to haunt the corridors of power in Jerusalem for many a year, and were ultimately to prove fatally illusory, the issue was decided in principle in the year 605 BC at the battle of Carchemish in north Syria. Babylon replaced Assyria as the scourge of the small states of the Ancient Near East. In spite of attempts to prove otherwise, the book of Habakkuk makes sense as the product of one prophetic personality, struggling to understand God's purpose in this period of international upheaval.[29]

The book begins with a typical complaint (1.2–3):

> How long, O Lord, have I cried to thee, unanswered?
> I cry 'Violence', but thou dost not save.
> Why dost thou let me see such misery,
> why countenance wrongdoing?

The prophet's complaint is about the society in which he lives, a society characterized by violence, by strife and social confusion, a society in which people ignore God's instruction, in which justice is a scarce commodity and the wicked flourish. It is a critique of society, which in its general theme any other prophet might have proclaimed. Behind the 'How long' and the 'Why's' there lies the conviction that the judgment of God must fall on such a community. The prophet's complaint is answered in verses 5–11. The Lord speaks to declare that he is about to act in a way that will stun an incredulous people. Judgment is coming in the shape of the conquering Babylonians, whose military juggernaut is scything its way across the world, crushing everything and everyone. Fair enough, replies Habakkuk; you are in control, Lord, you always have been; the Babylonians are your chosen instrument. But does this not leave a morally ambiguous situation? Is this not simply a classic illustration of using the devil to cast out the devil? You are supposed to be a God of awesome purity (v. 13), why then do you allow the power-drunk, ruthless Babylonians to do as they like?

> Why keep silent when they devour men more righteous than they? (v. 13)

The agent of God's judgment upon the wicked in Jerusalem, turns out to be none other than 'the wicked' who themselves deny justice to others. It is a world in which the righteous never seem to win – a crazy system which cries out for some explanation. And for an explanation the prophet is prepared to wait, to wait till God's word comes to him; only then will he know whether there is a satisfactory answer to his complaint. The pattern so far is clear. A question is raised, the answer given; the answer, satisfactory as far as it goes, immediately becomes the basis for a deeper question to which the prophet still awaits an answer.

'Then the Lord made answer:' so begins 2.2, and although the details of the answer are unclear because of some difficult textual problems in verses 2–4,[30] the main thrust of the argument is reasonably clear.

(a) There *is* an answer, an answer contained in a vision which the prophet is ordered to record. The meaning of this vision will one day be so crystal clear that every Tom, Dick and Harry will understand it. What the content of this vision is, we are not told. The Good News Bible by introducing verse 4 with the words 'and this is the message' assumes that the content of the vision is given in verse 4. But this is unlikely; verse 4 is pointing to the way in which people ought to act in the interim situation before the vision is made known.

(b) The answer is 'not yet'. It awaits the appointed time. It may seem slow in coming. Patience is required. The answer is for the moment hidden, the appointed time known only to God.

(c) Meanwhile the urgent questions centre not on God, on how or when he will act, but on man, on how he must live in this time of waiting. Waiting does not mean an inactive, passive acquiescence in whatever is going on. There are values for which, whatever the circumstances, men must be prepared to fight and live. The first line of verse 4 is difficult textually, though it is a reasonable assumption that it stands in contrast to the second line; hence the Good News Bible 'Those who are evil will not survive' and the New English Bible 'The reckless will be unsure of himself'. Over against the man who is 'evil' or 'reckless' 'the righteous man will live by his faith/faithfulness' (2.4b) a statement destined to have a long and varied history of interpretation.[31] Paul uses it, following the Greek text of Habakkuk, in both Romans and Galatians (Rom. 1.17; Gal. 3.11) in the context of contrasting man's futile attempt to put himself in the right with God by what he does, by 'the works of the law', with the grace of God offered in the gospel to which a man responds in faith, in trust. But such an antithesis is not implied in the original context in Habakkuk. The Hebrew word translated faith/faithfulness, *emûnāh*, carries a wide range of meanings in the Old Testament, but not faith in the sense of believing or trusting.[32] Steadfastness, steadiness, firmness often seem to underlie its usage. The word occurs, for example in the well-known picture of the coming kin in Isaiah 11.5:

> Righteousness shall be the girdle of his waist,
> And faithfulness the girdle of his loins,

which the Good News Bible simplifies into 'He will rule his people with justice and integrity'. 'Integrity' is defensible as a translation since it points to the quality in the coming king which will ensure that his actions are consistent and dependable, unlike those of the weak, vacillating monarch with whom the prophet had to deal. In context in Habakkuk 2.4, faithfulness is a more adequate translation than faith. Given that God's answer to the perplexing questions of the day is 'not yet' what must God's people do? When what is happening in the world seems meaningless and threatening, when rampant evil seems to terrorize the world, the true worshipper of God must hold on. He must firmly close the door in the face of despair. There may not seem to be any meaning, but meaning there must be. One day all will be clear. Meanwhile, says Habakkuk, the man who is in a right relationship with God will maintain his integrity, remain faithful, and never give up.

In this threefold response to the situation of crisis, (*a*) there is an answer, (*b*) the answer is not yet, (*c*) meanwhile hold on – we see the seed out of which a fully developed apocalyptic theology was in due course to be born. But it is wrong to assume that Habakkuk is a late apocalyptic work. Certain characteristic features of apocalyptic are missing. Habakkuk has not yet drawn a sharp line between this present age of struggle and darkness and the totally new coming age which God will inaugurate, nor does he employ any esoteric symbols or numbers which would encourage speculation as to the when of that new age. Rather he is struggling to maintain faith in God in a world where questions cannot be avoided unless men are prepared to bow down before naked power.

Does this then mean that Habakkuk is simply shutting his eyes, hoping for the best, keeping his spiritual fingers crossed? Not at all: there are certain theological convictions from which he refuses to depart:

(*i*) *The reality of judgment*

The mills of God may grind exceeding slow, but Habakkuk is convinced that they do grind. In 2.6b–17 we find four passages each beginning with the phrase 'Woe to him who. . . .' and each containing, explicitly in three instances, and implicitly in one, a declaration of judgment (cf. Isa. 5.8, 11, 18, 20, 22, where the NEB renders the same Hebrew 'Shame on you').

(*a*) 6b–8: Woe to the oppressor, he himself will one day be on the receiving end of oppression.

(*b*) 9–11: Woe to whoever seeks security through greed and power; such security is wholly illusory.

(*c*) 12–14: Woe to the exploiter; the world hinges not on exploitation, but on 'the glory of the Lord'. The logic of judgment is not so clear in this section and for this reason, among others, many modern commentators, think that verse 17 should be transferred to come immediately after verse 14, as an effective contrast to verse 12. This is not strictly necessary. Judgment is implicit in the sharp contrast between what men do, and what God does and will do.

(*d*) 15–17: Woe to him who degrades others; he will end up in degradation.

In the concluding section of the chapter, verses 18–20, a 'woe' is contained within a typically satirical attack on idols and those who worship them, (cf. Jer. 10.1–16; Isa. 41.18ff.; 44.9ff.). In all cases in the Old Testament such attacks have one primary purpose, to underline the essential character of Israel's God, as a living, active God, in contrast to the powerless nonentities whom other nations worship. Such gods are always satirized as being utterly devoid of life or breath (Heb. *ruaḥ*), the dynamic, life-giving energy which called creation into being and characterizes the control that Israel's God exercises over all history (cf. Gen. 1.2; Isa. 40.7). In worship Israel is in touch with this living God:

> But the Lord is in his holy temple;
> let all the earth be hushed in his presence (2.20).

For Habakkuk the reality of judgment corresponds to the reality of God. He is not thinking in abstract terms about inevitable laws of retribution operating in the world. He is talking about the certainty of judgment given the fact that this is God's world, still and always under his control. A resounding 'no' is being said to human exploitation, oppression, degradation and pride because the true character of the world is to be revealed when 'the earth shall be full of the knowledge of the glory of the Lord as the waters fill the sea' (2.14, cf. Isa. 11.9).

(ii) The Transcendent God

Chapter 3 contains liturgical material, as is evident from the liturgical rubrics found at the beginning and the end of the chapter (vv. 1, 19), rubrics similar to those found in many of the headings to the Psalms, and from the echoing 'selah' found at the end of verse 3, 9 and 13 (cf. Ps. 4 etc.). Central to the chapter is a powerful hymn (vv. 2–15) celebrating the majesty and the greatness of God, who came and comes to his people. Although the text is at points very difficult,[33] not least since the hymn seems to draw upon ancient mythological material, the precise details of which is not always clear, the overall significance of the hymn is clear. It divides into three sections:

(a) *Introduction* (v. 2) – an appeal to the past as the ground for present hope (cf. Ps. 44). Act again, O Lord, as you have acted in the past, so that we may discover anew your compassion.

(b) *God's coming* (vv. 3–7) – God comes from his southern home (cf. Judg. 5.4); his glory, awesome in power and splendour, fills the universe; nature and man tremble before him.

(c) *The 'why' of God's coming* (vv. 8–15). Beginning with the picture of God's conflict with 'rivers' and 'sea', the traditional forces of chaos in Ancient Near Eastern mythology, this section culminates in the declaration of God's sovereignty over all the forces which shape life and history (vv. 12) a sovereignty revealed in Israel's history as God's saving concern for his people.

To attempt to summarize this hymn is virtually to destroy it. To take it out of its context in worship is to rob it of its power. It is the language of devotion clothed in evocative poetry. It is the language of a great mediaeval cathedral soaring heaven-wards, pointing to the transcendent God. It is, of course, no coldly logical answer to the questions with which the prophet wrestles, but it is the point of reference without which there is neither answer nor problem. For the problem is precisely how to hold together this transcendent mystery and the grim power of evil, with its threat of meaninglessness. The problem could have been eased by denying this transcendent mystery. That Israel did not take this way out, it owed not primarily to its theologians or its thinkers, but to worship, to worship which, whatever its defects, refused to trivialize God.

(iii) *The meaning of faith (vv. 16–19)*

The chapter concludes by describing the prophet's response to this God who is present in worship. The response is twofold:

(a) there is a trembling, shuddering sense of awe, which makes it possible, indeed reasonable, to wait quietly for this God to act in judgment.

(b) there is an exultant cry of faith, which comes close to the experience of the author of Psalm 73.[34] Suppose there are no immediate signs of faith being vindicated in the confused pattern of events, what then?

> Although the fig-tree does not burgeon,
> the vines bear no fruit,
> the olive crop fails,
> the fold is bereft of its flock
> and there are no cattle in the stalls,
> yet I will exult in the Lord
> and rejoice in the God of my deliverance (3.17–18).

Recall for a moment the ending of one of the wisdom psalms we looked at, Psalm 144.[35] Happy are we . . . it declares,

Our barns are full and furnish plentiful provision;
our sheep bear lambs in thousands upon thousands;
the oxen in our fields are fat and sleek;
there is no miscarriage or untimely birth,
no cries of distress in our public places.
Happy are the people in such a case as ours;
happy are the people who have the Lord for their God
    (Ps. 144.13–15).

Happy am I . . . claims Habakkuk; the barns are empty, the crops
have failed, the fold is bare: happy am I, I still have the Lord as my
God, and that is the true and indestructible reason for rejoicing.

The vindication of faith lies in faith itself. But that certainty only
comes to those who have questioned and discarded the meritri-
cious trappings in which faith is often decked.[36]

7

VOCATIONAL CRISIS – THE
WITNESS OF JEREMIAH

We have already noted that behind the outward assurance of
Amos's sombre theology of doom there probably lies an inner
struggle. The probability of such a prophetic spiritual and mental
turmoil becomes a certainty when we come to Jeremiah, whose
ministry spanned the last forty fateful years of the kingdom of
Judah. Within the present book of Jeremiah there are a series of
passages which have been varyingly called his 'Confessions', his
'Personal Diary', his 'Laments and Complaints'. Although voices
have been raised in recent years arguing that these passages are
liturgical and/or late additions to the text, which tell us nothing
about Jeremiah's inner struggle,[1] J. Bright is still justified in
insisting that however much these passages may employ conventional, cultic forms and language such as we find in the psalms of
lament, 'we are forced to see behind the conventional forms a
prophetic individual persecuted because of the word, suffering
mental and physical anguish, and lashing out at his persecutors
– and God'.[2] The passages which throw light on Jeremiah's stormy
pilgrimage are: 11.18–23; 12.1–6; 15.10–21; 17.14–18; 18.18–23 and
20.7–18. In view of the complex problems which are raised by the
book of Jeremiah in its present form, it is impossible to assign
such passages with any degree of certainty to any particular
period in Jeremiah's ministry. It has been suggested that such
personal memoirs must come from the middle period of the
prophet's life; when he had been a prophet long enough to face
disillusionment, but before he became deeply involved in the
national crisis which led to the destruction of Jerusalem in 587 BC,

since, when we look at the activities of Jeremiah in the reign of
Zedekiah, the last king of Judah, we are seeing 'a man for whom
inner struggles are over'.[3] But outward courage and assurance
are compatible with inner turmoil and doubt. It is possible that
Jeremiah never fully resolved the tensions which surface in these
passages. Throughout a career that lasted over forty years, if the
editorial introduction to the book correctly gives the date of his
call,[4] Jeremiah seems to have been involved in conflicts which in
his case 'inevitably led to self-interrogation, a situation far more
agonising than all other battles. This inner struggle forced the
prophet to ask whether the voice he "heard" was not the sound
of thunder, the vision of a nightmare . . . the prophet could not
escape the inner doubts forced upon him by the unbelieving
populace, his disagreeing and often disagreeable colleagues, and
a God who refused to be a slave even to his own word.'[5]

Every attempt to schematize the material in these passages of
self-interrogation runs into trouble since part of the fascination of
it lies in the variety of its emphasis and insight. There are,
however, certain recurring themes, notably a strong sense of
failure. The initial hesitation which Jeremiah voiced when the call
came to him 'I do not know how to speak; I am only a child' was
countered by words of commanding assurance, '. . . you shall go
to whatever people I send you and say whatever I tell you to say'
(1.7). So he went and he spoke the word given to him. His
expectation seems to have been rather different from that ascribed
to Isaiah in the context of his call:

> This people's wits are dulled,
> their ears are deafened and their eyes are blinded,
> so that they cannot see with their eyes,
> nor listen with their ears
> nor understand with their wits,
> so that they may turn and be healed (Isa. 6.10).

Certainly in Jeremiah's case there was no stoical acceptance of a
response which breathed suspicion, misunderstanding, open
hostility and indifference:

> Alas, alas, my mother, that you ever gave me birth!
> A man doomed to strife, with the whole world against me.
> I have borrowed from no one, I have lent to no one,
> yet all men abuse me (15.10).

Violently he protests to the Lord about the unacceptable reward
he has received for proclaiming the word given to him:

> I have become a laughing stock all the day long,
> Everyone mocks me.
> Whenever I cry out I must needs cry out
> and proclaim violence and destruction.
> I am reproached and mocked all the time
> for uttering the word of the Lord (20.7b–8).

This mockery has its roots in the fact that to many of his contemporaries Jeremiah must have seemed a classic illustration of a
failed, false prophet. If he began preaching a message, which had
in it the note of doom upon Judah and Jerusalem, from about 627
BC, then twenty five years later nothing had happened except that
the city, having purged its conscience in a national reformation
under king Josiah in 621 BC (cf. II Kings 22.23), seemed more
politically self-confident and more spiritually complacent than it
had ever been. What clearer illustration could there be of the
Deuteronomic test: 'When a word spoken by a prophet in the
name of the Lord is not fulfilled and does not come true, it is not
a word spoken by the Lord. The prophet has spoken presump-
tuously; do not hold him in awe' (Deut. 18.22). And they didn't.
People say to me, protests Jeremiah:

> Where is the word of the Lord?
> Let it come, if it can . . . (17.15).

It is hard to live with such a sense of failure particularly when
the failure is evident in the response of those who might well
have been expected to show some sympathy or understanding.
Those whom he regarded as his friends sought to stab him in the
back:

> . . . I heard many whispering,
> 'Denounce him! We will denounce him.'
> All my friends were on the watch for a false step,
> saying, 'Perhaps he may be tricked, then we can catch him
> and take our revenge' (20.10).

Although the New English Bible deletes after 'whispering' the
phrase 'Terror all around' (Heb. *māgôr-missābîb*) it is possible
that this phrase was a cliché in the prophet's preaching which
certain people applied to him sarcastically as a nickname. Jeremiah

had applied the phrase to Pashur, the temple guardian of law and order, who had had Jeremiah flogged and put into stocks for prophesying the downfall of the nation (20.3). The words were hurled back derisively at the prophet himself: here comes old 'Terror all around'; at it again, and nothing ever happens (cf. 6.25). The atmosphere of hostility and suspicion was there at times even within his own family circle:

> All men, your brothers and kinsmen, are traitors to you,
> they are in full cry after you:
> trust them not, for all the fine words they give you (12.6).

There is good reason to believe that his sense of failure was compounded the longer his ministry lasted. If, as seems likely, he had at one time placed high hopes in the reformation of 621 BC, he was soon to be disillusioned. An enlightened statute book, a purified temple; but a people who remained the same . . . or worse. In 3.6–10 Israel and Judah are compared to two sisters, both of them harlots. Israel the Lord had divorced but Judah learned nothing from that example:

> In spite of all this that faithless woman, her sister Judah, has
> not come back to me in good faith, but only in pretence (3.10).

This coming back 'only in pretence' makes most sense as the prophet's verdict on the outcome of Josiah's reformation. Post-reformation euphoria, allied to a theology with roots in the inviolability of Mount Zion and the temple[6] and a belief in an everlasting covenant between the Lord and the Davidic royal family, proved an effective barrier against the prophet's words. He failed . . . and he knew it.

Closely related to this experience of failure was an awareness of *loneliness*. That this should be part of his agony is hardly surprising when we consider the extent to which he felt alienated from the main stream religious attitudes of the day, and from the political aspirations of the community. You do not openly attack the temple (7.1–15) and get invited to the Jerusalem priests' fraternal; you do not walk through the streets of Jerusalem advocating desertion to the enemy and then go for a drink in the officers' mess. Jeremiah seems to have realized that such loneliness was part of the inevitable cost of his prophetic vocation:

> I have never kept company with any gang of roisterers,
>   or made merry with them;

Because I felt thy hand upon me I have sat alone;
  for thou has filled me with indignation (15.17).

Although a comparison is sometimes made with Psalm 26.4–5 where the Psalmist protests:

I have not sat among (or kept company with) worthless men,
  nor do I mix with hypocrites.
I hate the company of evildoers,
  and will not sit among the ungodly,

the comparison simply points up the difference. The Psalmist sees himself as one of the righteous, the true worshippers of God, washing his hands of all who threaten the faithful; in Jeremiah's case his sitting alone is the consequence of his commitment to his prophetic ministry, 'because I felt thy hand upon me I have sat alone'. By a society which he declared unacceptable to God he was not accepted. There are those who can come to terms with loneliness, who can be almost coldly analytical in their detachment from other people, but the passionate and intense imagery and language which Jeremiah uses do not suggest that this was his nature. In the words

. . . I have sat alone,
  for thou has filled me with indignation

we may well be hearing the hurt cry of a man who longed to be accepted, but was not prepared to pay the price of such acceptance.

There is another personal factor the full effects of which we can only surmise.

The word of the Lord came to me: You shall not marry a wife; you shall have neither son nor daughter in this place. For these are the words of the Lord concerning sons and daughters born in this place, the mothers who bear them and the fathers who beget them in this land: When men die, struck down by deadly ulcers, there shall be no wailing for them and no burial; they shall be like dung lying upon the ground. When men perish by sword or famine, their corpses shall become food for birds and for beasts (16.1–4).

Even if the hand of later Deuteronomic editing is to be seen in the language of this prose passage, 'the passage by its very nature has autobiographed data at its heart'.[7] Jeremiah's renunciation of marriage was part of his prophetic vocation and an act of prophetic symbolism. He was dramatically communicating his message. Marriage was not optional in ancient Israel; it was arranged by family negotiation, obligatory, if for no other reason, to continue the family name into the future. Jeremiah's celibacy noticeably marked him off from other men. It was a break with the conventions of the society in which he lived. It was almost certainly done with the same intent as we find in Ezekiel's strange conduct when his wife died:

> These were the words of the Lord to me: Man, I am taking from you at one blow the dearest thing you have, but you must not wail or weep or give way to tears. Keep in good heart, be quiet and make no mourning for the dead; cover your head as usual and put sandals on your feet. You shall not cover your upper lip in mourning nor eat the bread of despair (Ezek. 24.15–17).

In other words, ignore all the social conventions which surround the public proclamation of mourning, in order to invite the question 'why'? And when people automatically asked Ezekiel that question, it became the occasion for his proclaiming a word concerning the coming destruction of temple and community and a consequent greater mourning. Jeremiah's renunciation of marriage was a similar prophetic sign declaring 'there is no future for this community'. To commit yourself to a course of action in obedience to the Lord does not, however, exempt you from the personal consequences of such action. Jeremiah's celibacy must have intensified his loneliness, his sense of alienation from the community around him. It is arguably one of the psychological factors behind the outbursts of vindictiveness and bitterness which are one of the most marked features of the confessional passages. The most bitter such passage is 18.21–23 where Jeremiah prays to the Lord for vengeance on his opponents:

> . . . give their sons over to famine,
>   leave them at the mercy of the sword.
> Let their women be childless and widowed,
>   let death carry off their men.
> Let their young men be cut down in battle.
> Bring raiders upon them without warning,
>   and let their screams of terror ring out from their houses.

For they have dug a pit to catch me,
   and have hidden snares for my feet.
Well thou knowest, O Lord,
   all their murderous plots against me.
Do not blot out their wrongdoing
   or annul their sin;
when they are brought stumbling into thy presence,
   deal with them on the day of thy anger (cf. 12.3; 15.15;
17.17–18; 20.11–12).

We have already noted that such cursing of the enemy is a feature of some of the psalms of lament; but the fact that we find in such passages in Jeremiah conventional forms and at times stereotyped language does not mean that such experience is unreal. Personal experience can clothe itself in conventional forms. The intensity of denunciation in such passages probably corresponds to the intensity of the prophet's commitment and the depths of his loneliness.

Peter Berger, discussing the secularizing pressures which play upon the theologian today, says, 'Unless our theologian has the inner fortitude of a desert saint, he has only one effective remedy against the threat of cognitive collapse in the face of these pressures. He must huddle together with like-minded fellow deviants – and huddle very closely. Only in a counter community of considerable strength does cognitive deviance have a chance to maintain itself. This counter community provides continuing therapy against the creeping doubt as to whether after all one may not be wrong and the majority right.'[8] The desert saint is hardly an Old Testament concept; for Jeremiah there seems to have been no 'counter community of considerable strength' – and there is evidence that Jeremiah went to the very brink of cognitive and spiritual collapse.

This collapse took several forms:

(*i*) We find Jeremiah in the grip of moods of deep personal despondency. The dark shadow of failure seemed to blight his life. This surfaces in its most dramatic form in 20.14–18 where the prophet calls down a curse. Again it is interesting to note that although the curse is not uncommon in the psalms of lament, there is no curse in such psalms remotely similar in content to this curse.

A curse on the day when I was born!
Be it forever unblessed,
   the day my mother bore me!
A curse on the man who brought word to my father,
'A child is born to you, a son',
   and gladdened his heart!
That man shall fare like the cities
   which the Lord overthrew without mercy.
He shall hear cries of alarm in the morning
   and uproar at noon,
because death did not claim me before birth,
   and my mother did become my grave,
      her womb great with me for ever.
Why did I come forth from the womb
   to know only sorrow and toil,
      to end my days in shame?

This 'before birth death wish' is very uncharacteristic in the Old Testament. Life comes as God's gift, a gift to be enjoyed and lived to the full. Even the author of Psalm 22 in the dark night of his soul, surrounded by scorn and abuse, draws strength from remembering:

But thou art he who drew me from the womb,
   and laid me at my mother's breast.
Upon thee was I cast at birth;
   from my mother's womb thou hast been my God
      (Ps. 22.9–10).

The only parallel to Jeremiah's cry in the Old Testament is to be found in Job 3, in a passage which may well have been influenced by Jeremiah's words:

perish the day when I was born,
and the night which said, 'A man is conceived'!
May that day turn to darkness; may God above not look for it,
nor light of dawn shine on it. (Job 3.3).

   . . .

Why was I not stillborn,
why did I not die when I came out of the womb?
Why was I ever laid on my mother's knees
or put to suck at her breasts?
Why was I not hidden like an untimely birth,
like an infant that has not lived to see the light?

For then I should be lying in the quiet grave,
asleep in death, at rest . . . (Job 3.12, 13, 16).

Why should a man be born to wander blindly?
hedged in by God on every side? (Job 3.23)

Such 'whys' are wrung from a man who like Jeremiah, though for different reasons, feels that he has reached the end of his tether. There is deep despondency in Jeremiah's curse, but also an element of defiance as if he were shaking an angry fist at God as he screams 'why?'. His whole life seemed on the point of collapse; the spiritual resources which had carried him so far had vanished, and he was left with apparently nothing. Such moods were almost certainly involuntary. Dietrich Bonhoeffer has left us a vivid description of something similar, which he calls a spiritual trial: 'Quite suddenly . . . the peace and placidity which had been a mainstay hitherto began to waver, and the heart, in Jeremiah's expressive phrase, becomes that defiant and despondent thing one cannot fathom. It is like an invasion from outside, as though evil powers were trying to deprive one of life's dearest treasures.' Bonhoeffer adds 'But it is a wholesome experience which helps one to a better understanding of human life.'[9] Presumably Jeremiah reached a similar conclusion, or at least learned to live with such experiences since he sustained a ministry which lasted for forty difficult years.

(*ii*) There is, however, another level of Jeremiah's experience in which we find him consciously and self-reflectively raising questions about the meaning of his relationship with God, opening the door to doubts which the bitter ambiguity of his ministry forced him to face.

(*a*) The apparent failure of his ministry and the all-too-obvious success of those who defied or ignored the word of the Lord on his lips, raised for him the issue of why, in a God-ordered world, such things should happen. This problem is aired in 12.1–6. It begins with the language of the law court. Jeremiah has a perplexing case which he wishes to bring for decision before the Divine Judge, who he knows must be righteous, i.e. who can be depended upon to give right decisions: why, he says

Why do the wicked prosper
and traitors live at ease? (12.1)

He holds God directly responsible for this situation, since God allows them to flourish:

> Thou has planted them and their roots strike deep,
>   they grow up and bear fruit (12.2),

hypocrites though they are.[10] Then pleading his own innocence and devotion he demands that the wicked be condemned:

> Drag them away like sheep to the shambles;
>   set them apart for the day of slaughter (12.3).

If verse 4 is in its correct context – and many commentators doubt this[11] – Jeremiah backs up his case by appealing to the sad plight of the drought-stricken nation, being ruined by such irresponsible people who pursue their evil ways and claim that 'God will not see what we are doing'.

It is important to recognize that when Jeremiah makes his complaint about the prosperity of the wicked he is not raising a general theoretical issue. He is not inviting God to enter into a philosophical discussion on the problem of evil in the world, nor is he looking for a demonstrable intellectual answer to this problem. Gerard Manley Hopkins captures the spirit of the passage when he renders:

> Thou art indeed just, Lord, if I contend
> With thee; but, Sir, so what I plead is just
> Why do sinners' ways prosper? and why must
> Disappointment all my endeavour end?[12]

The prophet is raising a sharply personal question. The 'wicked' are those who ignore the Lord and the word of the Lord on the prophet's lips. Instead of wilting under divine judgment, they prosper; while the prophet, strenuously striving to remain faithful to his divine commission, makes no impact at all. What is at stake is the meaning and effectiveness, if any, of the prophet's ministry. Only this interpretation makes any sense of the answer which the prophet is given in verse 5:

> If you have raced with men and the runners have worn you
>   down,
>   how then can you hope to vie with horses?
> If you fall headlong into easy country,
>   how will you fare in Jordan's dense thickets?

It is unnecessary to try to find in these words any veiled references to Jeremiah's conflicts with other prophets (cf. 23.12 where such prophets are said to 'run') or to the impending threat of Babylonian occupation as a harsher reality than that which the prophet has yet faced. The meaning of both the pictures sketched in this verse is clear. If you think the going is hard at present, and just cause for complaint, says the Lord to Jeremiah, then you better be prepared for it getting harder. Jordan's dense thickets or jungle growth was the home of marauding lions who struck at the flocks in the open hill country around (cf. 49.14; 50.44) – a fit symbol of danger as opposed to the comparative security of the easy, open countryside. Cheer up, says the Lord in effect to Jeremiah, the worst is yet to be. There is greater threat coming to you, including a threat from an unexpected quarter, from within your own family circle (v. 6). If this seems cold comfort it nevertheless penetrates to what lies behind Jeremiah's initial question. Faced with seeming failure, the prophet is wrestling with the question 'Is it worth continuing?'. Yes, comes the reply, you must, you will continue, knowing that you are going to have to swim in even more troubled waters. [13]

(*b*) That answer, however, has built into it the assumption that, in spite of appearances, the Lord can be trusted. But can he? One section in the confessions (15.15–18) which begins with a cry for vengeance then moves into self-justification, ends with the words:

> Why then is my pain unending,
>> my wound desperate and incurable?
> Thou art to me like a brook which is not to be trusted,
>> whose waters fail (15.18).

There is a very poignant and almost despairing undertone in these words. If we look at some of the themes in Jeremiah's early preaching – assuming these to be preserved in the early chapters of the book – we find the prophet persistently attacking the futility of people worshipping any other God than the Lord, the God of Israel. All other deities are powerless nonentities. One of the most striking ways in which he draws this contrast between the one true God and all other false gods is to be found in 2.13, where he depicts the Lord accusing the people of two evils:

> They have forsaken me,
>> a spring of living water,

and they have hewn out for themselves cisterns,
      cracked cisterns that can hold no water.

In a land of uncertain rainfall the storage of water for irrigation
and other purpose (cf. Eccles. 2.6) is essential; but to store water
in cracked cisterns is an exercise in futility. The water drains
away, and when water is most needed the cistern is mockingly
empty – fit symbol for the futility of other gods who cannot satisfy
the needs of their worshippers. The truly fortunate community is
one which has access to a continuous, dependable supply of
running water, bubbling forth from a spring, 'a spring of living
waters' – fit symbol for the dependable God of Israel's faith. But
suppose this trustworthy 'spring of living water' turns out to be:

           like a brook that is not to be trusted,
              whose waters fail

like one of these Palestinian wadis or gorges down which water
runs in the rainy season, but which are totally dry in the heat of
summer when the traveller is in most need of water? To put it in
other words, what happens if you reach the point where what
you have been most confidently preaching to others about the
reality of God, no longer makes sense in your own experience?
Accept cognitive collapse, pack in . . . or what?

    This was the Lord's answer
              If you will turn back to me, I will take you back
                 and you shall stand before me.
              If you choose noble utterance and reject the base,
                 you shall be my spokesman.
              This people will turn again to you,
                 but you will not turn to them
              To withstand them I will make you impregnable,
                 and a wall of bronze.
              They will attack you but they will not prevail,
                 for I am with you to deliver you
                    and save you, says the Lord;
              I will deliver you from the wicked,
              I will rescue you from the ruthless (15.19–21).

This passage ends with a promise, with the confident assertion
that Jeremiah's ministry will not only continue, but will be fruitful.
The promise, is, however, conditional, and the conditional element is interesting:

If you turn back to me, I will take you back . . .

The Hebrew word rendered 'turn back' is the verb *shûbh*, which may be variously rendered 'turn', 'return' or 'repent' in the sense of doing a right-about turn in attitude. Jeremiah 3–4.2 contains a series of linked passages, all of which use or play upon difference nuances of this word *shûbh*. The impossibility of a wife, once divorced and remarried, 'returning' to her first husband is used to stress the difficulty of a faithless people 'turning back' to God (3.1–5): there is the pretence 'return' of faithless Judah who had apparently learned nothing from the fate of apostate (literally 'turned away') Israel (3.6–11): a moving appeal is made to 'turned away' Israel to 'turn back' to a God whose nature is love unfailing (3.12–13), a theme which is to be further developed at a later date in verses 14–18. Against the background of Israel's infidelity:

> . . . like a woman who is unfaithful to her lover,
> so you, Israel, were unfaithful to me (v. 20),

a further appeal is made;

> Come back to me, wayward sons;
> I will heal your apostacy (v. 22),

with forms of the root *shûbh* being used in 'come back', 'wayward' and 'apostacy'. The opening verses of chapter 4 emphasize what is involved in any genuine return:

> If you will but come back, O Israel,
> if you will but come back to me, says the Lord . . . (4.1);

such a return must involve a radical break with the worship of other gods, and a realignment of life which will express itself in the great prophetic demands of justice and righteousness.

This whole section, however much it may have been reshaped and edited by other hands, must preserve an important element in Jeremiah's own preaching. He had again and again called on his people to 'turn', now the same word is directed against him in an implied rebuke. He is being told that he is not exempt from the demands of the message he proclaims to others:

> If you will turn back to me, I will take you back . . . (15.19).

When Jeremiah calls on the people to turn, it is usually to turn back from the worship of other gods, from apostacy, from dabbling in religious practices which are inconsistent with the true

worship of the Lord. But from what has Jeremiah to turn? This is
not at all clear from the passage. Is the reference back to the bitter
words of verse 18, i.e. only if you turn from self-indulgent pitying
and despair, will you be restored to be my spokesman? Is the
charge that he had given up too soon, too easily? Or is the clue to
be found in the immediately following words:

> If you choose noble utterance and reject the base,
> you shall be my spokesman?

But that simply leaves us asking, what is 'noble utterance' and
what is 'base'? The Good News Bible paraphrases this as 'If
instead of talking nonsense you proclaim a worthwhile message'.
But when and how did Jeremiah talk nonsense? His message
seems to have been always characterized by an uncompromising
bluntness, which he knows will not be acceptable to the people,
but which he believes to be the only authentic word for the day.
Is it possible that when opposition and misunderstanding were at
their fiercest, he was tempted to ease his troubles by trimming his
message to make it slightly more palatable? Is a warning against
this implicit in the promise of verse 19c?

> This people will turn again to you
> but you will not turn to them.

There is no evidence of such trimming in the extant authentic
oracles of the prophet, but it is not impossible that behind the
outward integrity of the message, there lay an inner personal
struggle. If the clue to Jeremiah's need to 'turn' is to be sought not
in the immediate context of 15.19, but in the wider setting of the
confessions than other possibilities arise.

J. Skinner, noting that we find in the confessions a process of
self-examination at work, a scrutinizing of his own motives, a
protesting, for example, that he took no secret delight in the doom
of others (17.16) but had sought to mediate on their behalf of God
(15.11; 18.12), suggests that there may be an undue element of
morbidity in all this. Is he really protesting too much? 'Had he
crossed the line between a holy zeal for the manifestation of the
divine righteousness and a selfish desire for his own vindication;
or between an avid submission to Yahweh's purposes of judgment and a gloomy satisfaction in being its instrument and
herald?'[14] Preaching judgment and coming doom can be for some
people a thoroughly self-satisfying, indeed enjoyable experience.

Had Jeremiah put his foot on the road to Pharisaism, that occu-
pational disease of the devout in every generation? A closely
similar view is powerfully advocated by J. Muilenburg.[15] 'Precisely
because he (i.e. Jeremiah) is so intensely religious, so intensely
near to God, he is in most need of repenting. His intensely
religious mood has actually separated him from the men to whom
he ministered and, more astonishingly, it has actually separated
him from God.' Inevitably we are groping here in the realm of the
probable and the psychologically reasonable. It is perhaps safer
to admit that we do not know the why of this call to the prophet
to 'turn'; but at least this call ensures that Jeremiah is being placed
firmly under the burden of his own message. He is being reminded
that the world cannot be neatly divided into sinners in need of the
prophetic message on the one hand, and on the other the one
perfect prophet exempt from such a need.

The challenge to the prophet to turn is backed up by a promise.
He is to be:

> . . . impregnable,
>   a wall of bronze,
> They will attack you but they will not prevail,
>   for I am with you to deliver you,
>   and save you, says the Lord (15.20);

The language of this promise is closely echoed in 1.18–19, in the
expansion of the call and vision material at the beginning of the
book:

> This day I make you a fortified city,
>   a pillar of iron, a wall of bronze,
> to stand fast against the whole land,
>
> . . .
>
> They will attack you, but they will not prevail,
>   for I am with you to deliver you,
>   and save you, says the Lord.[16]

Although the hand of a Deuteronomic editor is often seen in the
detail of 1.18–19, the core of this promise is also found in 1.8, in
the context of the prophet's call experience:

> Fear none of them for I am with you to deliver you.

There is therefore good reason for believing that the promise
Jeremiah now hears is no new promise. It is the reaffirmation of
a promise made to him at the outset of his ministry. The promise

was never one of any easy ride; it was the promise of the
continuing presence of God even in the midst of the storm. It is as
if God is saying to Jeremiah, don't go looking for further spiritual
credit, cash the cheque you have already been given. This may be
sound advice, unless you begin to seriously question whether the
cheque you have been given may not be a forgery or a cruel hoax.

> O Lord, thou hast deceived me, and I have been deceived;
>   thou hast outwitted me and hast prevailed.
> I have been made a laughing stock all the day long,
>   everyone mocks me.

There is no more bitter cry of disillusionment in all prophetic
literature than these words from 20.7. The closest linguistic
parallel to the opening words of this verse are to be found in the
Micaiah son of Imlah story in I Kings 22 where the Lord asks the
members of the heavenly council 'Who will deceive Ahab. . . ?'
When one spirit offers to become a lying spirit in the mouth of all
Ahab's prophets the Lord responds, 'You shall deceive him . . .
and you shall succeed' (I Kings 22.22); the same Hebrew word
being translated by the New English Bible 'succeed' in I Kings
22.22 and 'prevailed' in Jeremiah 20.7. There the Lord is depicted
as deliberately sending and using false prophets to toy with Ahab
and lure him to his doom.[17] Jeremiah may well be giving voice
here to the suspicion that the Lord is deliberately toying with him
to lead him to destruction, especially since his preaching has
provoked from the community at large only opposition and
derision. Can we go further and wonder whether the thought
had perhaps crossed Jeremiah's mind that just as the Lord had
used false prophets filled with a lying spirit to achieve his ends
with Ahab, so now he himself might be just that, a false prophet
filled with a lying spirit? Since he repeatedly found his footsteps
dogged by other prophets boldly declaring 'Thus says the Lord'
and contradicting his message; since the Deuteronomic tests for
prophecy in Deuteronomy 13 and 18 for identifying 'the prophet
whom the Lord did not send' were just as likely to apply to him as
to them,[18] it would hardly be surprising if he began to wonder,
'suppose I am wrong after all'. There was so much he did not
understand and could not come to terms with.

> Wert thou my enemy, O thou my friend,
> How wouldst thou worse, I wonder, than thou dost
> Defeat, thwart me?[19]

Whatever the explanation his doubts, his disillusionment, were serious enough to take him to the point of saying, 'I quit' – only to find that he couldn't.

> Whenever I said, 'I will call him to mind no more,
> nor speak in his name again'.
> Then his word was imprisoned in my body,
> like a fire blazing in my heart,
> and I was weary with holding it under,
> and could endure no more (20.9).

These words make little or no sense except on the assumption that there were occasions in Jeremiah's life when he was so obsessed by the failure of his ministry, so shaken by opposition and indifference, so unsure of God, that he lapsed into silence and decided to renounce his prophetic ministry. Then he discovered that the choice he faced was grim; either he had to go on, haunted by the thought that he might be no more than a plaything in the hands of an inscrutable God, or he had to face being burned up from within by ceaseless spiritual torment. He thought that he had reached the point where it was impossible to go on; he discovered instead that it was impossible for him not to go on. His doubts about God were serious, but the alternative, the attempt to suppress God's demand upon his life, was soul-destroying.

If that were all that the confessional passages revealed then we would have to assume that for the prophet life was always a grim and desperate struggle for some kind of spiritual integrity. But that is not the whole picture. At several points we find him reaching out beyond the confusions and the uncertainties, beyond the sense of failure and his unanswered questions, in search of some ultimate confidence . . . and finding it. He gazes into the confusions of his own mind, and turns away perplexed:

> The heart is the most deceitful of all things,
> desperately sick; who can fathom it? (17.9)

The answer comes:

> I, the Lord, search the mind,
> and test the heart,
> requiting man for his conduct,
> and as his deeds deserve (17.10).

Over against the baffling uncertainties of his own thought and motives, he places the certainty of a God who knows what is happening, and who must, and can be, relied upon – with whatever misgivings – to do right and vindicate his servant prophet. So we find him praying for healing:

> Heal me, O Lord, and I shall be healed,
> save me and I shall be saved;
> for thou art my praise (17.14).

He urgently pleads with God to keep a tight grip on him in the midst of the conflicts he faces:

> Do not become a terror to me;
> thou art my sole refuge on the day of disaster (17.18).

Most remarkable of all is 20.13, which in the present context flashes like a shaft of lightning dissecting the darkness of bitter revenge and cursing:

> Sing to the Lord, praise the Lord;
> for he rescues the poor from the hand of those
>   who would do them wrong.

The whole section, 20.7–13, of which these words are the climax is reminiscent in form of the psalms of lament, with the complaint element in verses 7–10, being followed by a confession of faith in verses 11–12, a confession which breaks into a song of praise in verse 13. There is, therefore, nothing incongruous about this verse in its present context. To dismiss it in principle as being inconsistent with other elements in the confessions is the fruit of an arid academicism which has not probed the depths of spiritual experience. Bishop Berggrav of Oslo, one of the leaders of the Norwegian church struggle against the Nazi-occupying forces, wrote to an English friend, '. . . during such periods as that of 1942, half of your soul was in a hell of anxieties, doubt and fear; the other half of your soul is in heaven, carried on the wings of the faith which God bestows on you.'[20] This corresponds to Jeremiah's experience. He was caught somewhere between heaven and hell in that struggle for faith which cannot eliminate the darkness, yet discerns in the darkness a flickering light which the darkness is never able completely to extinguish.

Apart from a few brief sections which are in the form of words from the Lord to Jeremiah (11.21–23; 12.5–6; 15.19–21) all the material in the confessions is in the form of prayers. This is not a man thinking his own thoughts as in some Shakespearean soliloquy; this is a man pouring his whole self out to God; his despondency, his doubts, his disillusionment, his curses, his unanswered questions, his hurt cries for healing and vindication. In such prayers we find the same kind of raw honesty which we noted in the psalms of lament, an honesty intensified by a sharply personal edge which we can relate to conflict situations in the prophet's life. If we find the honesty too raw, in some of its expressions, particularly in the prayers for vengeance, let us remember two things:

(a) it is not easy for those of us who live carefully in the shallows to enter sympathetically into hurt cries which come to us from the depths;

(b) it was of no little importance that Jeremiah, following the psalms of lament, shaped the totality of his experience into prayers. He might otherwise have ceased to pray, or have so carefully shaped his prayers that they expressed only a pseudo piety which would have hurt no one but himself. He would have understood Gerard Manley Hopkins words:

> A warfare of my lips in truth;
> Battling with God is now my prayer.[21]

But at least if you are 'battling with God' you still believe that there is someone there with whom it is important and worthwhile to do battle . . . in truth.

8

JERUSALEM – SYMBOL OR SNARE?

'From the moment when a national catastrophe appears inevitable, and especially after it has become a reality, it can like every
other great torment become a productive force from a religious
point of view: it begins to suggest new questions and to stress old
ones. . . . But the new acting force is nothing less than the force
of extreme despair, a despair so elemental that it can have but one
of two results; the sapping of the last will of life, or the renewal of
the soul.'[1] To respond to such elemental despair was the challenge
which faced the Jewish community in the aftermath of the events
of 587 BC when Jerusalem the city and its temple on Mount Zion
were destroyed by the Babylonians. We have already looked at
Psalms 44 and 74 as examples of typical community laments.[2]
Whether they were originally related to this crisis situation or not
hardly matters. What they provide is an opportunity for the
community to relive a shattering national disaster in the context
of worship, and thus to find at least emotional release from its
trauma. What they do not provide is any positive answer to the
question which they both raise, 'why?'. There is faith implicit in
the urgent appeal to God which comes at the end of each psalm:

> Bestir thyself, Lord; why dost thou sleep?
>   Awake, do not reject us forever.
>
> . . .
>
> Arise and come to our help;
>   for thy love's sake set us free (Ps. 44.23, 26).
>
> Rise up, O God, maintain thy own cause;
>   remember how brutal men taunt thee all day long.
> Ignore no longer the cries of thy assailants,

the mounting clamour of those who defy thee
(Ps. 74.22, 23).

But in both psalms this is a faith which admits that it does not understand what has happened. Psalm 44 is very conscious of the tension between the community's witness to the great things God did in the past, and a present in which his people are defeated and rejected:

All this has befallen us, but we do not forget thee
and have not betrayed thy covenant (Ps. 44.17).

God must somehow be responsible for what has happened, but why is not clear.

Psalm 74 surveys the desolation of a ruined temple and complains:

We cannot see what lies before us, we have no prophet now;
we have no one who knows how long this is to last
(Ps. 74.9).

'No prophet now', and therefore no one to interpret the meaning of what has happened or to tell them how to respond to it.

It is perfectly possible – as we have noted[3] – for people to live with many questions unanswered; but this question, the question as to why Jerusalem and the temple of the Lord had been destroyed demanded an answer since it placed in jeopardy much that had been considered close to the heart of the nation's faith. To grasp the urgency of the question we must understand what Jerusalem and Mount Zion meant to the faithful. Jerusalem was not merely another city, not merely the capital of the nation, it was 'the city of God'; the temple on Mount Zion was not merely a sacred building, a national shrine, it was the place where the Lord had chosen to dwell on earth. From this belief in the Lord's presence in city and temple there grew the doctrine of the inviolability of Jerusalem. Other cities might perish, but not this city. This evoked from the community a deeply-held and moving confidence for which men were prepared to die, and did die. This confidence receives powerful expression in worship in some of the 'Songs of Zion', notably Psalms 46 and 48:

God is our shelter and our refuge,
a timely help in trouble;
so we are not afraid. . . . (Ps. 46.1, 2a).

not even when the ordered structure of the world seems threatened by the forces of chaos, not even when other nations are in uproar (cf. verses 2b, 3, 6). Why? . . . because Jerusalem is:

> . . . the city of God,
> which the Most High had made his holy dwelling,
> God is in that city; she will not be overthrown,
> and he will help her at the break of day (Ps. 46.4–5).

This is the God who controls all the forces of history, the God who is:

> high over the nations, high above the earth (Ps. 46.10b)

and this God is 'with us'. We still sing this psalm as a psalm of confident faith, but in a form which has given it a more generalized, spiritual meaning:

> A safe stronghold our God is still,
> A trusty shield and weapon;
> He'll help us clear from all the ill
> That hath us now o'ertaken.[4]

It is important, however, to realize that the original reference of the psalm is earthy and literal; the city is no heavenly ideal, it is the earthly city of Jerusalem.

Psalm 48 is very similar, though it makes more explicit reference to the temple (v. 9) and to the hill of Zion (vv. 2, 11).

> The Lord is great and worthy of our praise
>   in the city of our God, upon his holy hill.
>
> . . .
>
> All we had heard we saw with our own eyes
>   in the city of the Lord of Hosts,
>   in the city of our God,
>   the city which God plants firm for evermore (Ps. 48.1, 8).

Kings gather to attack Jerusalem, only to be:

> . . . struck with amazement when they see her,
>   they are filled with alarm and panic;
> they are seized with trembling,
>   they toss in pain like a woman in labour,
> like the ships of Tarshish
>   when an east wind wrecks them (Ps. 48.5–7).

So the Psalm ends with an invitation to a faith-strengthening pilgrimage:

> Make the round of Zion in procession,
>> count the number of her towers,
>
> Take good note of her ramparts,
>> pass her palaces in review,
>
> that you may tell generations yet to come:
>> Such is God,
>
> our God for ever and ever;
>> He shall be our guide eternally (Ps. 48.12–14).

The fact of this Jerusalem-centred faith is not in doubt; equally important, however, are the roots from which it sprung. We may identify two.

1. *Mythology*. Associated with Jerusalem there is a cluster of ideas which find their home in religious mythology current in the Ancient Near East before Israel ever existed as a nation. They are part of Israel's religious heritage from her cultural environment, a heritage which she was not afraid to adapt and use for her own purposes. The description of the Zion, the temple mount, in Psalm 48 contains the following words:

> Fair and lofty, the joy of the whole earth
>> is Zion's hill, like the farthest reaches of the north,
>
> The hill of the great King's city (v. 2).

Whatever the phrase 'like the farthest reaches of the north' may mean, it can hardly be a geographical pointer. Jerusalem was in the southern kingdom of Judah, and from no point in Judah would it have made sense to talk of the city as being 'like the farthest reaches of the north'. The Hebrew word for the north, however, as the New English Bible footnote indicates is *Zaphon*.[5] We know from the Canaanite texts from Ras Shamra (fourteenth century BC) that the traditional abode of the gods, the place where they met to take decisions, was Mount Zaphon, a mountain whose location was only vaguely indicated as being somewhere far distant probably in the north. 'Like the farthest reaches of the north', therefore, is not in any way intended to send us map hunting; it conveys a religious idea, it is identifying Mount Zion with the traditional abode of the gods.

The same may very well be true of Psalm 46.4, which talks about

> . . . a river whose streams gladden the city of God[6]

But there is no river as such in Jerusalem. It is possible, of course to spiritualize this language and talk about 'the life-giving fountain of God's presence'.[7] But this river has a much more specific source. Closely associated with the dwelling place of the gods in Ancient Near Eastern mythology there is a complex of ideas, one of which focusses upon the river or the water of life. We can trace this in the Ras Shamra texts where the head of the Ugaritic pantheon, the god 'El, sits:

> at the source(s) of the rivers
> [and the springs of the] two [oceans]

This may well have been thought of as the place where the subterranean waters surface into streams and hence flow outwards to fertilize the earth. So in the religious symbolism of the garden of Eden tradition, from Eden there flows 'a river' (Gen. 2.10). Ezekiel in his vision of a restored world says: 'I saw a spring of water issuing from under the terrace of the temple towards the east, for the temple faced east' (Ezek. 47.1). From the temple it flows outwards in an ever-deepening stream till it eventually negates the deadness of the Dead Sea (Ezek. 47.8–10).[8] Associated with this river-gladdened city there is a title for God 'the Most High' (Heb. *'Elyon*), a title found mainly in liturgical texts in the Old Testament, particularly the Psalms, and often closely linked to the Jerusalem temple. There is, however, one interesting narrative which features this divine title, Genesis 14, where Melkizedek, a pre-Israelite priest-king in Salem, is described as the 'priest of God the Most High' (Gen. 14.18, cf. vv. 19, 20); and in Genesis 14.22 there seems to be a deliberate attempt to identify Yahweh, the God of Abram, with this God Most High, and thus to associate Israel's God with a long tradition of worship in Salem, probably Jerusalem.[9] The temple site in Jerusalem, therefore, was believed to have a long pre-history as a place of worship, a pre-history which takes us back beyond any Hebrew associations with the site; and round the site there clusters a complex of religious, mythological ideas which enhanced its importance and its sanctity.

2. *History*. Jerusalem fell into Hebrew hands thanks to the political shrewdness and the military skill of David (see II Sam. 5), who quickly seized upon its potential as the political and religious centre of his kingdom. The city, therefore, was closely associated with the Davidic dynasty, and with the promises and expectations

which surrounded that dynasty.[10] The temple which Solomon built in Jerusalem was partly a national shrine and partly a chapel royal. Psalm 132, for example, keeps these royal and temple motifs interlocked;

> The Lord swore to David
>   an oath which he will not break:
> 'A prince of your own line
>   will I set upon your throne.
> If your sons keep my covenant
>   and heed the teaching that I give them,
> their sons in turn for all time
>   shall sit upon your throne.'
> For the Lord has chosen Zion
>   and desired it for his home:
> 'This is my resting place for ever;
>   here will I make my home, for such is my desire'
>   (Ps. 132.11–14).

A royal dynasty which will last 'for all time' goes hand in hand with a temple which will be God's 'resting place for ever'.

For a period historical events seemed to vindicate this ideology. The chronically unstable northern kingdom of Israel, its capital Samaria and all its religious sites, perished before the Assyrians in 721 BC. But in the year 701 BC Jerusalem survived when an Assyrian army led by Sennacherib marched through Judah. The narrative in II Kings at this point presents complex and much discussed problems. It is generally recognized that II Kings preserves at least two accounts of the Assyrian confrontation with Jerusalem: (A) II Kings 18.13–16, an account which in all essentials agrees with Sennacherib's own account in his annals,[11] and describes King Hezekiah's submission to his imperial Assyrian overlord with the payment of tribute. (B) II Kings 18.17–19.37 which contains, *inter alia*, a prophecy from Isaiah declaring that the Assyrians would not enter the city:

> This is the very word of the Lord.
> I will shield this city to deliver it,
> for my own sake and for the sake of my servant David
>   (II Kings 19.33b–34).

And culminates in the account of the miraculous deliverance of the city as the result of divine intervention:

That night the angel of the Lord went out and struck down a
hundred and eighty five thousand men in the Assyrian camp;
when morning dawned, they all lay dead. So Sennacherib king
of Assyria broke camp, went back to Ninevah and stayed there
(II Kings 19.35–36).

Whether it is possible to trace the theological assumptions which
have shaped account B back to the end of the eighth century BC or
to find them in the authentic oracles of Isaiah of Jerusalem, must
remain doubtful.[12] There is no doubt, however, that when Jerusalem was facing the ultimate threat to its existence as the capital
of an independent kingdom at the beginning of the sixth century
BC what happened in 701 BC was being interpreted as the classic
illustration of the Lord defending his own city, and oracles
attributed to Isaiah were propounding the doctrine of the inviolability of the city.

> This is what the Lord has said to me:
> As a lion or a young lion growls over its prey
>   when the muster of shepherds is called out against it,
> and is not scared at their noise
>   or cowed by their clamour,
> so shall the Lord of Hosts come down to do battle
>   for Zion and her high summit.
> Thus the Lord of Hosts, like a bird hovering over its young,
>   will be a shield over Jerusalem;
> He will shield her and deliver her,
>   standing over her and delivering her (Isa. 31.4–5).[13]

Twice in these verses God is described as 'the Lord of Hosts' (vv.
4, 5). The same title occurs twice in Psalm 46 'The Lord of Hosts is
with us' (vv. 7, 11) and once in Psalm 48 where Jerusalem is
described as 'the city of the Lord of Hosts' (v. 8). The 'hosts'
referred to in this title may mean many different things in various
contexts in the Old Testament, culminating in the picture of a
God who controls all the forces in nature and history, in heaven
and earth. There is, however, a good deal of evidence to suggest
that it began life closely associated with the ark, the symbol of the
Lord's presence in the midst of his wandering people, the ark
which was carried into battle by the tribes of Israel. To counteract
growing Philistine power, the people send to the sanctuary at
Shiloh for 'the Ark of the Covenant of the Lord of Hosts' (I Sam.
4.3), the 'hosts' referred to being almost certainly the armies of

Israel. So David faces Goliath, 'in the name of the Lord of Hosts, the God of the army of Israel which you have defied' (I Sam. 17.45). However this phrase developed,[14] it seems for long enough to have retained powerful national and military overtones. The Lord of Hosts was the one who could be depended upon to deliver his people from their enemies. He dwelt in the temple in Jerusalem, yet he was king over all the earth. His universal sovereignty is celebrated in Psalm 47, a psalm which because of its present position was believed to be closely related to Psalms 46 and 48. This sovereignty is exercised in favour of his people Israel:

> He lays the nations prostrate beneath us,
>   he lays people under our feet;
> he chose our patrimony for us,
>   the pride of Jacob whom he loved (Ps. 47.3–4).

Eighty years after the Assyrian withdrawl from Jerusalem the city witnessed the most thorough and far-reaching reformation in the nation's history. It was led by the young king Josiah, supported by the religious establishment, and had wide popular acclaim. There was a strong political motivation behind the reform movement. It represented a bid for freedom from Assyrian domination by a revival of the nation's religious heritage. An attempt was made to eliminate popular paganism by closing all local shrines. The purified Jerusalem temple would alone remain the centre of the nation's devotion. Henceforth there would be one God, worshipped in one temple by one people who had heard the Deuteronomic call to repent and to love the Lord (II Kings 22–23). There are still good grounds for believing that 'the book of the law', discovered while repairs were being undertaken to the temple precincts is closely related to the central legislative portion of Deuteronomy (chapters 12–26), a book probably brought from the north by Yahweh loyalists after the destruction of Samaria and deposited for safe keeping in the Jerusalem temple archives. Deuteronomy 26 ends on a note of high expectations:

> This day the Lord your God commands you to keep these statutes and laws; be careful to observe them with all your heart and soul. You have recognised the Lord this day as your God; you are to conform to his ways, to keep his statutes, his commandments, and his laws, and to obey him. The Lord has recognized you this day as his special possession, as he promised you, and to keep his commandments; he will raise you

high above all the nations which he has made, to bring him praise and fame and glory, and to be a people holy to the Lord your God, according to his promise (Deut. 26.16–19).

Thus various strands – age-old mythology, religious ideology surrounding the Davidic dynasty and the Jerusalem temple, the past history of the community and a contemporary reformation – came together towards the end of the seventh century BC to produce in Jerusalem a mood of confident faith, a faith in whose name men were prepared to fling defiance in the face of threatening totalitarianism, convinced that the God who was present in their midst would crush all the powers of evil which opposed him.[15] As they prepared the defences of Jerusalem against the gathering Babylonian storm, their mood echoed the thought of a psalm of very uncertain date, Psalm 124.

> If the Lord had not been on our side,
>   Israel may now say.
> if the Lord had not been on our side
>   when they assailed us,
> they would have swallowed us alive
>   when their anger was roused against us.
> The waters would have carried us away
>   and the torrent swept over us;
>   over us would have swept
>   the seething waters.
> Blessed be the Lord, who did not leave us
>   to be the prey between their teeth.
> We have escaped like a bird,
>   from the fowler's trap;
>   for the trap broke and so we escaped.
> Our help is in the name of the Lord,
>   maker of heaven and earth.

The Babylonian torrent did sweep over them; they did not escape; the trap did not break. The high expectations were shattered. The Lord did not seem to have been on their side. The stunnedbewilderment of some of the survivors of this Jerusalem holocaust is voiced by a group who came to the prophet Jeremiah to plead;

Pray to the Lord your God on our behalf and on behalf of this remnant for, as you see for yourself, only a few of us remain out

of the many. Pray that the Lord your God may tell us which
way we ought to go and what we ought to do (Jer. 42.2–3).

If they expected instant answers to their questions they were in
for a shock. It was ten days later before Jeremiah had anything to
say to them (Jer. 42.7), and what they heard then was unpalatable.

In response to this crisis of faith, the most severe that the Old
Testament knows in community terms, there was to be no one
answer. There were to be many attempts to make sense of what
for most people, for the best of religious reasons, seemed to make
no sense. Without the asking of certain radical questions, without
the discarding of some hitherto accepted certainties, there was to
be no 'renewal of the soul'.

1. There is one response which we can dispose of fairly quickly,
since it represents a dead end, 'the sapping of the last will of life',
as far as continuing faith in the God of Israel is concerned.
According to Jeremiah 44 some of the Jewish survivors who fled
down to Egypt laid the blame squarely on the shoulders of the
reform movement which had eliminated all other religious cults
in Jerusalem and committed the community to the worship of
Yahweh alone. The women in particular seemed to wish to revert
to the good old days when they had worshipped a beneficent
mother goddess, the queen of heaven.

> . . . we will burn sacrifices to the queen of heaven and pour
> drink offerings to her as we used to do, we and our father, our
> kings and our princes, in the cities of Judah and in the streets of
> Jerusalem. We then had food in plenty and were content; no
> calamity touched us. But from the time we left off burning
> sacrifices to the queen of heaven and pouring drink offerings to
> her, we have been in great want, and in the end we have fallen
> victims to sword and famine (Jer. 44.17–18).

It is important to recognize that there is an element of truth in
this. Politics and religion were essentially indivisible in the world
of the Ancient Near East. When Josiah led his people in a
reformation whose sincerity we have no right to question, he was
at the same time asserting his nation's independence. By banishing all other gods and goddesses, including Assyrian deities, from
Jerusalem he was throwing down the gauntlet to his Assyrian
overlords. He died at Megiddo in 609 BC fighting against Egyptian
forces which were attempting to bolster up the tottering power of
the Assyrian empire (II Kings 23.29). The Deuteronomic ideal was

that of a purified national religion, with nationhood and theology walking hand in hand. It was this religious nationalism which tried to defy the Babylonians, and lost. If the community had been more tolerant; if it had been content to accept a pluralistic religious situation, this confrontation with Babylon might never have taken place. In the short term the people might well have been better off continuing to worship the queen of heaven. Historical pragmatism has its advantages. Peace and security can always be purchased, at a price. If reversion to religious syncretism had been the sole response to the Jerusalem holocaust, however, the Jews would have nothing distinctive to offer to the world, and instead of the Old Testament we would presumably have had a few Hebrew documents surviving in a collection of Ancient Near Eastern Texts.

2. The prophet most intimately involved in the political and religious tensions which led up to the confrontation with Babylon, the prophet who lived through the crisis of national collapse, was Jeremiah. Thanks to the presence of a disciple and scribe called Baruch,[16] we are singularly well informed of Jeremiah's activities in this period. Two aspects of the prophet's activity are particularly relevant to our theme.

(*a*) The first is the so-called Temple Sermon, of which we have two accounts, the one is chapter 7.1–15, concentrating upon what the prophet is believed to have said, the other in chapter 26 which shifts attention to the divided audience reaction. At a great national religious occasion, perhaps celebrating the accession of king Jehoiakim (cf. 26.1), Jeremiah takes his stance at the gate of the Lord's house and harangues those assembling for worship:

> These are the words of the Lord of Hosts, the God of Israel: Mend your ways and your doings, that I may let you live in this place. You keep saying, 'This place is the temple of the Lord, the temple of the Lord, the temple of the Lord!' This catchword of yours is a lie; put no trust in it. Mend your ways and your doings, deal fairly with one another, do not oppress the alien, the orphan, and the widow . . . (Jer. 7.3–6).

It may seem at first glance as if this is a head-on theological clash, Jeremiah simply denying out of hand a theology which asserts the mystic presence of God in the temple on Mount Zion, the negation of the theology of Psalms 46 and 48. But this is not so. Let us continue with the passage for a moment:

You gain nothing by putting your trust in this lie. You steal, you murder, you commit adultery and perjury, you burn sacrifices to Baal, you run after other gods whom you have not known; then you come and stand before me in this house, which bears my name, and say, 'We are safe', safe you think to indulge in all these abominations (vv. 8–10).

What Jeremiah is attacking is not the statement 'this is the temple of the Lord' *per se* but the unwarranted corollary of that statement that no matter what people do or how they act in their attitude to other people, they can still go to this temple and say 'We are safe': this is the temple of the Lord and he, present with us, will protect city and temple. Far from denying the presence of the Lord in the temple, Jeremiah is affirming it, affirming it to stress that in certain circumstances that very presence makes judgment inevitable. He is doing what Amos did with the doctrine of election,[17] accepting it, yet drawing from it a challenging and uncomfortable conclusion to which other people seemed blind.

This challenge is underlined in verses 12–15, which have an added interest when read in the light of Psalm 78. Reviewing the history of God's people from the exodus onwards, Psalm 78 sees it as being on the one hand the story of God's continuing grace and patience, and on the other the story of a nation's continuing ingratitude, rebellion and apostasy. As far as the northern kingdom of Israel is concerned this culminates in God's decision to reject and to abandon his people. So God is depicted as leaving one of the tradition hallowed cultic centres of the north:

He forsook his home at Shiloh,
    the tabernacle in which he dwelt among men (Ps. 78.59).

But if the north were rejected, the true life of the people of God flowed on in the south, in Judah, where there was a sanctuary which would last for ever;

He chose the tribe of Judah
    and Mount Zion which he loved;
He built his sanctuary high as the heavens,
    founded like the earth to last for ever (Ps. 78.68–69).

Not so, claims Jeremiah; just as God abandoned Shiloh because of the continuing wickedness of the people, so the Jerusalem temple 'this house which bears my name, the house in which you put your trust' (Jer. 7.14) will be destroyed, to become like Shiloh a grim reminder of human perversity. Jeremiah does not speak of God forsaking the Jerusalem temple, he speaks of God throwing the people out of his sight (v. 15), as if to stress that it is God's presence which guarantees that the Jerusalem temple will no longer be a place of worship for the community. He was shattering the comforting conclusions which were being drawn from a religious tradition which thought of Jerusalem as 'the city of God' and Mount Zion as God's dwelling place on earth, in a temple which would last for ever. He is asserting the freedom of God to act against the very institutions and indeed against the theology by which men believed they were honouring him. One of the most effective ways of domesticating God is to lock him into a theology, particularly if that theology can claim powerful support from tradition and enshrines a genuine insight, in this case a belief in God's presence. Jeremiah sounds the death-knell for a deep-rooted, tenaciously held theology, in order that God may live and continuing realistic faith be possible.[18]

(*b*) The second aspect of Jeremiah's activity is his involvement in the crisis political issues of his day. Although the evidence is not clear, it seems likely that Jeremiah supported, perhaps publicly advocated, the reform movement which culminated in the events of 621 BC.[19] He had called for repentance and here was a national movement with a positive programme for repentance. The reformation had two tangible results:

(*i*) an increase in the mystique and significance of the Jerusalem temple, henceforth to be the sole legitimate sanctuary for the worship of Yahweh;

(*ii*) the inauguration of a period of increasingly self-confident religious nationalism on a Deuteronomic basis.

We have looked at Jeremiah's critique of the first, we now turn to the second. The first question mark against this self-confident nationalism must have come in 609 BC when the reforming king Josiah, still comparatively young, died in battle seeking to secure his people's independence. A more serious jolt came in 597 BC when, after an unsuccessful attempt to revolt against Babylon, king Jehoiachin and the political and religious leaders of the community were exiled to Babylon. Judah was now in a novel situation, a divided community, partly in exile, partly in and around Jerusalem. Those who remained in Jerusalem seem to have adopted an attitude of mingled pity and scorn towards those in exile. To be in Jerusalem, was to be assured of God's continuing presence and grace; to be in exile was to be deprived of the means of grace – but no doubt the exiles deserved their fate. This is the context of Jeremiah's vision of the two baskets of figs, the 'good figs' and the 'bad figs' in chapter 24. The explanation of the vision given in verses 4–10 may well have been annotated and expanded by later editors in the light of the fact that it was out of the Babylonian exile that the new leadership of the community came, but in essence the vision and its interpretation go back to the prophet. The adjectives 'good' and 'bad' are in no sense a judgment on the character or the spirituality of the groups identified as the 'good figs' and the 'bad figs'. The 'good figs', fit to eat and therefore acceptable as an offering in the temple, are analogous to 'the exiles from Judah whom I (i.e. the Lord) sent away from this place to the land of the Chaldaeans . . . I will look upon them meaning to do them good' (Jer. 24.5, 6a). The 'bad figs', fit only to be thrown out are analogous to those who remain in Jerusalem and Judah; they are doomed to destruction. Jeremiah is here undermining the religious nationalism, based on the continuing existence of Jerusalem, by affirming that the exile is not only within the Lord's purposes, but that it is a liberating experience upon which a new future can be built. Without this shattering, yet liberating experience, there is no future.

It is this conviction, and this conviction alone, which makes sense of Jeremiah's activity in the last ten years of the independent Judaean state. It is this that accounts for his clash with Hananiah (ch. 28), spokesman of the prophets who believed that the Lord would break the stranglehold of the Babylonians and bring the exiles back to their rightful spiritual home in Jerusalem. It is this that leads him openly to commit high treason, counselling his fellow citizens, in the middle of the final grim siege of the city, to desert to the enemy:

> These are the words of the Lord: Whoever remains in this city shall die by sword, by famine, or by pestilence, but whoever goes out to surrender to the Chaldaeans shall survive; he shall survive, he shall take home his life and nothing more (Jer. 38.2).

It is small wonder that he was arrested on a charge of undermining the morale of both soldiers and civilians; he was lucky to escape with his life (cf. Jer. 38.4–13). It is this which explains the brutal frankness he displays in a series of interviews with the last king of Judah, Zedekiah, a man bullied into disastrous policies by the Jerusalem Pentagon and pathetically anxious to know whether there is any word from the Lord. When the Babylonians momentarily lift the siege of Jerusalem to settle scores with an Egyptian army threatening their rear, Zedekiah sends a message to Jeremiah requesting him 'Pray for us to the Lord our God' (Jer. 37.3). Perhaps another eleventh hour miracle would occur. The response is stark and uncompromising:

> These are the words of the Lord the God of Israel: Say to the king of Judah who sent you to consult me, Pharaoh's army which marched out to help you is on its way back to Egypt, its own land, and the Chaldaeans will return to the attack. They will capture this city and burn it to the ground. These are the words of the Lord: Do not deceive yourselves, do not imagine that the Chaldaeans will go away and leave you alone. They will not go; for even if you defeated the whole Chaldaean force with which you are now fighting, and only the wounded were left lying in their tents, they would rise and burn down the city (Jer. 37.7–10).

Notice the total lack of political realism in the concluding words. Jeremiah has not sat down, done his military and political sums and come to the conclusion that the Babylonians were bound to win. The real enemy of Jerusalem is not the Babylonians, but the Lord. He has decreed the destruction of the city and temple. The God whom they had lost amid the ordered beauty and security of city and temple, they would find again amid the disordered ugliness of national disaster. They had to find blessing in the midst of what seemed to be a curse, life in the midst of what seemed to be death.

In the light of this we might expect to find Jeremiah very chary of using as a description of God the title 'the Lord of Hosts', a title which, as we have seen, has powerful nationalistic and military overtones. In fact the phrase 'the Lord of Hosts' or 'the Lord, the God of Hosts' occurs with greater frequency in the book of Jeremiah than in any other book in the Old Testament with the exception of the Psalms; and in passages which cannot be attributed easily to later redactional activity.[20] This may seem paradoxical until we examine the contexts in which the phrase occurs. In every case, with the exception of two personal confessional passages (11.20 and 15.16) the title 'the Lord of Hosts' or 'The

Lord the God of Hosts' occurs at the beginning or the end of a statement whose theme is God's coming judgment upon the community or where that judgment is already a reality. Thus

> It is your own wickedness that will punish you,
>   your own apostasy that will condemn you.
> See for yourselves how bitter a thing it is and how evil,
>   to forsake the Lord your God and revere me no longer.
> This is the very word of the Lord God of Hosts (2.19).

> These are the words of the Lord of Hosts:

> Cut down the trees of Jerusalem
>   and raise siege-ramps against her,
> the City whose name is Licence,
>   oppression is rampant within her (6.6, cf. 6.9).[21]

This is the 'Lord of Hosts' of Psalms 46 and 48, yet the theological content of the title is very different. It was only by someone having the courage to question the theology of such psalms and the way in which that theology was being understood, that it was possible for there to be a creative response to events which were incomprehensible in terms of such a theology. A new theology of the Lord of Hosts was struggling to be born. Jeremiah remained in the city as it reaped the bitter harvest of political folly and theological myopia; he remained to act in the midst of travail as the midwife of a new and more realistic faith.

3. That Jeremiah's hopes were not in vain can be seen in the book of Lamentations, a book of uncertain date and authorship. It contains a collection of five poems, for which unity of authorship is difficult to prove, but which share a common background. The blow has fallen, Jerusalem has been destroyed; how now does the faith of the people survive? Although the tradition of Jeremiah's authorship can hardly be sustained, nowhere does prophetic faith, the faith which Jeremiah proclaimed and for which he lived, shine more brightly than in this book.[22] The five poems correspond to the five chapters in the book. Poems, one two and four begin with the exclamation which is characteristic of the funeral dirge or oration, the word translated 'how' (Heb. *'ēkhāh*)

> How solitary lies the city, once so full of people (1.1).

> What darkness (lit. how he darkens) the Lord in his anger
>   has brought upon the daughter of Zion (2.1).

How dulled is the gold,
  how tarnished the fine gold! (4.1)

But if these poems begin as funeral dirges almost imperceptibly
they change into 'laments' with the poet speaking in the first
person as personified Jerusalem, describing the agony of present
suffering, appealing to the Lord, and sometimes calling down
vengeance on the brutal enemy, cf. 1.12–22; 2.11–22; 4.6ff., with
4.17–20 a typical community lament, beginning

Still we strain our eyes,
  looking in vain for help.

Poem three, on the other hand, is from beginning to end a typical
lament such as we find in the psalms, and as is the case in some
of the psalms it varies between using the first person singular 'I'
and the plural 'we': verses 1–39 'I', verses 40–47 'we', verses 48ff.
'I'. In such cases it is likely that the 'I' who speaks is a representative
of the community, king, priest or prophet, giving voice to the
community's experience.[23] Poem five is throughout a community
lament, beginning with a call to God to remember what has
happened, and ending with a characteristic appeal to God to do
something to remedy the situation.[24]

Behind Lamentations there lies a long literary tradition. We
have several examples from Sumerian sources of laments over
the destruction of cities, laments which go back to the third and
second millenia BC.[25] The most complete text to survive, although
it has had to be carefully pieced together from fragments, is the
so-called 'Lament over the Destruction of Ur'.[26] This lament is
more than a thousand years older than the book of Lamentations,
but more than time separates the outlook of the two documents.
Both describe with grim realism the horrors of the siege and the
last days of the city. Desolation and destruction have replaced
order and joy. Hunger and death stalk the streets. Worship has
come to an end; the great temple ruined and silent. The situation
described is similar, the imagery in the two poems has many
common links, but there the similarity ends. If we think of
historical events in Toynbeean terms of challenge and response,[27]
the challenge is the same, community disaster; the response is
markedly different. This becomes clear when we approach the
two documents with the recurring questions which feature in the
psalms of lament – 'why?' and 'how long?'

(a) Why? Why did it happen? The background to the Ur lament is polytheistic. In so far as any answer is given to the question 'why?', it is this: the destruction of Ur was decreed by two of the most powerful deities in the pantheon, Anu and Enlil. The patron goddess of Ur, the goddess Ningal, bitterly complains:

> They have pronounced the destruction of my city,
>> they have pronounced the utter destruction of Ur.

But no plea of Ningal's can make them alter their decision. No reason is given for the decision. The gods who belong to the inner divine council are under no obligation to explain their decisions to other gods or goddesses. Perhaps the question 'why' can never be an urgent question in this context. What we are left with is the picture of the patron goddess of the city appealing against the destruction of the city to other deities who for reasons best known to themselves have decreed its destruction. If the problem has something to do with personal rivalries and tensions in the divine family, then that is not something that can or need be justified before mortal men. Lamentations has a very different answer. There is only one God, the Lord who, as we have seen, was regarded by a powerful religious tradition as the patron god of Jerusalem, the Lord of Hosts, the God of Jacob, the one who could be depended upon to guarantee the continuing existence of his abode on Mount Zion. Hence the dilemma: to whom can Zion appeal? Only to her protector, now turned executioner:

> Zion lifted her hands in prayer,
>> but there was no one to comfort her;
> the Lord gave Jacob's enemies the order
>> to beset him on every side (Lam. 1.17).

The God of Jacob had become the destroyer of Jacob. In picture after picture in 2.1–8 the point is hammered home. It is the Lord who decided the fate of Jerusalem; This is the expression of his anger (v. 1), his fury (v. 2), his blazing anger (v. 3), his indignation (v. 4), his grim anger (v. 6). These verses ransack almost the entire Hebrew vocabulary of anger. What had happened was 'the day of his anger' (v. 1), the day on which the Lord had acted like an enemy to his own people:

> Sorrow upon sorrow he brought
>> to the daughter of Judah (v. 5c).

Lamentations has broken irrevocably with any purely patron
deity concept common to Ur and to popular theology in Judah
right up to the destruction of the city. But this gives added urgency
to another question: why this fury and anger of the Lord? Here
Lamentations stands firmly within prophetic tradition, the tradition which spans the period from Amos to Jeremiah:

> The Lord has cruelly punished her
> because of misdeeds without number (1.5).

> Jerusalem has sinned greatly,
> and so she was treated like a filthy rag (1.8).

> The Lord was in the right;
> it was I who rebelled against his commands (1.18).

And in communal lament:

> We ourselves have sinned and rebelled,
> and thou hast not forgiven (3.42).

> The garlands have fallen from our heads;
> woe betide us, sinners that we are (5.16).

Jerusalem and Judah stand judged and condemned in the light of
the prophetic doctrine of responsibility and moral accountability.
There is nothing remotely similar to this in the Ur lament.

(b) How long, O Lord? or to put it in other terms; what of the
future? where do we go from here? Is there any glimmer of hope
amid the darkness?

The Ur lament begins by describing how the various deities
worshipped in the city abandoned their temples as the city went
up in flames. Even Ningal the patron goddess is addressed as
follows:

> . . . O my queen,
> you too have departed from your house,
> you too have departed from the city.

Since the future of the patron goddess is intimately bound up
with the future of her city, the question is raised as to how Ningal
can hope to exist, once her city is destroyed. If there is any hint of
hope it comes in a prayer towards the end of the poem which
gives voice to the possibility that perhaps Anu and Enlil may
change their decision, allow Ningal to return to her home, and
revitalize the life of the community. But no reason is given as to

why this should take place, no more than any reason was given for the initial decision to destroy.

What of Lamentations? The community accepts that it is under the judgment of God, the Lord's fury and anger being the inevitable corollary of the people's sinfulness. But such fury and anger are not the Lord's true nature as that had been revealed to the community in the past:

> the Lord's true love is surely not spent
>> nor has his compassion failed;
> they are new every morning,
>> so great is his constancy.
> The Lord, I say, is all I have;
>> therefore I will wait for him patiently (3.22–24).

Suffering, tragedy may, indeed must, be patiently endured:

> for the Lord will not cast off
>> his servants forever.
> He may punish cruelly, yet he will have compassion
>> in the fulness of his love;
> he does not willingly afflict
>> or punish any mortal man (3.31–33).

The darkness of disaster, though richly deserved, cannot be God's final word to the community. They remain his servants, his people, who may confidently expect to experience in the future, as they have done in the past, his steadfast-love and his dependability.

At least two theologies coexisted in Judah in the days leading up to the destruction of Jerusalem; a dominant theology of confidence whose catchwords might well have been 'Hallelujah, all will be well', and the theology of a prophetic minority who insisted that all would not be well.[28] It is this theology of prophetic realism which we see rising Phoenix-like from the ashes of Jerusalem in the book of Lamentations. Paradoxically it had discovered that there was more creative faith to be found in confessing:

> In anger thou hast turned and pursued us,
>> and slain without pity;
> thou hast hidden thyself behind the clouds
>> beyond the reach of our prayers (3.43–44);

than in singing with untroubled certainty:

God is in that city; she will not be overthrown.
  . . .
The Lord of Hosts is with us,
  the God of Jacob is our refuge (Ps. 46.5, 7).

Yet this faith is no easy option. The closing section of Lamentations
is a blend of confident affirmation and continuing questions:

O Lord, thou art enthroned forever,
  thy throne endures from one generation to another.
Wilt thou quite forget us
  and forsake us these many days?
O Lord, turn us back to thyself, and we will come back;
  renew our days as in times long past.
Hast thou utterly rejected us,
  has your anger been great indeed against us? (5.19–22)

The Rabbis insisted that when Lamentations was being used
liturgically, the second last verse, 'O Lord, turn us . . . times long
past', should be repeated after the last verse. But it is a sound
insight which ends the book with a question or a continuing
possibility.[29] Only those who have faced, and continue to face,
the fact that God cannot be identified with self or national interest,
can have hope for the future.

   4. Lamentations probably reflects the outlook of some of the
survivors of the Jerusalem holocaust who remained in their
homeland in and around Jerusalem. We turn now to certain voices
from exile, or speaking to those who have been physically as well
as spiritually ejected from their homeland. Two passages highlight the struggle for faith. The first is Psalm 137, a psalm probably
written by a man who had just returned from exile. Looking at the
still ruined temple, he summarizes in deeply moving words the
experience of many of his fellow exiles. The psalm clearly shows
how something of the mystique of Jerusalem and its temple had
survived national catastrophe.

By the rivers of Babylon we sat down and wept
  when we remembered Zion.
There on the willow trees
  we hung up our harps,
    for there those who carried us off
      demanded music and singing,
and our captors called on us to be merry:

'Sing us one of the songs of Zion.'
How could we sing the Lord's song in a foreign land? (vv. 1–4)

We can almost hear the catch in this man's voice. The unthinkable had only too grimly happened. How in distant Babylon could they be expected to sing the joy-filled confident songs of that city of God which could not be overthrown? Yet Jerusalem cannot simply be eradicated from this man's religious consciousness. It had been as much religious symbol as place on the map; and although the place lay in ruins the power of the symbol, as expressing much that is central to his faith, remains:

> If I forget you, O Jerusalem,
>   let my right hand wither away;
> let my tongue cling to the roof of my mouth
>   if I do not remember you,
> if I do not set Jerusalem
>   above my highest joy (vv. 5–6).

At worst we might accuse this man of unrealistic nostalgia; at best we see a hurt sensitive spirit seeking to preserve lasting values in a cruel and uncertain world. Then comes the explosion of unconcealed anger. The gentle sensitivity is drowned in a raw, embittered cry for vengeance:

> Remember, O Lord, against the people of Edom
>   the day of Jerusalem's fall,
> when they said, 'Down with it, down with it,
>   down to its very foundation!'
>   O Babylon, Babylon the destroyer,
> Happy the man who repays you,
>   for all that you did to us!
> Happy is he who shall seize your children
>   and dash them against the rock (vv. 7–9).

Our pagan captors want a song; let them have one – a curse. Our temptation is to say 'amen' to verses 1–6, and to consign the bloody sequel in verses 7–9 to what we consider a well-deserved oblivion. To do this, however, is to destroy the psalm and to prevent us from seeing the fundamental issues which it raises; and that for two reasons:

(*a*) Psalm 137 does not stand alone in this respect. As we have seen it is not uncommon to find within the psalms of lament curses being called down upon the wicked or the enemy,[30] and the same is true of the confessional material in Jeremiah.[31]

(b) The two sides of this Psalm must not be seen as spiritually incompatible, but rather as the opposite sides of one coin.

This may become clearer if we listen to another voice to the exiles in Jeremiah 29.1–15. This contains a letter written by the prophet to the first group of exiles deported from Jerusalem to Babylon in 597 BC. It was written to counteract the activity among the exiles of certain prophets whose message seems to have been roughly this – Babylon is not your home; Jerusalem still stands; the Lord will soon crush the Babylonians and bring you triumphantly back to the city of God; meanwhile adopt a policy of non-cooperation with the Babylonian authorities. Jeremiah writes:

> These are the words of the Lord of Hosts the God of Israel: To all the exiles whom I have carried off from Jerusalem to Babylon: Build houses and live in them; plant gardens and eat their produce. Marry wives and beget sons and daughters; take wives for your sons and give your daughters to husbands, so that they may bear sons and daughters and you may increase there and not dwindle away. Seek the welfare of any city to which I have carried you off, and pray to the Lord for it; on its welfare your welfare will depend (Jer. 29.4–7).

Don't be deceived, says Jeremiah, by prophets who fill you with false hopes; settle down, prepare for a long stay, it is the Lord who has sent you to Babylon. Here we find our first point of contrast with Psalm 137. Curse Babylon, says Psalm 137; seek its welfare (Heb. *shālôm*), says Jeremiah, pray for it, for your welfare is bound up with its welfare. One day, continues Jeremiah, a generation or two off,[32] there will be a return but meanwhile God's purpose in bringing you here can be summed up in one word 'shālôm', not tragedy or disaster:

> If you invoke me and pray to me, I will listen to you: when you seek me, you shall find me; if you search with all your heart, I will let you find me, says the Lord (Jer. 29.12–13).

Jeremiah is defining the essence of true faith as a dedicated seeking which leads to finding, and he is claiming that this can happen as surely by the rivers of Babylon as in the temple at Jerusalem. In losing Jerusalem, nothing has been lost which is essential to faith. Thus the contrasts:

Psalm 137	*Jeremiah 29*
1. Jerusalem, central to faith.	No Jerusalem, but still God present.
2. Curse Babylon.	Pray for Babylon.

It is the very intensity of Psalm 137's devotion to Jerusalem that makes it react negatively to the world which has destroyed Jerusalem and hence threatened faith. The enemies of Jerusalem must be the enemies of God. The more deeply pious this psalmist is, the more he will look forward to the coming doom of Babylon. There is nothing strange in this. It is often the most passionately committed religious enthusiasts who are most bitterly judgmental in their attitudes to the world or to anything or any person who seems to pose a threat to their faith. It is Jeremiah's openness to the presence of God, even in Babylon, which enables him to say 'pray for the welfare of Babylon'.

The two voices we hear are discordant. Jeremiah gives voice to an attitude which keeps open the possibility of spiritual growth. But such an attitude was only possible for someone who had come to terms with Jerusalem as a religious symbol, so that whatever its religious significance it was no longer a threat to a wider vision. God had to be set free to wander the world; and his people set free to find him – or to be found by him – out there, once they had been ejected from false religious securities.

5. The anonymous author of Isaiah 40–55, the so-called Second Isaiah, speaks to his fellow exiles in Babylon. The vision of Jerusalem and Jerusalem restored is an important element in his theology, (e.g. 44.26–28; 51.1–3, 11; 51.17–52.2; 52.7–12; 54); but this is a vision tempered by a new realism. The people have lived through a crisis of faith. Much that they had regarded as indispensable to their faith, – the inviolable city of the Lord and its temple, the unquestioning validity of certain promises to the Davidic dynasty – had been destroyed. There was no going back beyond that destruction; the questions it posed had to be faced. The prophet's opening words:

> Comfort, comfort my people,
> – it is the voice of your God (Isa. 40.1),

and the echoing 'fear not' in his poems (e.g. 41.10, 14; 43.1, 5; 44.2, 8) are both directed towards meeting this crisis of faith.[33] The nature of the crisis, as the exiles experienced it, is expressed

in 40.27 in words which the prophet must have heard his fellow
exiles saying:

> Why do you complain, O Jacob,
>   and you, Israel, why do you say,
> 'My plight is hidden from the Lord,
>   and my cause has passed out of God's notice'?

A logical explanation of national defeat in the ancient world was
to say that the gods of the conquerors had triumphed over the
gods of the conquered. When Jerusalem and the temple were
destroyed, therefore, the God whose abode was in that holy
temple had gone under before the gods of Babylon. It is the
powerlessness of Israel's God, rather than his lack of knowledge
of what is going on, which is the basis of this bitter complaint.[34]
He may know of the plight of his people, but he is incapable of
doing anything about it. He seems unable to keep the promises
once made to his people (cf. 49.14).

In such a situation how is faith to be rebuilt? First by appealing
to the traditional faith of the community and that within it which
ought to have enabled the community to face crisis. The trouble,
argues the prophet, is that your God is too small – and he should
not have been. In question after rhetorical question he appeals to
what they ought to have known:

> Do you not know, have you not heard,
>   were you not told long ago,
> have you not perceived ever since the world began,
>   that God sits enthroned on the vaulted roof of earth,
>   whose inhabitants are like grasshoppers?
> He stretches out the skies like a curtain,
>   he spreads them out like a tent to live in;
> he reduces the great to nothing
>   and makes all earth's princes less than nothing
>   (Isa. 40.21–23).

Unwearingly he recalls the central certainties of Israel's faith –
creation (40.12, 28; 42.5; 44.24; 45.18–19; 48.13), the Abraham
traditions (41.8; 51.1–2), the exodus theme (43.2–3, 16–17; 51.9–
11), the wilderness wandering (43.19–20; 48.12) – and insists that
the God of Israel always has been in control of human history,
still is and always will be (cf. e.g. 41). He ridicules the powerlessness of all other gods, symbolized by their lifeless, if aesthetically

pleasing, idols (40.18–20; 41.6–7; 44), and affirms that there is only one God:

> Thus says the Lord, Israel's King,
>> the Lord of Hosts, his ransomer:
> I am the first and I am the last,
>> and there is no god but me (44.46);
>
> . . . I am God, there is no other,
>> I am God there is no one like me (46.9);
>
> Hear me, Jacob,
>> and Israel whom I called:
> I am He, I am the first,
>> I am the last also (48.12).

Much of Second Isaiah's theological stance can be summed up in a word which he uses on several occasions 'remember' (e.g. 44.21; 46.8, 9), remember, not as a piece of escapist nostalgia, but remember so that, through the past relived, the living God of the past becomes the living God of the present and the future.[35] But where was the living God of the past in the darkness of the present, and how was he at work?

> Thus says the Lord,
>> who opened a way in the sea
>>> and a path through mighty waters,
> Who drew on chariot and horse to their destruction,
>> a whole army, men of valour;
> there they lay, never to rise again;
>> they were crushed, snuffed out like a wick (43.16–17).

There is the appeal to the past, the remembering of the mighty deeds of the Lord in the exodus events: then comes the unexpected word:

> Cease to dwell on (lit. remember not) days gone by
>> and to brood over past history.
> Here and now I will do a new thing;
>> this moment it will break from the bud.
> Can you not perceive it? (43.18–19)

Instead of clinging to the past and to the past pattern of God's dealings with his people, they are being challenged to be open to the present and the future in which the same God will act again, but in ways which may be novel and surprising: 'a new thing' . . . . 'Can you not perceive it?' And the answer of most of the people to whom the prophet spoke was 'No, we can't'![36] Much of what the prophet has to say about the community and the positive way in which it must respond to present crisis is contained in his picture of Israel as the 'servant of the Lord'.[37] However high the calling of the servant, the prophet has no illusions; the servant is blind and deaf:

> Hear now, you that are deaf;
> you blind men look and see:
> yet who is blind but my servant.
> who so deaf as the messenger whom I send?
> Who blind as the one who holds my commission,
> so deaf as the servant of the Lord? (42.18–19).

But why is it that servant Israel does not see or understand what is happening? Because of her doubts? No, on the contrary, because of her blinding certainties. This is the claim of an interesting passage, not free from textual difficulties, in 45.9–13:[38]

> Will the pot contend with the potter,
> or the earthenware with the hand that shapes it?
> Will the clay ask the potter what he is making?
> or his handiwork say to him, 'You have no skill'?
> Will the babe say to his father, 'What are you begetting?'
> or to his mother, 'What are you bringing to birth?'
> Thus says the Lord, Israel's Holy One, his maker:
> Would you dare question me concerning my children,
> or instruct me in my handiwork?
> I alone, I made the earth
> and created man upon it;
> I, with my own hands, stretched out the heavens
> and caused all their host to shine.
> I alone have roused this man in righteousness,
> and I will smooth his path before him;
> he shall rebuild my city
> and let the exiles go free –
> not for a price nor for a bribe,
> says the Lord of Hosts.

Think, says the prophet, a piece of clay does not turn round and argue with the potter or accuse him of doing a poor job; no more does a child at the moment of conception or birth ask his parents what they think they are doing: why then do you believe that you can tell the creator of the universe how he ought to act? 'This man' (v. 13) the agent of God's deliverance of his people, God's 'anointed' (45.1) the 'shepherd' of God's people (44.28) is none other than Cyrus of Persia, a pagan emperor, claims the prophet. We must imagine some of the prophet's fellow Jews in exile, longing for, praying for, a new exodus, a new deliverance from enslavement, and when the prophet comes to them and says 'Now is the moment – and Cyrus is God's chosen agent' they turn to him and say 'You must be joking'. Of course God had used non-Jews, Assyrians and Babylonians, in the past as the agents of his judgment upon his rebellious people; but that was something different from inviting them to enrol Cyrus in the hall of fame of the great deliverers of Israel. Were they to place him alongside Moses, Joshua, David. . . ? Were their lively expectations of a coming messiah to end in this? Surely not.[39] The problem was that, based on the past they already had too clear a picture of the way in which they expected God to work. They had mapped out the contours of God's presence in the world; and God, if the prophet were right, had disappeared off their map. What Second Isaiah is trying to do is to get them to question some of their basic religious certainties, so that they may see God at work in the world, in a new and surprising way. He had to destroy elements in the faith they held; he had to sow doubts in order to make continuing faith possible. What was blinding them to God was not their doubts but their certainties; what was deafening them was not the harsh discordant voice of the pagan world, but the melodies of their own faith. They were too sure of God to find God.

In the third 'servant' passage in 50.4–9, the servant confesses his faith as one who has found vindication by remaining faithful in the midst of the darkness of persecution, degradation and insults. In the light of this the community is faced with a choice:

> Which of you fears the Lord and obeys his servant's
>   commands?
>   The man who walks in dark places with no light,
>   yet trusts in the name of the Lord and leans on his God.
> But you who kindle a fire and set fire-brands alight,
>   go, walk into your own fire,
>   and among the fire-brands you have set ablaze (50.10–11a).

Following in the way of the servant means' walking in dark places with no light' and learning in the darkness to trust and to lean on God. The alternative is to avoid the darkness, kindle, a fire-brand and walk confidently forward in that light to destruction.[40] Notice how in this context true obedience, true faith is being described as 'walking in dark places with no light', while its opposite is walking in the light which is self-kindled and self-destructive. There is no need to claim that this was always or even normally Israel's experience, but there were situations in which those who claimed to see clearly were blind, and those who claimed to have all the answers had none. In such situations the way of faith was marked by the risk of walking in darkness with previous certainties destroyed.

9

REWRITE OR RETHINK

The destruction of Jerusalem and the temple caused a fundamental shift in Jewish thinking which has left its mark on much of the literature in the Old Testament.[1] Although, after the exile to Babylon, city and temple were restored to become again important in the life and faith of the people, it could never be forgotten that they had been destroyed. A prophetic theology of judgment had been vindicated; a theology centring upon the inviolability of Zion had been found wanting. There was no longer any independent monarchy, no Davidic ruler. Any religious stance which claimed: 'I will protect this city for my own sake and for my servant David's sake' (II Kings 20.6) had proved to be at best a partial truth. The Davidic-Zion theology had 'relied too heavily upon the human institutions in which it rejoiced rather than in the God who lay behind them'.[2] Much of the history of the Hebrew monarchy in I Samuel–II Kings was reshaped and rewritten in the light of the Deuteronomistic theology which sought to take seriously the fact of national disaster and exile. That such rewriting should have taken place in an attempt to provide a valid theological response to experience was natural and necessary, but there is always the possibility that such rewriting may be used as a means of avoiding awkward facts and thus concealing the need for a more radical theology.

One of the themes of the Deuteronomic history is the operation of the word of God in Israel's history and the need for total obedience to the known demands of that word. On such obedience hangs the future of the kingdom. To 'obey the voice of the Lord your God' brings tangible blessings (Deut. 28.1–14), not to obey brings innumerable curses (Deut. 28.15–68). But do the facts preserved in the history itself always support this thesis? Do not the narratives themselves sometimes leave awkward questions unanswered? Let us examine the way in which II Kings deals with two sharply contrasted kings of Judah. II Kings 21.1–18 deals trenchantly with Manasseh who in the eyes of the narrator is the arch heretic and traitor, the epitome of all that evil in the life of Judah which ensured the downfall of the kingdom. He actively encouraged religious pluralism (vv. 3–5), offered his son as a sacrifice in pagan rites, and 'practised soothsaying and divination and dealt with ghosts and spirits' (v.6). The prophetic word of judgment was heard in the land because 'Manasseh misled them into wickedness far worse than that of the nations which the Lord had exterminated in favour of the Israelites' (v. 9). If anyone ought to have experienced the destructive curse of the Lord it was Manasseh. Yet he died peacefully at a ripe old age, after reigning fifty-five years in Jerusalem. Not only so, but for half a century he ensured that his people enjoyed the fruits of peace. No foreign armies burned or pillaged the countryside. He succeeded in convincing his Assyrian overlords that he could on the whole be trusted as a loyal vassal, although he may have been tempted on occasion under Egyptian influence, to flirt with rebellion.[3] At the opposite end of the religious spectrum stands Josiah (II Kings 22–23, 30), the reforming king, antithesis to Manasseh, the epitome of all that is to be commended in the eyes of the narrator. He suppressed all forms of religious pluralism, 'got rid of all those who called up ghosts and spirits' (II Kings 23.24), and led the nation into renewing its exclusive loyalty to the Lord. As the narrator comments: 'No king before him had turned to the Lord as he did, with all his heart and soul and strength, following the whole law of Moses; nor did any king like him appear again' (II Kings 23.25). Yet he died comparatively young, at the age of thirty nine, and he died a violent bloody death on the field of battle in a vain attempt to defend his religious policies and his nation's independence (II Kings 23.29–30). So much for promised blessing. Does this mean that 'the death of Josiah proved to be a relatively small but sharp-edged rock on which the Old Testament concept of divinely motivated history foundered'?[4] It would be wiser to claim, somewhat more modestly that both the reign of Manasseh and the death of Josiah raised theological questions of which the Kings narrative itself seems to be aware, but which it had no adequate means of handling though it tried to blunt the edge of the questions. On the one hand Manasseh may have survived long and successfully, but twice in the concluding chapters of Kings the narrative claims that it was the fatal legacy of Manasseh's apostasy which sealed the fate of Judah and Jerusalem. Josiah may have been the ideal king, 'Yet the Lord did not abate his fierce anger; it still burned against Judah because of all the provocation which Manasseh had given him. 'Judah also I will banish from my presence', he declared, 'as I banished Israel; and I will cast off this city of Jerusalem which I once chose, and the house where I promised that my Name should be' (II Kings 23.26–27). On the other hand Josiah's premature death is regarded by the narrative as a blessing in disguise; his piety ensured that he did not live to witness the final agony of his people as they experienced the just judgment of the Lord (II Kings 22.20).

Such attempted explanations in the Kings narrative do not, however, seem to have been unquestioningly accepted or acceptable in certain circles. The Chronicler, for example, whose theological outlook tends to stress even more firmly the immediacy of divine retribution, makes no reference to the held-over guilt of Manasseh as being responsible for the fate of Judah and Jerusalem.[5] How then, in the light of such a theology are the respective histories of Josiah and Manasseh to be explained? The Chronicler's account of the reign of Josiah is contained in II Chronicles 34–35 and extensively overlaps its major source material in II Kings 22–23. But there are differences, not least in the way in which the narratives deal with the death of Josiah. Whereas II Kings 23, 29 simply notes that Josiah died fighting at Megiddo against Pharaoh Necho of Egypt, II Chronicles 35.20–25 contains an interesting expansion which claims that Pharaoh Necho tried to dissuade Josiah from opposing him on the grounds that:

I have no quarrel with you today, only with those with whom I am at war. God has purposed to speed me on my way, and God is on my side; do not stand in his way, or he will destroy you (II Chron. 35.21).

But Josiah refused to listen to Necho's words 'spoken at God's command' (v. 22) and went on to be fatally wounded. Thus apparently for the first and last time, Josiah disobeyed the word of God with immediate and tragic consequences. But did he so disobey or is this perhaps history being rewritten to make it fit more easily into theology? I Esdras, a second-century BC document, takes the Chronicler's clue a step further:

> And the king of Egypt sent word to Josiah saying, 'What have we to do with each other, King of Judea? I was not sent against you by the Lord God, for my war is at the Euphrates. And now the Lord is with me. The Lord is with me urging me on. Stand aside and do not oppose the Lord'. But Josiah did not turn back to his chariot, but tried to fight him, and did not keep the word of Jeremiah the prophet from the mouth of the Lord (I Esdras 1.26–28).

There are two significant developments here; (*a*) the Chronicler speaks of Josiah disobeying 'God'. While the Chronicler almost certainly meant by this the God of Israel, there is a possible ambiguity. The reference could be interpreted in terms of an Egyptian 'god' whose command Josiah would presumably have been amply justified in ignoring. I Esdras makes it explicit that it is the Lord who speaks through Pharaoh, and that Josiah is deliberately refusing to conform to the purposes of the Lord. (*b*) Josiah's action is no longer merely violation of a word of the Lord that comes through an Egyptian Pharaoh, it is equally direct disobedience of the word of the Lord which had come through the true prophet in his reign, Jeremiah. No further vindication of the immediacy of judgment is thus needed. Instead of being potentially 'a sharp-edged rock' on which a theology of judgment may founder, Josiah's death is now a perfect illustration of the outworking of such a theology.

The Chronicler's account of Manasseh's reign is to be found in II Chronicles 33.1–20. II Chronicles 33.1–9 corresponds, with minor variations, to II Kings 21.1–9 and depicts Manasseh as the arch fiend, corruptor of the nation. According to II Chronicles 33.10–12 Manasseh paid the penalty for his misdeeds; he was captured by the Assyrians and forcibly taken to Babylon. That Manasseh, along with other Assyrian vassal kings, paid such a forced visit to Assyria – no doubt to have the dangers of flirting with Egypt personally impressed upon them – is confirmed by Assyrian documents.[6] The Chronicler then goes on to claim that in this situation of distress Manasseh

> prayed to the Lord his God and sought to placate him, and made his humble submission before the God of his fathers. He prayed, and God accepted his petition and heard his

supplication. He brought him back to Jerusalem and restored him to the throne; and thus Mannaseh learned that the Lord was God (II Chron. 33.12–13).

Thereafter not only did Manasseh see to the physical security of Jerusalem, but he carried through a thorough religious reformation, totally reversing his previous apostate inclinations. Truly, this was a sinner come to repentance. Yet neither the Kings narrative nor the book of Jeremiah (Jer. 15.4) hint at any such conversion. There is indeed something inherently improbable in the story. Is it likely that the man who has just been forcibly dragged to Assyria to have the consequences of any anti-Assyrian activities spelled out to him, would return to Jerusalem and, *inter alia*, carry through a religious reformation involving the ejection of all foreign, including presumably Assyrian gods, from Jerusalem, a policy which could only be construed as open rebellion against his imperial overlord?

The rehabilitation of Manasseh gathered momentum in certain circles. Among the documents in the Apocrypha there is 'The Prayer of Manasseh'. It purports to give substance to the brief statement in II Chronicles 33.12 that 'he prayed to the Lord his God'. This prayer is a model of penitence and piety. It begins:

> O Lord Almighty,
>> God of our fathers
>> God of Abraham and Isaac and Jacob
>>> and of their righteous posterity . . .

it concludes:

> I earnestly beseech thee,
>> forgive me, O Lord, forgive me,
> Do not destroy me with my transgressions.
> Do not be angry with me for ever
>> or lay up evil for me;
> Do not condemn me to the depths of the sea.
> For thou, O Lord, are the God of those who repent,
>> and in me thou wilt manifest thy goodness;
> for, unworthy as I am, thou wilt save me
>> in thy great mercy,
> and I will praise thee continually
>> all the days of my life.
> For all the host of heaven sing thy praise,
>> and thine is the glory for ever, Amen.

But did Manasseh repent or did the Chronicler – and those dependent upon him – rewrite history in an attempt to avoid the more challenging task of rethinking a theology to make it flexible enough to face honestly the challenge which events and experience brought? Not all later sources were happy with this total rehabilitation of Manasseh. The so-called 'Apocalypse of Baruch' claims that Manasseh prayed but did not repent.[7] Later rabbinic sources claimed: 'The angels stopped up the windows of heaven that the prayer of Manasseh might not ascend to God, and they said, "Lord of the world, art thou willing to give a gracious hearing to one who has paid worship to idols and set up an idol in the temple?" "If I did not accept the presence of this man" replied God, "I should be closing the door in the face of all repentant sinners." God made a small opening under the Throne of his Glory and received the prayer of Manasseh.'[8] There is a curious, but not uncommon, ambivalence reflected in this passage. Yes, God had to accept the prayer of the penitent, but it did not come to him through the normal channels, but almost, as it were, by the back door. Arguments were to continue as to whether Manasseh had or had not forfeited his share in the world to come.

Whatever our judgment may be on certain details in the narrative traditions and their later developments, the accounts of Manasseh and Josiah focus attention upon a problem. Where doctrine and history, either communal or personal, clash, an attempt may be made to resolve the tension in one of two ways: either by rewriting the history in such a way that it conforms more closely to what doctrine demands or by taking a long, hard look at doctrine, being prepared to rethink it in the light of experience. It is sometimes easier to rewrite history.[9]

In its starkest form this issue is faced in the book of Job. 'Great literature', it has been well said, 'is a universe framed in words.'[10] This universe, framed in the powerful poetry of the book of Job is complex, fascinating and capable of being interpreted on many different levels. The rich complexity of the literary structure and the thought patterns of the book have too often been sacrificed in an attempt to make it more amenable to Western logical criteria. There are, however, increasing signs of a new willingness to accept the integrity of the book as it now lies before us and ask what it is seeking to say as a whole.[11] The theological significance of the book as a whole, however, is not our immediate concern. At the risk of distorting or ignoring important elements in the book, let us concentrate on what divides Job from his three friends, Eliphaz, Bildad and Zophar in the dialogue which extends from chapters 3 to 27. The scene is set in the prologue in chapter 1, in which Job is introduced as 'a man of blameless and upright life' (1.1), a man in whom the ideal of piety and material prosperity walking hand in hand is perfectly realized. The prologue also indicates clearly what the ensuing tragedy is all about. This is a man being tested, with God's permission, to see whether he truly 'fears God' (cf. 1.9; 2.3), to discover whether there is such a thing as wholly disinterested faith. One by one the material props to his piety are removed. He himself is afflicted with 'running sores from head to foot' (2.8). The reader knows what is at stake, but Job does not, neither do the three friends who come silently to share his grief and to comfort him.

Job's initial response is one of quiet acceptance:

> Naked I came from the womb,
>   naked I shall return whence I came.
> The Lord gives and the Lord takes away;
>   blessed be the name of the Lord (1.21).

The extremity of his suffering, however, demands some explanation. Echoing through his first bitter complaint in chapter 3 is the demand for some answer to the niggling question 'why?':

> Why was I not still-born,
>   why did I not die when I came forth from the womb?
> Why was I ever laid on my mother's knee
>   or put to suck at her breasts? (3.11, 12)

>   . . .

> Why should the sufferer be born to see the light?
> Why is life given to men who find it so bitter? (3.20)

The why is acute for Job because of a theological premise which both he and his friends share, a premise concerning the relationship between the divine ordering of the universe and human suffering which is to be found widely not only in the Old Testament, but which had for centuries prior to the book of Job been normative in Mesopotamian thought.[12] It is stated in its most persuasive form in Eliphaz's first speech to Job in chapters 4 and 5, and is intended to give both comfort and hope. Job had often in the past spoken the helpful word to others in their experience of

affliction, can he not now apply the same teaching to his own
condition?

> Is your religion no comfort to you?
>   Does your blameless life give you no hope?
> For consider, what innocent man has ever perished?
>   Where have you seen the upright destroyed?
> This I know, that those who plough mischief and sow trouble
>   reap as they have sown;
> They perish at the blast of God
>   and are shrivelled by the breath of his nostrils (4.6–9).

Stated thus baldly, this is a theological stance which leads to
inevitable questioning as we have seen in our study of the Psalm.[13]
But Eliphaz qualifies it by an appeal both to religious experience
and to observation of life. Claiming the authority of a strange
nocturnal vision, graphically described in 4.12–16, Eliphaz declares that no man can be wholly righteous or pure in the sight of
God (4.17f.). It follows therefore by implication that suffering,
which is related to sin, is an element in all human experience. It
does not grow naturally like weeds out of the ground; it is human
conditioned, an inevitable part of what it means to be human (5.6–
7). Further, it is not necessarily true that wicked men meet with
immediate retribution, nor that retribution falls solely on themselves. They may seem for a time to flourish, to take root, but one
day the crash comes engulfing family and dependents in misery
and suffering.[14] Human calamities abound, but there is still God,
dependable in his generosity and his goodness; and it is part of
that goodness that he 'frustrates the plots of the crafty' (5.12) and
rescues 'the needy from the grip of the strong' (5.15). For a man
whose conscience is clear, therefore, suffering may be accepted
as part of God's discipline. But for such a man it can only be
temporary. Job can trust God to see to it that once again all will be
well in his life (5.17–26). It is important to do justice to Eliphaz's
position. It has a strong claim to be taken seriously, otherwise it
would hardly have been so widely and tenaciously held. It
recognizes that, and seeks to explain why, suffering is a part of
human experience. At the same time it insists that this is God's
world, a world that makes moral sense, a world in which the
righteous flourish and the wicked do not. Such is the theme,
which, transposed into different keys and subject to a profusion

of variations, increasingly strident variations, is sounded by the three friends throughout their dialogue with Job.

When Job responds to Eliphaz in chapters 6 and 7, it is almost as if he had not heard what Eliphaz had been saying. What Eliphaz says may well be true, but it makes no point of contact with a man struggling to find meaning in the midst of extreme physical and spiritual agony. Eliphaz may speak calmly of suffering as God's discipline, but Job can only cry out:

> The arrows of the Almighty find their mark in me,
>   and their poison soaks into my spirit;
> God's onslaughts wear me away (6.4).

The pain-wracked 'whys' of chapter 3 remain unanswered and unaswerable on Eliphaz's premise, except on the assumption that Job must have committed crimes in some sense commensurate with his suffering:

> 'Tell me plainly' he cries, 'and I will listen in silence,
>   show me where I have erred' (6.24).

Job makes no claim to be perfect; yet he insists on his integrity. He has not wilfully offended God or man. He belongs to the righteous rather than to the wicked, yet he is experiencing a fate appropriate to the wicked, not to the righteous. Nothing can shake him from this conviction, and in the light of it the theological certainties of his friends bring him neither comfort nor hope.

As the dialogue develops there is evidence of increasing exasperation in the minds of the friends, and an ever-deepening sense of alienation from Job. Who is he to subvert traditional theological teaching? Yet they cannot persuade him either to deny or to reinterpret what he believes to be the clear witness of his own personal experience. There is also evidence, however, of something much more sinister at work. A comparison between Eliphaz's first speech in chapters 6 and 7 and his third and final speech in chapter 22 is instructive. Both speeches hold out to Job the hope that he will experience a happy and joy-filled future, if only he will submit to God's discipline (5.8–27; 22.21–30). Yet the basis for such hope has shifted. In his first speech Eliphaz assumes that Job is 'blameless', 'innocent' and 'upright' (5.6, 7) and that as such he has, under God, an assured, successful future, no matter what temporary upsets may intervene. In his final speech Eliphaz reiterates a theme which has been frequently on the lips of the friends – the wicked and the inevitable fate which befalls them, e.g. 18.5–21; 20.4–26 – and pointedly applies it to Job by cataloguing the crimes of which he is guilty;

> Do not think that he reproves you because you are pious,
>   that on this account he brings you to trial.
> No: it is because you are a very wicked man,
>   and your depravity passes all bounds.
> Without due cause you take a brother in pledge,
>   you strip men of their clothes and leave them naked.
> When a man is weary, you give him no water to drink
>   and you refuse bread to the hungry.
> Is the earth, then, the preserve of the strong
>   and a domain for the favoured few?
> Widows you have sent away empty-handed,
>   Orphans you have struck defenceless.
> No wonder that there are pitfalls in your path,
>   That snares are set to fill you with sudden fear (22.4–10).

Yet these words cannot be anything other than a baseless slander. In his noble and impassioned *apologia pro vita sua* in chapter 31 Job categorically denies that he has been guilty of such crimes:

> If I have withheld their needs from the poor
>   or let the widows' eyes grow dim with tears,
> If I have eaten my crust alone,
>   and the orphan has not shared it with me –
> . . .
> If I have seen anyone perish for lack of clothing,
>   or a poor man with nothing to cover him,
> . . .
> then may my shoulder-blade be torn from my shoulder,
>   My arm be wrenched out of its socket! (31.16, 17, 19, 22)

Indeed the whole drama of the book depends on Job speaking the truth in these words. If it were not so there would be no problem. And that is precisely the point. Because in the light of the friends' theological outlook there *ought* to be no problem, then there will be no problem. If Job's experience does not fit in with the religious script they are following, so much the worse for Job's experience. Their theology insists that Job must have sinned grievously, therefore he has sinned grievously. Rather than revise their script, they are prepared to rewrite Job's life – not the first or the last time that truth has been sacrificed upon the altar of deeply-held theological convictions.

What of the attitude of Job? Job shares with his friends the conviction that he lives out his life in a world ruled by God, and that therefore God is the ultimate source of his problems. But whereas to the friends God is trustworthy, his ways morally justifiable and understandable, even though his greatness transcends full human comprehension, to Job God is complex, enigmatic, elusive and apparently irrational. The more the attitude of the friends hardens against him, the more Job appeals from them and their theology to God: yet far from easing his problems, this appeal increases his spiritual travail. Certain things, however, become clear.

1. With increasing clarity Job senses that life does not always fit the religious script from which the friends are working. Not only is he convinced of this in terms of his own experience, but he is prepared to throw down the gauntlet by an appeal to human experience in general. No matter with what impassioned repetition the friends seek to defend the thesis that in God's world the righteous flourish and the wicked perish, Job with icy logic insists that this is not a verifiable presupposition, and that there is much evidence pointing in the opposite direction. To Zophar's assertion in 20.4 that 'the triumph of the wicked is short-lived, the glee of the godless lasts but for a moment', Job retorts:

> Why do the wicked enjoy long life,
>   hale in old age, and great and powerful?
> They live to see their children settled,
>   their kinsfolk and descendants flourishing;
> their families are secure and safe;
>   the rod of God's justice does not reach them (21.7–9).

Often it is the wicked who seem to escape when tragedy strikes. They live life to the full and are as honoured in death as they are during their lifetime. They have no hesitation in using power to further their own interests, often at the expense of the poor and the defenceless in society who struggle, often in vain, to keep body and soul together:

> Naked and bare they go about their work,
>   and hungry they carry the sheaves;
> they press the oil in the shade where two walls meet,
>   they tread the winepress but themselves go thirsty.

> Far from the city, they groan like dying men,
>   and like wounded men they cry out;
> but God pays no heed to their prayer (24.10–12).

Flinging such evidence in the face of the confident, pious asser-
tions of his friends, he challenges them to prove that he is wrong:

> If this is not so, who will prove me wrong
>   and make nonsense of my argument? (24.25)[15]

Job's words to his friends climax in a dramatic and uncompromising declaration of innocence:

> I swear by God who has denied me justice,
>   and by the Almighty, who has filled me with bitterness:
> So long as there is any life left in me
>   and God's breath is in my nostrils,
> no untrue word shall pass my lips
>   and my tongue shall utter no falsehood.
> God forbid that I should allow you to be right;
>   till death, I will not abandon my claim to innocence.
> I will maintain the rightness of my cause, I will never give up;
>   so long as I live, I will not change (27.2–6).[16]

But something must give. If Job's innocence is not to be sacrificed,
then the theology of the friends stands in need of radical revision.
If they are not to be allowed to rewrite Job's life, then the reader
is compelled to recognize the inadequacy of their theology,
however hallowed it may be by tradition.

2. What is at stake in all this, however, is not merely an
argument about the respective fortunes of the wicked and the
righteous in a God-ordered world, it is rather a doctrine of God.
What kind of God is it possible to believe in, in a world where the
traditional religious script no longer makes sense, and where
there seems no explanation of the harshness of life's experience?
Job hardly seems to know. His attitude to God is characterized by
wildly fluctuating moods, with bitterness and trust, hope and
despair struggling within his soul. The friends may speak to God
calmly; Job's relationship with God is tempestuous and volcanic.
The God whom he once knew as a friend, he now thinks of as a
cruel capricious enemy:

> God had left me at the mercy of malefactors
>   and cast me into the clutches of wicked men.

I was at ease, but he set upon me and mauled me,
    seized me by the neck and worried me.
He set me up as his target;
    his arrows rained upon me from every side;
pitiless, he cut deep into my vitals,
    he spilt my gall on the ground.
He made breach after breach in my defences;
    he fell upon me like a fighting man (16.11–14; cf. 6.4).

The pent up bitterness in his soul bursts forth into a bitter parody of Psalm 8, that Psalm which expresses the special place of man in God's creation:

What is man that thou makest much of him
    and turnest thy thoughts towards him,
only to punish him morning by morning
    or to test him for every hour of the day? (7.17–18)

Pleading with God to stop hounding him, he contemplates the brief, troubled frailty of human life and lapses into despair (cf. chapters 14 and 17). But even on the edge of despair, he remains convinced of his innocence, convinced that what alienates him from God must be some tragic misunderstanding and that if only he could break through to God all would be well. It is as if two warring visions of God were tearing Job apart. God cannot be made to account for his actions to man. Although it seems to Job that God flouts justice indiscriminately (ch. 9), yet Job insists in appealing to this alien God:

I am sickened of life;
I will give free reign to my griefs,
I will speak out in bitterness of soul.
I will say to God, 'Do not condemn me,
    but tell me the ground of thy complaint against me' (10.1–2).

There must be some way in which his appeal will be heard. An arbitrator would surely be able to bridge the gulf between himself and God and remove misunderstanding (9.33–35). There must be someone in heaven prepared to act as witness in his defence (16.18–22). Although he finds his friends totally devoid of human pity, determined only to break him, he firmly believes that one day he will be vindicated (19.25–26).[17] Yet he is reaching out in hope to a God who remains elusive:

If only I knew how to find him,
  how to enter his court,
I would state my case before him
  and set out my arguments in full;
Then I should learn what answer he would give
  and find out what he had to say.
Would he exert his great power to browbeat me?
  No; God himself would never bring a charge against me.
There the upright are vindicated before him,
  and I shall win from my judge an absolute discharge.
If I go forward he is not there;
  if backward, I cannot find him;
when I turn left, I do not descry him;
  I face right, but I see him not (23.2–9).

Job does not doubt the power, the omnipotence of God; but he is
driven to wonder whether he is not merely a plaything in the
hands of a capricious God who for ever eludes his grasp, and
whose ways he can neither understand nor justify.[18]

To what extent the issues raised in the dialogue between Job
and his friends find any resolution in the book depends largely on
what significance we assign to the speeches of the Lord to Job
which come as the climax to the book in chapters 38–41. Certainly
they provide no obvious answer to the problem of unmerited
human suffering and meaningless agony. Indeed they are conspicuous by the absence of any reference to this issue. The tables
are now reversed. The Job who had hurled his questions at God,
now finds himself on the receiving end as, in rhetorical question
after rhetorical question, God confronts Job with the mysteries of
creation and life which surpass all human comprehension. The
poetry is superb, the meaning and purpose far from clear. Do
these chapters leave us with Job crushed by naked power,[19] with
a God who is beyond morality?[20] Do they celebrate not only the
mystery but the miracle of life which enables men, even in the
midst of oppressive evil 'to refuse to yield either to self-deception
or to despair'?[21] Do they speak of a God no longer elusive, a God
who comes to Job in the midst of his suffering, no longer an
enemy but a companion banishing his sense of alienation?[22] Such
questions can be multiplied, and they are best left as questions,
since there is little consensus as to the answers – nor is there likely
to be. One of the most ironic statements in the whole of the Bible,
however, is surely to be found in the epilogue to the book at 42.7,

where the Lord, at the end of his speeches with Job, turns to Eliphaz and says, 'I am angry with you and your two friends, because you have not spoken as you ought about me, as my servant Job has done'. The friends are then told to go to Job, to offer sacrifices, and to ask Job to intercede for them. There is irony in the fact that in his final speech to Job Eliphaz has demanded that Job should 'come to terms with God' (22.21), repent, and has promised that if he does he will prosper and God will hear his prayers. Job did come to terms with God (42.2–6), but little did Eliphaz suspect that Job's prayers that God would hear would be prayers designed to divert God's anger away from Eliphaz and his friends. There is irony in the fact that the friends, who unquestioningly believed that they were defending the ways of God against the disturbed protests of a man who had lost faith, are described as not speaking about God as they ought, while the angry, agonized protests of that man are apparently acceptable to God. It is not necessary to assume that all that the friends said about God was erroneous – far from it; nor that everything that Job said was correct: but on the central issue as to whether Job's suffering could be explained in terms of his sinning against God and whether, in general, merit and experience walked hand in hand, the theology of the friends, however hallowed by tradition, was inadequate, and the protests of Job were justified. It is of the essence of Job's position that he is depicted not as locked into assured certainties, but as on pilgrimage, a troubled, stormy pilgrimage, searching for a faith which will make sense of his experience. H. H. Rowley has commented: 'For tortured spirits theology is less satisfying than religion, and religion is encounter, encounter with God. It is in the sphere of religion rather than theology that the meaning of the book is to be found.'[23] But theology and religion are not so easily separated. The nature of Job's encounter with God was inseparable from his protest against an over-simplistic theology. He refused to allow his friends to rewrite his life to preserve that theology. Instead he challenged them and himself to rethink. He struggled to grasp the God who was beyond the God of current theology. In the outcome his hurt protests, his bitter wrestling with God, were justified. There was more faith in such deeply questioning protests and scepticism than in the pious affirmation of untroubled, but blind, certainty.

10

THE RADICAL CONSERVATIVE

If Job is the story of a man whose relationship to God drove him into a whirlwind of spiritual turmoil, the author of the book of Ecclesiastes, Qoheleth,[1] portrays himself as a very different and somewhat enigmatic character; though his attitude to much in the religious tradition which nurtured him is equally radical. How enigmatic Qoheleth is, the history of the interpretation of the book across the centuries amply demonstrates. In 1861 Christian D. Ginsburg concluded a monumental survey of both Jewish and Christian exegesis of the book with the following words: 'What a solemn lesson for the pious and for the learned to abstain from dogmatism, and what an admonition not to urge ones own pious emotions and religious conceits as the meaning of the Word of God.'[2] Ginsburg's own commentary amply illustrated his own warning, and the history of interpretation ever since has provided further illustration. It is not difficult to imagine the ghost of Qoheleth flitting around Sheol thinking, with a wry smile on his face, that the way commentators have handled his book is a beautiful example of his central conviction, 'Vanity of vanities, all is vanity' (1.2).

Before we can begin to analyse the book there are two major critical issues about which we have to take decisions.

1. To what extent can we regard the book of Ecclesiastes as reflecting the thought of one man? What allowance must we make for the possibility that the thought of a man who may have been radically sceptical has been modified by later, more orthodox thinkers, to make it more palatable? There are scholars who have seen as many as four or five different hands at work in the book in its present form. Almost all introductions to the book provide

lists of verses which are taken to be later additions.[3] While each case must be judged on its merits any fragmentary approach to the book is far from convincing. The passage which has the strongest claim to come from someone other than Qoheleth is 12.9–12, perhaps added by a friend of, or at least a sympathizer with, Qoheleth, who was only too conscious that some of the words of Qoheleth were liable to give offence to more timid and pious minds. He defends Qoheleth on the ground that what he had to say was nothing other than the truth, and that if the reader does not like it, that only witnesses to the fact that the truth is often uncomfortable: 'The sayings of the wise are sharp as goads, like nails driven home . . .' (12.11).[4]

2. The other, and indeed related, problem is the extent to which the book in its present form contains quotations. Since Hebrew does not use quotation marks, how do we know in certain cases whether Qoheleth is giving us his own thoughts, or whether he is quoting someone else's opinions and then commenting upon them perhaps by way of disagreement? Chapter 2.13–14 provides an interesting example of the problem. The New English Bible translates, 'Then I perceived that wisdom is more profitable than folly, as light is more profitable than darkness: the wise man has eyes in his head, but the fool walks in the dark. Yet I also say that one and the same fate overtakes them both.' This translation assumes that these verses contain two considered conclusions held by Qoheleth:

(a) it is better to be wise than to be a fool;
(b) in the end, however, one fate (i.e. death) comes to both wise and fool alike.

Robert Gordis, however, translates: 'I have heard it said, "Wisdom is more profitable than folly . . .". But I know that one and the same fate comes to both.' In this case Qoheleth begins by quoting what may well have been a traditional wisdom saying about the superiority of wisdom over folly, and quotes it to reject it, or at least severely to qualify it, on the grounds that death is the great leveller.[5] A variation on this approach is to see in 2.13–14 a shift in Qoheleth's own thinking, without assuming that he is necessarily quoting anything: 'I once thought that wisdom was more profitable than folly . . . but now I realise that. . . .'[6] Where we insert quotation marks, and what particular nuance we give to certain words and phrases, has a profound effect on how we understand the book. Thus Jerome put some of the inconveniently sceptical passages into quotation marks. They are, he claims, the utterances of opponents to the truth whom Qoheleth proceeds to refute with impeccable orthodoxy and vibrant faith. Jerome indeed used the book to try to persuade a certain young lady of his acquaintance to betake herself to a nunnery. Qoheleth's purpose is 'to show the vanity of every earthly enjoyment and hence the necessity of betaking oneself to an ascetic life devoted entirely to the service of God'. He got round the problem of the recurring passages which advocate that one should 'eat and drink and enjoy oneself' (e.g. 2.24; 3.13; 5.18), by referring them to the eucharist![7] Many modern commentators tend to do the opposite. They put what seem to be inconveniently orthodox passages into quotation marks and allow Qoheleth to comment on them with eager and acid scepticism. We are caught here in an inescapable circle. The placing of quotation marks, the flavour we give to certain statements, depends upon certain prior assumptions that we have about the main drift of Qoheleth's teaching; and the conclusions we reach about the main drift of that teaching depends upon what we think ought to go into quotation marks and what particular flavour we give to certain statements in the book.

One thing is reasonably clear; both from the standpoint of language and content, Ecclesiastes is one of the latest books in the Old Testament. Although it was traditionally assigned to Solomon,[8] to say that Solomon wrote it is like saying, in the words of R. B. Y. Scott, that 'a book about Marxism in modern English idiom and spelling was written by Henry VIII'.[9] Qoheleth stands near the end of a long tradition of faith, and with respect to that tradition he is both cautious and rebellious. To some parts of the tradition he is prepared to say firmly 'amen'. He accepts, for example, the picture in Genesis 2 of man in his creaturely finitude, man who receives from God the same breath of life as the animals, man from whom at the end this breath of life is withdrawn, and who then returns to the dust from whence he came (3.19, 9.10). Both socially and religiously there is a strong conservative streak in Qoheleth.[10] But in the main he gives the impression of being a man for whom much in the religious traditions of his people no longer has the power to convince. The God of his forefathers was dead, though Qoheleth would have been shocked if it had been suggested to him that he no longer believed in God. Atheism was hardly a live intellectual option for a Jew of his day.

There is an intensely personal, confessional element in the

book. Although standing within the wisdom tradition, Qoheleth is not content merely to pass general wisdom-style comments on life, on the distinction between wise and foolish, righteous and wicked. The book is full of statements of personal attitudes and conclusions: e.g. 'I applied my mind to study and explore all that is done under heaven (1.12, cf. 1.17; 2.13). . . . I said to myself (2.1, 14 etc.) . . . I perceived . . . yet I also saw (2.13). . . . I turned and gave myself up to despair (2.20)'. Such personal reflections and questioning are encapsuled in the thematic text within which he begins – and probably ends his book at 12.8 – and which occurs at point after point in the course of the book,

> Vanity of vanities, says Qoheleth, vanity of vanities, all is vanity.[11]

The varied attempts of modern translations to render this phrase only serve to reveal how elusive it is:

> It is useless, useless, said the Philosopher. Life is useless, all is useless (Good News Bible).

> In my opinion, nothing is worthwhile: everything is futile (The Living Bible).

> Emptiness, emptiness, says the Speaker, emptiness, all is empty (NEB).

The key Hebrew word which lies behind these varied renderings is *hebel*, a word which basically seems to mean breath, vapour or wind. Its primary meaning is well preserved in Isaiah 57.13, where it is said of idols:

> The wind shall carry them away, one and all,
>   a puff of air shall blow them away.

The word translated 'wind' (*rûaḥ*) can indicate a strong powerful wind – and hence by analogy, the spirit of God powerfully at work in the world – but *hebel*, the 'puff of air' never develops this meaning. It always has the idea of weakness, of something which is insubstantial, often futile. As such it can be applied to specific experiences or things in life. Thus 'making a fortune by telling lies' is characterized as *hebel* in Proverbs 21.6 (cf. Prov. 13.11) or as the Good News Bible paraphrases 'The riches you get by dishonesty soon disappear'. Job, in the grip of despair, can cry out:

> Leave me alone, for my life is but a vapour (*hebel*) (7.16, cf. 7.3).

The servant of the Lord in Isaiah 49.4 complains:

> I have laboured in vain, I have spent my strength for nothing
> and to no purpose;

i.e. my ministry has been an exercise in futility. Here, in the phrase 'for nothing and to no purpose' the word *hebel* is linked to one of the words commonly used in the Old Testament to describe the disorderly nothingness of chaos. In Isaiah 30.7, the prophet describes the military help, on which the people are depending, from Egypt as *hebel*, meaningless, irrelevant to the crisis situation; help which is in fact no help. Psalm 78.32 speaks of the effect of the judgment of God on a stubbornly rebellious people in the following terms: 'he made their days vanish like a breath (*hebel*)', which the New English Bible felicitiously renders, 'So in one moment he snuffed out their lives'. It is hardly surprising that *hebel* gained popularity as a word suitable to use to describe idols, and the activity of those who worship idols. The gods of other nations are *hebel*, false, lacking all substance (e.g. Jer. 14.22; Deut. 32.21; Jonah 2.9). Jeremiah complains that the forefathers of the nation, when they proved faithless to the Lord in the wilderness, pursued *hebel* and became *hebel*: 'pursuing empty phantoms and themselves becoming empty' (Jer. 2.5). Thus specific situations, and in particular the turning to other gods, are described as *hebel* in Old Testament tradition prior to Qoheleth. But no one, as far as we can see, before Qoheleth had dared within this tradition to look at the whole of life, all experience, everything, and pass on it the verdict 'completely *hebel*'. It is important to realize how radical a break this is with the tradition in which Qoheleth had been nurtured. Genesis 1 surveys the world, sees everything as created by God, and passes on it all the verdict 'good, very good' (Gen. 1.31). Book after book in the Old Testament insists, or assumes, that life is meaningful. Deuteronomy will sum up this meaning in the words 'Hear, O Israel, the Lord is our God, one Lord, and you must love the Lord your God with all your heart and soul and strength' (Deut. 6.4–5). Both Jeremiah and Job, caught up in situations which they cannot understand and which drive them to near despair, still insist that there must be meaning, that life must make sense, even if that means questioning or dissenting from what other people say about God. They defiantly affirm meaning in face of the apparent meaninglessness of life. Along comes Qoheleth and coolly says: 'It is all *hebel*', you are wasting your time looking for meaning; there is none.' This does not mean that Qoheleth finds life uninteresting. He is in fact intensely interested in the rich variety of human experience and in the many faceted diamond of life which he examines in his own quizical way. Nor does it mean that life is not enjoyable. Qoheleth had come to terms with life and found much that was positive in it to enjoy. What it does mean is that life to him was an insoluble puzzle, and the more he wrestled with it the more puzzling it became. Beside the whole of life he places a large question mark. It is as if he had taken a long cool look at life, turned away, shrugged his shoulders and said 'well I don't know'. Life had for him a will o' the wisp quality. To try to penetrate its inmost secrets was – to use another phrase which Qoheleth often uses in conjunction with *hebel* – like 'chasing the wind' (e.g. 1.17; 2.11, 17,26; 4.4; 6.9). Perhaps the New English Bible 'emptiness' comes near to catching the flavour of what Qoheleth intends by *hebel*, provided we take such emptiness to mean 'empty of ultimate meaning'. In this sense the thought of emptiness pervades the entire book.

Let us trace this idea as, in Qoheleth's thinking, it impinges upon different aspects of Israel's religious traditions.

1. *The attitude to the natural world*

The hymn of creation in Genesis 1, whatever its date, celebrates an ordered universe created by God out of chaos, a universe which reflects the activity and purposes of a God upon whose work the verdict 'good, very good' is passed. In line with this we find in many Psalms hymns which approach the world with a sense of awe and gladness, and see reflected in its ordered structure something of the character of God. Thus Psalm 8,

> When I look up at thy heavens, the work of thy fingers,
>   the moon and the stars set in their place by thee,
> what is man that thou shouldst remember him,
>   mortal man that thou shouldst care for him? (Ps. 8.3–4)

In Psalm 136, among the great marvels of God which call for a grateful celebration of the divine love which endures for ever, are:

> In wisdom he made the heavens;
>   his love endures for ever.

> He laid the earth upon the waters,
>   his love endures for ever.
> He made the great lights,
>   his love endures for ever,
> The sun to rule by day,
>   his love endures for ever,
> The moon and the stars to rule by night;
>   his love endures for ever (Ps. 136.5–9).

Psalm 104 invites the worshipper joyfully to celebrate the greatness of God:

> Bless the Lord, my soul:
> O Lord my God, thou art great indeed,
>   clothed in majesty and splendour,
>   and wrapped in a robe of light.
> Thou hast spread out the heavens like a tent
>   and on their waters laid the beams of thy pavilion;
> who takest the clouds for thy chariot,
>   riding on the winds of the wind;
> who makest the winds thy messengers
>   and flames of fire thy servants;
> thou didst fix the earth on its foundation
>   so that it can never be shaken (Ps. 104.1–5).

In all such hymns there is a mood of positive appreciation, of confidence, of joyful response to a God whose goodness and dependability are writ large across the world of his creating, the world which is man's home.

Qoheleth looks out on the same world, but he views it very differently.

> The sun rises and the sun goes down; back it returns to its place and rises there again. The wind blows south, the wind blows north, round and round it goes and returns full circle. All streams run into the sea, yet the sea never overflows; back to the place from which the streams ran they return to run again (1.5–7).

No longer is the sun in its daily routine a witness to 'the love that endures for ever'; no longer does God ride on the winds, making the winds his messengers. The joy, the confidence, the positive appreciation are missing. The only message that the sun and the wind convey, is the message of the relentless, unceasing and wearying monotony which characterizes the world, a monotony which reduces men to silence and underlines that no human experience can ever be fully satisfying. Sun, wind and rivers are parables of a dull uniformity, signs that there is nothing new, nothing unexpected or exciting in human experience. The same things which made the psalmist cry out, 'Bless the Lord, my soul' make Qoheleth say, 'I have seen it all before'. In this Qoheleth seems to be ploughing a lonely furrow, not only in the light of other Old Testament hymns, but also in the light of earlier and later wisdom teaching.[12]

2. *Prophetic tradition*

Qoheleth also parts company from what are certain strong emphases in prophetic teaching. Again and again he insists that life is what it is, and that there is little use getting uptight or complaining about it. We may not like it, but we must accept *inter alia* that

> What is crooked cannot become straight; what is not there cannot be counted (1.14).

But it is the repeated prophetic claim that the crooked can and must be made straight, and that in a society where justice and righteousness are missing, it is God's will, and man's responsibility to struggle, to establish a right order of society in which the needs of all are met. Qoheleth disagrees. He is well aware that there are anomalies and injustices in the world; '. . . I saw here under the sun that, where justice ought to be, there was wickedness, and where righteousness ought to be, there was wickedness' (3.16). To such a situation the prophetic response would be the challenge 'repent'; 'hate evil, love good' . . . 'Let justice roll on like a river and righteousness like an ever-flowing stream (Amos 5.24). Qoheleth, however, simply throws up his hands and says, 'no doubt God will judge one day, but meanwhile there is nothing that can be done; that is just how it is in life. There is no point in being either shocked or outraged'.

> If you witness in some province the oppression of the poor and the denial of right and justice, do not be surprised at what goes on, for every official has a higher one set over him, and the highest keeps watch over them all (5.8).

Blame it all on bureaucracy. It's the system and you can't beat or change the system. No revolutionary prophetic ethic stirs in Qoheleth's soul. Rather he advises us to accept the *status quo*; it is far from perfect but it is all that we have got. At this point Qoheleth may be reflecting, more or less uncritically, the aristocratic, upper-class mentality which finds strong expression in many strands of the wisdom tradition in the Old Testament, notably in Job and Ecclesiastes.[13] But where else in the Old Testament do we find such a passive, uncritical acceptance of the *status quo*?

3. *The authority of torah*

Torah, the law or revelation, particularly in its fixed written form contained in Genesis to Deuteronomy, had a unique authority in Israel before Qoheleth's day. He had pondered the implications of this authority and come to his own distinctive conclusions. Twice in Deuteronomy the absolute and final authority of the revelation given to Israel through Moses is underlined by emphasizing that it must not be tampered with in any way:

> Now Israel, listen to the statutes and laws which I am teaching you, and obey them; then you will live, and go in and occupy the land which the Lord the God of your fathers is giving you. You must not add anything to my charge, nor take anything away from it. You must carry out all the commandments of the Lord your God which I lay upon you (Deut. 4.1–2).

Again at the climax to a series of injunctions:

> See that you observe everything I command you: you must not add anything to it, nor take anything away from it (Deut. 12.32; Heb. 13.1).

This stress upon the integrity of the given revelation is intended in Deuteronomy to provide the community with a secure and unchanging framework within which they may respond in love to the God who comes to them in love. Qoheleth is well aware of this teaching: 'I know', he says 'that whatever God does (or wills) lasts for ever; to add to it or to subtract from it is impossible' (3.14). But this hardly evokes from him the kind of response which is intended in Deuteronomy. God has done it all, claims Qoheleth 'in such a way that men must feel awe in his presence'. Here

Qoheleth is dealing with a concept which appears widely in the Old Testament, particularly in the wisdom tradition, and is present in his thinking, 'the fear of the Lord' or the awe that men ought to feel in God's presence (cf. 5.6; 8.12; 12.13). It is a highly ambiguous concept which can range in meaning all the way from a gladly-given reverence and obedience – the Old Testament equivalent of what we mean by religion – to something much nearer to our popular sense of dread. R. Gordis thinks that behind the use of the phrase here there lies a primitive concept of the jealousy of God which threatens man; and that genuine faith having broken down for Qoheleth, all that is left for him is to revert to the primitive. But we do not need to go so far as that to understand Qoheleth's attitude here. Whereas in Deuteronomy the statement, 'you must not add anything to it, nor take anything away from it' affirms the need for total obedience to the given revelation, for Qoheleth this statement deepens his sense of fatalistic resignation in the face of life. God's will and intentions are fixed, inscrutable and totally unalterable. The trouble is that it is not clear what they are. We can only bow before what we cannot understand. We must accept, and such acceptance is part of what is meant for Qoheleth by 'the fear of the Lord'. Far from bringing him security and joy, however, this thought brings a chill into his sensitive soul.

4. *The meaning of worship*

In our study of the Psalms we have noted the many-sided, open and frank approach to God which was characteristic of worship in ancient Israel.[14] Qoheleth has a few well-considered words to say about worship in chapter 5.1–7 (Heb. 4.17ff.). He begins with a word of warning:

> Go carefully when you visit the house of God. Better draw near in obedience than offer the sacrifice of fools, who sin without a thought. Do not rush into speech, let thee be no hasty utterance of God's presence. God is in heaven, you are on earth; so let your words be few (5.1–2)

Again there is much that is traditional in this attitude. We can almost hear, echoing in his mind, some of the trenchant criticisms that the prophets had made of the superficial shallowness of

worship in Israel, an attitude crystalized in Samuel's words to
Saul:

> Obedience is better than sacrifice,
>   and to listen to him than the fat of rams (I Sam. 15.22).

And if when he says, 'do not rush into speech' all that he is asking
for is a little meaningful verbal economy in our approach to God,
there would be few to disagree with him. Likewise there is a
healthy realism in the advice he gives in verses 4ff.

> When you make a vow to God, do not be slow to pay it, for he
> has no use for fools; pay whatever you vow. Better not vow at
> all than vow and fail to pay.

There is no use, he says, promising something to God, and then
turning round and saying 'I did not really mean it' or 'I can't keep
my promise'. In that case it would have been better never to have
taken a vow at all. In this he is going no more than echoing the
words of Deuteronomy 23.21–23:

> When you make a vow to the Lord your God, do not put off
> its fulfilment; otherwise the Lord your God will require
> satisfaction of you and you will be guilty of sin. If you choose
> not to make a vow, you will not be guilty of sin; but if you
> voluntarily make a vow to the Lord your God, mind what you
> say and do what you have promised.

It is characteristic of Qoheleth, however, that even when he is
quoting or echoing traditional teaching, he tends to mean something different, because his experience is different. Verbal economy in worship – yes, but if you ask whether Qoheleth would
have joyfully and meaningfully sung, 'Bless the Lord, my soul;
my innermost heart, bless his holy name', (Ps. 103.1) or shouted
'hallelujah, praise the Lord' without embarrassment, then the
answer is almost certainly 'no'. His attitude to worship is con-
trolled by his belief: 'God is in heaven, you are on earth; so let
your words be few.' God, for Qoheleth, is wholly transcendent,
unknowable; between God and man there is an impassable gulf,
which rules out the possibility of any living relationship. What is
there left to say, except 'You must fear God' (v. 7). It is as if
Qoheleth was trying to hold on firmly to religious conventions,
after the vital flame of religion had gone out in his own soul. Yet
even the religious conventions which remained had a chill side to

them. As has been well said, 'For Qoheleth there can be no talk of a vital prayer relationship with God. . . . For other sages, the fear of the Lord is the beginning of wisdom; it is the Israelite equivalent of our term "religion". For Qoheleth it signifies cold terror; the fear of the Lord means that one is in mortal danger when dealing with God who interferes in human affairs only at the point of judgment'.[15] From the worship of such a God much of the rich and warm variety of Israel's authentic worshipping experience is excluded.

5. *The wisdom tradition*

It is in his attitude to the wisdom tradition that Qoheleth reveals most clearly where he stands. We cannot come to grips with Qoheleth unless we see him as one brought up within, and thoroughly familiar with, the wisdom tradition in Israel. It is indeed quite likely that Qoheleth himself functioned as a teacher in some wisdom academy, where seekers after wisdom would gather to be instructed in the traditions of the wise, and where there would be lively discussion of the issues raised by traditional wisdom teaching. In certain sections of the book, notably in chapters 7 and 10, there are collections of wisdom sayings, which tersely and vividly draw attention to varied aspects of human experience, e.g.:

Better the end of anything than its beginning;
 better patience than pride.
Do not be quick to show resentment;
 for resentment is nursed by fools.
Do not ask why the old days were better than these;
 for that is a foolish question (7.8–10).

If a snake bites before it is charmed,
 the snake-charmer loses his fee (10.11).

Do not speak ill of the king in your ease,
 or of a rich man in your bedroom;
for a bird may carry your voice,
 and a winged messenger may repeat what you say (10.20).

He who watches the wind will never sow,
 and he who keeps an eye on the clouds will never reap
 (11.4).

Similarly we find the characteristic wisdom contrast being drawn
between the wise man and the fool, e.g.:

> Wise man's thoughts are at home in the house of mourning,
>   but a fool's thoughts in the house of mirth (7.4).

> It is better to listen to a wise man's rebuke
>   than to the praise of fools (7.5).

> The mind of the wise man faces right,
>   but the mind of the fool faces left (10.2).

> A wise man's words win him favour,
>   but a fool's tongue is his undoing (10.12).

Yet even as a wisdom teacher Qoheleth gives the impression of
being something of a cuckoo in wisdom's nest. It is difficult
sometimes to know whether Qoheleth is simply transmitting
proverbial wisdom sayings or whether he is adding to them his
own heavily ironic comment. At the beginning of chapter 7, for
example, there is grouped together a series of sayings, each in the
form A is better than B. It is possible that each of these sayings has
had added to it an ironic comment by Qoheleth. Thus:

'A good name is better than the finest ointment' (7.1 – four brief
alliterative words in Hebrew); to which the comment has been
added, 'yes, and the day of death is better than the day of birth'.

'Better to visit the house of mourning than the house of feasting'
(7.2) yes, says Qoheleth, 'for to be mourned is the lot of every
man, and the living should take this to heart'.

Like Job, and the author of Psalm 73, Qoheleth enters a sharp
dissent from any view which claims that the righteous enjoy
shālôm, while the wicked men meet with trouble in this life. 'In
my empty existence', says Qoheleth, 'I have seen it all, from a
righteous man perishing in his righteousness to a wicked man
growing old in his wickedness' (7.15) – so much for the belief that
righteousness guarantees long life and wickedness leads to a swift
and unpleasant end. Nor is there any correlation between merit
and success in life:

One more thing I have observed here under the sun: speed does
not win the race, nor strength the battle. Bread does not belong
to the wise, nor wealth to the intelligent, nor success to the
skilful; time and chance govern all. Moreover no man knows
when his hour will come; like fish caught in a net, like a bird

taken in a snare, so men are trapped when bad times come suddenly (9.11–12, cf. 9.1–13).

Chapter 8.11–13 is an excellent example of a passage which takes on new meaning, and underlines the same point, once we recognize the existence of quotation marks. The Good News Bible gets the flavour of it very well:

> Why do people commit crimes so readily? Because crime is not punished quickly enough. A sinner may commit a hundred crimes and still live. Oh yes I know what they say, 'If you obey God everything will be all right, but it will not go well for the wicked. Their life is like a shadow and they will die young because they do not obey God'. But this is nonsense. Look at what happens in the world; sometimes righteous men get the punishment of the wicked, and wicked men get the reward of the righteous. I say it is *hebel*.

The fact that the anomalies of life make nonsense of certain traditional claims is, however, for Qoheleth a minor irritant, compared with certain more fundamental issues on which his wisdom teaching seems to cast no light. Rightly he has no time for a fool, be he a moral or an intellectual fool. Wisdom does bring many advantages to men, but it is important, he claims to recognize that there are *frontiers* beyond which wisdom cannot take you.

The first is the *frontier of death*. We have already had occasion to note his statement in 2.12–14 that one fate comes to wise and foolish alike.[16] Notice how this passage continues in verses 15–16: 'So I have thought to myself, "I too shall suffer the fate of the fool. To what purpose have I been wise? What is the profit of it? Even this", I said to myself, "is emptiness. The wise man is remembered no longer than the fool, for, as the passing days multiply, all will be forgotten. Alas, wise man and fool die the same death".' In these closing words, we are hearing what R. Gordis has described as Qoheleth's 'authentic cry of protest and anguish'.[17] There is no 'alas' in the Hebrew, and perhaps 'alas' gives the statement a much more resigned character than it ought to have. Gordis translates 'Yet how *can* the wise man die like the fool' and this catches the undertone of puzzled protest in the statement. Beyond death there lies the great unknown.

For man is a creature of chance and the beasts are creatures of chance and one mischance awaits them all: death comes to both alike. They all draw the same breath. Men have no advantage over the beasts; for everything is emptiness. All go to the same place; all came from the dust, and to the dust all return. Who knows whether the spirit of man goes upward or whether the spirit of the beast goes downward to the earth? (3.19–22, cf. 9.10)

Who knows? Not wisdom, for wisdom cannot take you with any certainty beyond this frontier. It leaves you peering into the mists of an unexplored terrain.

But there is another frontier, a frontier equally clearly defined for Qoheleth, the *frontier of our knowledge of God* and our understanding of his purposes in the world. When we look at life, says Qoheleth, it seems like a rich tapestry of contrasting colours; with every thread in place and everything seeming to fit:

> a time to be born and a time to die;
> a time to plant and a time to uproot;
> a time to kill and a time to heal;
> a time to pull down and a time to build up;
> a time to weep and a time to laugh;
> a time for mourning and a time for dancing;
> a time to scatter stones and a time to gather them;
> a time to embrace and a time to refrain from embracing;
> a time to seek and a time to lose;
> a time to keep and a time to throw away;
> a time to tear and a time to mend;
> a time for silence and a time for speech;
> a time to love and a time to hate;
> a time for war and a time for peace (3.2–8).

The tapestry ought to be meaningful, yet it isn't. 'I have seen', he says, 'the business that God has given men to keep them busy. He has made everything to suit its time; moreover he has put *'olam* in men's hearts, without giving man any comprehension of God's purposes from beginning to end' (3.11). The word *'olam* has been left untranslated because there are several different approaches to this word; and which we take will colour our understanding of what we think the sentence means.[18] The traditional view has been to translate 'eternity', but eternity in the sense of timelessness is not an Old Testament concept. If we rule out eternity there remain several different possibilities.

(a) It has been argued that the word comes from a root meaning to hide. Early Aramaic translations found here a reference to the hidden, ineffable name of God. One of the great mediaeval Jewish commentators, Rashi, saw here a reference to the hidden time of a man's death: it is truly a beautiful thing, he says, that no man knows this hidden time. Coverdale translated 'ignorance' – 'He hath planted ignorance also in the heart of men.' Among modern commentators R. B. Y. Scott in the Anchor Bible continues this tradition by translating 'an enigma' – 'Yet he put in their minds an enigma' i.e. what purposes, if any, God had in weaving this tapestry is beyond our ken. It remains for ever an unsolved mystery.[19]

(b) In post-Biblical Hebrew and Aramaic one of the most common meanings of '*olam* is 'the world'. Thus man is faced by a world in which it is not possible to discern God's purposes. R. Gordis thinks that what is meant here is 'the love of the world',[20] i.e., man embraces the world, but can never understand what it adds up to.

(c) The normal Old Testament meaning of '*olam* is time, time as it stretches indefinitely into the past or into the future or into both. Thus the New English Bible renders, 'Moreover he has given man a sense of time, past and future, but . . .' Man sees life in which a rich variety of experiences seem to fit beautifully into place; he also has a sense of time, a feel for the panorama of events, but it all still does not make clear what divine purpose is in it.

It may well be that Qoheleth is deliberately playing upon different meanings of this word, particularly the time, past, present and future theme and the idea of hiddenness. Certainly for Qoheleth wisdom can pick out the contours of what looks as if it ought to be a meaningful pattern, but it cannot discover what that meaning is, God's purposes are hidden, hidden from even the wisest of men.

This is a theme to which Qoheleth returns again and again. The text of 6.10–12 is at points very difficult, but the general line of argument is clear enough. You cannot argue with God or with the forces which shape your life, says Qoheleth; they are outside your control, stronger than you are. Nor do you improve your chances by getting into deeper and deeper arguments about it. Multiply words and you merely multiply *hebel*. Another section, in which he has been musing on some of the strange anomalies in life, ends: 'All this I have put to the test of wisdom. I said, "I am resolved to be wise", but wisdom was beyond my grasp – whatever has happened lies beyond our grasp, deep down, deeper than man can fathom' (7.23–24). His considered verdict on wisdom, and its limitations, is given in the concluding verses of chapter 8: 'I applied my mind to acquire wisdom and to observe the business which goes on upon earth, when men never closes an eye in sleep day or night; and always I perceived that God has so ordered it that man should not be able to discover what is happening here under the sun. However hard a man may try, he will not find out; the wise man may think he knows, but he will be unable to find the truth of it' (8.16–17). Wisdom, says Qoheleth, has its place. It has an important contribution to make to the sensible living of life, but it does not, and it cannot, answer the ultimate questions. There is no use claiming or pretending that it does. This is not an attack on wisdom *per se*, nor is it a warning against being avid in the pursuit of wisdom. It is an attack on the pretensions of wisdom which may be tempted to claim more than wisdom can give.[21] No doubt there is a purpose behind the manifold events of this world; no doubt God knows what it is: but God alone knows, and it is stupid for men to pretend otherwise. So wisdom takes you again to a frontier, and leaves you gazing across the frontier at a great unknowable.

There is no reason to believe that Qoheleth regrets this. He accepts it; he comes to terms with it and says that since there are no answers to ultimate questions, it is our God-given duty to get on with the business of living. He is convinced that that, and that alone, is what God wants of us. 'There is nothing better for a man to do than to eat and drink and enjoy himself in return for his labours. This too comes from the hand of God' (2.24, this, or similar phrases echo across the book cf. 3.13; 5.18; 8.15; 9.7–10). Qoheleth would have been shocked to think that anyone would so misinterpret his attitude as to make it into an invitation to dissipation or uncontrolled hedonism. He is against excess in any form; he had found out by experience that it brought no ultimate satisfaction, whether in the form of wine, women or song. What he is affirming is this; take life as it comes to you day by day, live it to the full – that is God's gift. It is not an ignoble philosophy. It is one that we can trace back into the literature of the ancient world long before the time of Qoheleth.[22] It is one which many thoughtful and sensitive people subscribe to today. 'The important thing is to live, laugh, suffer, eat and love, and let the rest take care of itself. . . . If I have learned anything it is that life forms no logical patterns. It is haphazard and full of beauties which I try to catch as they fly by, for who knows whether any of them will ever return.'[23] Thus Dame Margot Fonteyn joins hands with Qoheleth across the centuries. If they seem strange allies, let it be remembered that both of them began life in a strong religious tradition which somewhere along the line lost its power to convince.

There is no use trying to make Qoheleth fit neatly into the central stream of Israel's religious traditions. At many points he goes far beyond any other thinker in the Old Testament. He rejects much that lies close to the beating heart of Israel's faith. But he does so with an honesty and integrity which are refreshing. He takes a long hard look at the faith in which he has been nurtured, and at point after point he has the courage to say, 'I can no longer believe that; it doesn't make sense to me'. Having said it, he then proceeds to make his peace with what is left, and tries to live responsibly in the light of what he can still affirm. The frontiers are drawn and beyond them he does not feel able to go – as the frontiers are drawn today for many people brought up in the biblical tradition. They still believe in God, even if he is somewhat less knowable than they once thought: they still try to live responsibly in the light of certain accepted standards of Christian conduct. Worship, however, is no longer particularly meaningful; and some at least of the traditional doctrines no longer ring bells. Instead of those whose faith is secure and untroubled becoming angry and judgmental about such people, it might make more sense if they were to say to them, 'Do you know that you have a fellow-traveller in the Bible?'

A comparison between Job and Qoheleth is instructive. They have much in common. Both stand within the wisdom tradition; both are intensely personal protests against certain over-simplifications of life's experience which that tradition helped to foster. But there are two crucial differences:

(*a*) Whereas the author of Job insists on struggling to save faith in a just world order, Qoheleth gives up the struggle. It doesn't make sense, cries Job, but it *must* make sense. It doesn't make sense, says Qoheleth, accept that it doesn't make sense.

(*b*) This difference is rooted in something that is perhaps more fundamental to the contrast between them. Job still believes that a living personal relationship between God and man is possible, even if God at times seems elusive. It is for him a stormy relationship. Job may accuse God of using him as a target at which to fire arrows (16.12–13); Qoheleth can no longer believe that God is interested enough to fire arrows. So the book of Job climaxes in God speaking to Job; and Qoheleth ends, where he begins, with a silent God, and the whole of life described as completely *hebel*. For Qoheleth the experiential side of religion has dried up; he believes still in religious etiquette, but no longer in personal faith. Perhaps when the experiential side of religion is gone, all that you can be is the joker in the Old Testament pack – but what a superb joker.

11

THE COURAGE TO DOUBT – THE OLD TESTAMENT CONTRIBUTION

We began by noting that the Old Testament comes to us in multi-dimensional form, with different literary and religious traditions coexisting within Israel. The traditions we have examined each point to the fact that within Israel's experience there was ample room for the expression of protest, the recognition of uncertainty and doubt, and the often painful rejection of hitherto accepted beliefs. This we can trace in worship as reflected in the Psalms, in the stories told about Israel's beginnings in the patriarchal and exodus narratives, in historiography, in prophetic material and in the wisdom literature. For the Old Testament at least faith in God is not so defined as to rule out the questioning of God or to deny the right to refuse to acquiesce in certain widely accepted beliefs about God. Israel, however, did not exist in a cultural or religious vacuum. To what extent may this element in Israel's experience be attributed to the heritage she received from the wider world of the Ancient Near East?

This is a difficult question to handle for several reasons.

(*a*) In spite of the ever increasing amount of literary material becoming available from the world of the Ancient Near East, notably within recent years material from the earliest Sumerian civilization in Mesopotamia, much of the material is either fragmentary or subject to considerable textual and interpretative problems; and no one scholar would dare to claim overall competence in Ancient Near Eastern studies. Even where there is substantial material whose meaning is reasonably clear it does not form part of a unified corpus of literary material such as we

have in the Old Testament. If, therefore, we find within the Old
Testament a variety of religious attitudes, not always easily
reconcilable with one another, and if at times we have to settle for
something less than certainty as to what the Hebrews believed,
how much more so is this true of the Sumerians, the Babylonians,
the Canaanites and the Egyptians?[1]

(b) The use of comparative material raises important and difficult questions of methodology. Even similar language and formally identical phrases may mean different things in different
cultural and religious contexts. The problems are nowhere more
clearly illustrated than in the use which has been made of extra-
biblical material to assess the religious function and significance
of kingship in Israel, with views ranging all the way from the view
that kingship was basically a secular institution to the view that
hedges it around with divinity, an indispensable link between
God and the community in pre-exilic Israel.[2] Much here depends
on the language of some of the Psalms, and to what extent that
language is to be interpreted in the light of suggested Ancient
Near Eastern parallels. There is a real danger that we become so
obsessed with trying to defend the distinctiveness of the Old
Testament material that we underestimate the significance of
comparative material from outside Israel, or that we become so
immersed in a patternist mentality that differences are blurred or
ignored.

In spite of the limitations within which the discussion must take
place, it is nevertheless clear that Israelite religion was neither the
only nor the earliest religion in the Ancient Near East to raise
questions about the way in which the divine impinged upon
human life. The earliest evidence for this is probably to be found
in the so-called *Sumerian Job*,[3] at least a thousand years earlier than
the biblical book of Job. This poem is essentially a lament in which
an unnamed and once prosperous man depicts himself as crushed
by illness and misfortune, despised by former friends and foes
alike:

Tears, lament, anguish and depression are lodged within me,
Suffering overwhelms me like one chosen for nothing but
    tears.[4]

Against this background he makes his urgent plea to god, and
confesses his guilt in the light of the fact that

> Never has a sinless child been born to its mother,
> . . . a sinless youth has not existed of old.[5]

The poem concludes by describing how the god listened to his lament, accepted his confession and withdrew the evil fate which had him in its grasp. Suffering turns into joy and into the praise of god.

The main thrust of this poem is its insistence that in the face of grave and inexplicable misfortune a man – recognizing the inevitable failings which are part of human experience – may turn in lament and plea to his personal god who presumably acts as his intercessor in the great assembly of the gods. Running throughout there is the note of acceptance. Lament and plea, yes – but the note of protest which is so characteristic of the biblical Job is noticeably absent. There is no demand to know the reason for undeserved calamity, no insistence that the ways of the gods ought to be understandable. How could there be since the poet writes against the background of a religion which acknowledged the existence of hundreds of deities – some of them mere names to us – organized in a hierarchical system presided over by four chief deities, Anu the heaven god, Enlil the air god, Enki the wise, the water god, and the mother goddess Ninhursag. These deities were essentially anthropomorphic. Even the most powerful among them act and think, love and hate like men and women. Normally they can be expected to support justice and order, but their motives are often obscure.[6] To demand total consistency in this divine world would be as unreasonable as to expect it from men.

The problem of life's anomalies, however, would not go away. The more that was expected from the gods, the more acute the problem became. To this two Babylonian documents bear witness.

1. The poem *ludlul bel nemeqi*, often misleadingly called the Babylonian Job,[7] is a lengthy monologue in which a man of standing relates how every conceivable calamity had befallen him, and how in the end he was restored to health and prosperity by the god Marduk. At many points, particularly in the descriptions of pain and suffering there are similarities in thought and language to some of the biblical lament psalms and to the book of Job. In other respects, however, the Babylonian poem is moving on a different level. Ultimately all it can say about the mystery of human suffering is that if the gods smite, the gods will also

restore. There is within the poem an element of resignation, inevitable resignation because of the inscrutability of the gods and the folly of believing that they can be made accountable to the human conscience.

> What is proper to oneself is an offence to one's god,
> What in one's own heart seems despicable is proper to one's
>   god
> Who knows the will of the gods in heaven,
> Who understands the plans of the underworld gods?
> When have mortals learned the way of a god?[8]

Against this background the poet places the sharply contrasting dimensions of the human condition, its height and depths, singing and groaning, joy and pain, life and death, and finds himself perplexed, unable to perceive any meaningful pattern. Lament and appeal to the gods are natural in the hour of crisis; joy and surprise at recovery lead naturally into the praise of Marduk: but of protest there is nothing. It is the failure to notice the absence of this note of protest which vitiates many of the attempts which have been made to stress the basic similarity in outlook between this poem and the book of Job.[9] For Job a doctrine of God is in the melting pot; there is no hint of this in the mind of this Babylonian sufferer.

2. From slightly later comes the *Babylonian Theodicy*,[10] a lengthy, twenty seven stanza acrostic poem in the form of a dialogue between a sufferer and his friend. The dialogue form and the acceptance of the causal relationship between piety and prosperity, wickedness and failure, provide points of contact with Job. Thus in response to the sufferer's initial *cri de coeur*, his friend replies:

> He who waits on a god has a protecting angel,
> The humble man who fears his goddess accumulates wealth
>   (stanza 2 lines 21–22).

Evidence to the contrary, however, is powerfully presented by the sufferer.

> Those who neglect the gods go the way of prosperity,
> While those who pray to the goddess are impoverished and
>   dispossessed (stanza 7, lines 70f.).

The sufferer insists through many examples that both in the

natural world and in human experience evil seems to pay dividends, while goodness often goes to the wall. This is ultimately admitted by the friend. The apparent contradiction, however, between belief and experience is never seriously explored since the friend takes refuge in the view that that is how it is, because that is how the gods made it. Since the contradiction is sidestepped rather than faced, there is little tension between the sufferer and his friend. They remain correctly polite, patient with each other, unlike the wild accusations which abound in the Job dialogues. A problem has been sensed, but there is little attempt to push awkward questions. The polytheistic setting, and the over-arching conviction about the inscrutability of the divine mind make such questions inappropriate.

Let us now turn to liturgical tradition. It was argued by G. Widengren in his study of *The Accadian and Babylonian Psalms of Lamentation as Religious Documents*[11] that both in terms of literature structure, imagery and religious outlook there was no significant difference between such Babylonian psalms and their biblical counterparts. He repeatedly complains of the tendency among Old Testament scholars to undervalue and to primitivize Babylonian thought. He himself seems to fall into the opposite trap of assuming that similar language and literary forms convey the same meaning in different cultural and religious contexts. In his pursuit of the thesis that throughout the Ancient Near East the basic features of the Semitic idea of the divine are the same, he underestimates differences, the difference, for example, between an essentially polytheistic and monotheistic context, or the degree to which magical formulas and rites control worship.[12] That there are substantial common features shared by the Babylonian and the Hebrew laments cannot be doubted. Both evince a strong sense of the compassionate activity of the divine, the concern for the weak and the oppressed; both provide evidence of the human sense of submission before the divine, but it is precisely in the area with which we are concerned that one of the major differences emerge. In both traditions the apparent aloofness of the divine features in the lament:

> How long, O my lady, wilt thou be angry,
>   and therefore thy face be turned away?
> How long, O my lady, wilt thou rage,
>   and therefore thy spirit be filled with wrath.[13]

Widengren himself, however, notes that the question form dominates in the Hebrew psalms to an extent to which it does not in
the Babylonian material. In particular we draw attention to the
fact that the urgent and repeated 'why' is absent from the
Babylonian material. The reason seems to be that in the Babylonian
laments it is believed that the problem stems basically from the
conduct and attitude of the worshipper. The nearest they come to
a 'why' question is a plea such as;

> What have I done, O my god and my goddess?
> It is done to me as to one who is not fearing my god and
>   goddess.[14]

In many of the Hebrew lament psalms the 'why?' stems not from
what the worshipper has or has not done, but from what it is
believed God has or has not done. The crisis is basically theocen-
tric. There must, therefore, be a reaching out not merely in
penitence and in submission, but in search of a doctrine of God
which will make greater sense to the worshipper in the light of his
experience than the beliefs in which he has been nurtured. In the
Babylonian laments protest is muted; in the Hebrew laments it is
often clamant.

The long and varied Egyptian literary tradition has little positively to contribute to our theme. In ancient Egypt both ethical
values and magical rites were often regarded as being subservient
to gaining access to the world beyond this present life. Not that
the anomalies and injustices of this present world went unnoted.
Particularly during the troubled period of the Middle Kingdom in
the first half of the second millenium BC there are vivid scribal
descriptions of social and political anarchy and corruption. The
times were often seen to be out of joint. No modern *laudator
temporis acti* has done better than the scribe Ipuwer in the eigh-
teenth century BC in bemoaning the faded glories of the past and
denigrating the degrading present:

> Crime is everywhere, there is no man of yesterday.

But the impression conveyed is that evil is a fact more than a
problem. It may lead to intellectual and emotional difficulties as
in the depression and disillusionment exemplified in the *Dispute
between a Man and his Ba* (soul). Occasional voices are heard
doubting the reality of the afterlife or the value of costly tombs.
This, however, does not provoke serious religious questioning,

and certainly no wrestling with the character or purposes of the gods.[15] From the New Kingdom (sixteenth to eleventh centuries BC) come three penitential hymns which bear certain formal and thematic resemblances to Old Testament lament and penitential psalms. The deity is praised in traditional hymnic style and appealed to in certain specific situations of crisis and illness. Since such illness is regarded as punishment for sins committed, it is believed that contrition will lead to restoration to health, this being the consequence of the renewed favour and mercy of the deity. As in the Babylonian material, however, there is no evidence of protest.

We are therefore left with the Old Testament giving expression to an area of religious experience – protest, questioning and doubt – which does not feature with any prominence in the surrounding cultures and religions. This suggests that there must be something in the Israelite understanding of God which makes such questions not only possible but acceptable as an authentic element in faith. But what is this something? Certain factors which we have already noted may have been influential. The thrust towards an ever more uncompromisingly monotheistic faith created, as we have seen,[16] tensions which might otherwise have been avoided. Likewise the insistence that the god must act in a way understandable to, and acceptable to man's moral sense leads to serious questions about how divine providence operates in a perplexing world. But perhaps the reasons for the Old Testament need to protest lie deeper.

If we go to the Old Testament looking for formal definitions of God or comprehensive credal statements, we shall look in vain. The nearest the Old Testament comes to a definition of God is in the story of the revelation of the divine name to Moses in Exodus 3.13–15, the name Yahweh. Old Testament tradition itself is ambivalent about the origin and history of this name for God. One tradition (J) traces the worship of God under the name Yahweh back to the beginning of human history; it being in the days of Enosh, the grandson of Adam, according to Genesis 4.26, that men first began to worship God under the name Yahweh. Another tradition in Exodus 6.2ff. is equally emphatic that God was not known by this name in Israel's experience prior to the exodus: 'God spoke to Moses and said, "I appeared to Abraham, Isaac and Jacob as God Almighty (El Shaddai). But I did not make myself known to them by my name Yahweh" ' (Exod. 6.3). The most natural interpretation of Exodus 3.13–15 is to see in this incident a new name for God being made known to Moses. Since a name for the Old Testament is not merely a formal identity disc but often a pointer to the character of the character who bears it, when Moses depicts the people as asking for God's name, he is claiming that the people have the right to know what kind of God this is. They are asking for a definitive clue to his character; they are looking for a basic theology. Exodus 3.14, 'God answered, "I am who I am (or I will be who I will be). Tell them that 'I am' has sent you to them" ' is one of the most discussed and disputed verses in the Old Testament. This verse, however, is linking the name Yahweh with some form of the Hebrew verb *hyh* to be or to become. R. de Vaux may well be right in arguing that Yahweh is here being explained as 'He who exists', not 'He who exists' in an abstract philosophical sense, but 'He who exists' to be in relationship with his people.[17] 'I will be with you'. . . . 'I will be your God and you will be my people' are typical of one common class of theological statements which we find echoing across the Old Testament. Two things would seem to follow from this.

1. If Yahweh means 'He who exists', far from defining his nature this name simply asserts his reality, a reality which impinges upon man. Instead of being offered a theology, the people are offered a presence now and in the future, the presence of one who lives in and beyond all experience, a presence which may, as S. Terrien has reminded us, be an elusive presence. Instead of neatly labelling and thus reducing the element of the unknown, this name contains within it a continuing recognition of the mystery and the transcendence of God. This is the reason Deuteronomy gives for the prohibition on any kind of carved-image representation of God:

> On the day when the Lord spoke to you out of the fire on Horeb, you saw no figure of any kind; so take good care not to fall into the degrading practice of making figures in relief . . . (Deut. 4.15–16).

If we ask what the people did see at Horeb, Deuteronomy replies:

> . . . the Lord spoke in a great voice to your whole assembly on the mountain out of the fire, the cloud and the thick mist. . . . When you heard the voice out of the darkness, while the mountain was ablaze with fire all the tribes and the elders came to me and said, 'The Lord our God has shown us his glory and

his greatness, and we have heard his voice out of the fire: today
we have seen that God may speak with men and they may still
live' (Deut. 5.22–24).

Fire . . . cloud . . . darkness, symbols which declare the presence
of God, yet assert the essential mystery of his being (cf. the
smoking fire-pot and the flaming torch of Genesis 15.17). Likewise
the word 'glory',[18] which when applied to man indicates his
standing or status in society, points to the presence of God, but
always a presence which is enveloped in splendour and mystery,
in a greatness which means that it must ever lie beyond human
rationalization or full comprehension. From the base of this
transcendent God who in his presence speaks to man, theology
sets out to speak about God. But if carved images are ruled out as
being inadequate or dangerously misleading symbols of this
transcendent God, what about verbal images? Is there not a real
danger that the mystery of God may disappear in a set of words
which seek neatly and definitively to map out what God is like
and how he acts? A theology of history or a dogmatic statement
as to how God works in the world, giving prosperity to the
righteous and destroying the wicked, can, in the very act of
attempting to witness to God, put him in a verbal strait jacket. As
G. von Rad has reminded us, 'Every period has its own conflict
with reality or, better, with the concepts it has formed of reality.
But there is always something that cannot be accommodated. The
search for knowledge in every age has only the confidence which
it has been given and is forced to halt at specific limits'.[19] There is
– and must always be – something about God which cannot be
accommodated to our stammering words. Again and again in
Israel's experience the need was felt to break out of the verbal
strait jackets which had proved inadequate to contain the reality
of God. You then either end up with Qoheleth, content to live
with broken verbal images and finding no urgent need to replace
them or you appeal from such broken images to a reality 'He who
exists' whose glory and greatness are such that any words can but
touch the fringe of his garments. Then, if I may use certain words
that Martin Buber uses concerning the distinction between the
god of the philosophers and the god of faith, then a man 'would
be compelled to recognize and admit the fact that the idea of God
was dissolving at the point where God *lives*: that it was dissolving
at the point where God is loved: because at that point God is no

longer 'the God' about whom one may philosophize, but 'He who exists'.[20]

2. 'He who exists' exists in relationship with his people. Many Old Testament statements of faith point to this relationship, and the initiative and the acts of God which give it birth e.g.:

> I am the Lord who brought you from Ur of the Chaldees (Gen. 15.7).

> I am the Lord your God who brought you out of the land of Egypt, out of the land of slavery (Exod. 20.2; Deut. 5.6).

> Comfort, comfort my people, says your God (Isa. 40.1).

Whether the word 'covenant' is the dominant or the correct word to use to describe this relationship, the relationship itself is fundamental to Israel's knowledge of God.[21] But the emphasis upon such a relationship, brought into being through events at a particular time in history brings with it its own problems. The community may meet to celebrate the mighty acts of God which gave it birth, but does it discern God's activity in the present? God came – hallelujah; but does he still come, and what are the signs of his coming? History is largely ambivalent and unrepeatable. It is much safer and surer to have a religion whose basic texts are mythological, in the sense that they tell stories about what the gods and goddesses do outside of history and thus plot their character, or to have a religion which focusses on the more or less recurring and predictable pattern in the world of nature. If you confess, on the basis of the past, faith in a God who delivers and saves, a God who brought his people out of slavery in Egypt, does this mean that in every situation God comes to deliver and to save, and if so, how? What of the physical symbols of God's gracious activity in the past – the promised land, the holy city, the temple – are they by their very existence the guarantee of God's gracious presence now? If they are, what response must be made to a situation where there is no land, no city, no temple?[22]

The problems become intensified when you try to hold together both the transcendence of God and his coming to his people. To confess God as transcendent means that he is not bound by history, but that, in his freedom, he may work in and through history to achieve his own purposes. But to take such freedom of God with full seriousness is to recognize that God cannot be programmed in advance; to face the possibility that you may find yourself arrested, when you least expect it, by a disturbing presence, or discover God disturbingly absent where you confidently expected him to find him. 'Religions' it has been well said, 'as complexes of popular practices and traditions are more or less "primitive" at all times and among all peoples. The inner conflict for faith, for the personally experienced reality, is non-primitive in all religions. A religious change, an interior transformation, which alters the structure, never takes place, however, without an inner conflict. Particularly as far as the religion of Israel is concerned, we cannot comprehend its ways and changes at all unless we pay attention to the inner dialectic, to the at various stages and in various forms, ever-recurrent struggle for the truth of belief, for revelation.'[23] There were always those – the majority – in ancient Israel who avoided such conflict and were content to remain with the confines of the primitive. But others discovered that such conflict was inherent in the very nature of the God who was central to Israel's experience. There are those today who wish to live unquestioningly within the security of inherited structures of belief and practice; for such people the Old Testament must be a very disturbing or a closed book, since it lives in the tension of faith and doubt. On the other hand the Old Testament gives no comfort to a radicalism which is arrogantly self-confident. 'The future', it has been claimed, 'belongs not to those who must have certainties, but to those who can live with uncertainty, who can calmly and self confidently explore the heritage of the past, the problems of the present, and the opportunities for the future, without the crutches of rigid and doctrinaire ideology.'[24] Calmness and self confidence are not the words that naturally spring to mind when we think of Jeremiah or Job or many of the psalms of lament. It is in the struggle to maintain certainties in the midst of uncertainty, in the painful groping for new light in the midst of a darkness that seems total, that the Old Testament bears its clearest witness to the courage to doubt.

NOTES

1. Worship and Questioning

1. See, for example, the essays in D. J. Knight (ed.), *Tradition and Theology in the Old Testament*, Philadelphia 1977. For a discussion of the different meanings of 'tradition', see R. E. Clements *Prophecy and Tradition*, Oxford 1975, pp. 4–7.

2. A. S. Kapelrud, 'The Role of the Cult in Old Israel' in J. P. Hyatt (ed.), *The Bible in Modern Scholarship*, Abingdon 1965, p. 55 cf. S. Terrien, *The Elusive Presence*, New York 1978, p. 4 and his general discussion of 'Culture and Faith in Biblical Research' ibid., chapter 1. The extent to which Israel's psalmody played a creative role in handing on and shaping Israel's faith has been underlined by A. R. Johnson in *The Cultic Prophet and Israel's Psalmody*, Cardiff 1979, see e.g., p. 433.

3. M. E. Marty, *Varieties of Unbelief*, New York 1964, in particular chapter 9, 'The Religious Varieties of Unbelief'.

4. W. Zimmerli, in D. Knight, op. cit., p. 100.

5. S. Terrien, op. cit., p. 4.

6. For a recent survey see J. H. Eaton, 'The Psalms and Israel's Worship', in G. W. Anderson (ed.), *Tradition and Interpretation*, Oxford 1979, pp. 238–73.

7. In addition to those mentioned Psalms 19, 24, 29, 33, 65, 68, 103–105, 111–117, 134–136, 145–150.

8. Cf. Psalms 18, 34, 66, 118, 138.

9. Psalms 46, 76, 84, 87, 122.

10. Psalms 60, 74, 79, 80, 83, 85, 90, 123, 137.

11. Cf. C. Westermann, 'The Role of the Lament in the Theology of the Old Testament' in *Interpretation* Vol. xxviii, 1974, p. 30. This volume of *Interpretation* is one of the few attempts to take this aspect of Old Testament thinking with *theological* seriousness.

12. F. Baumgartner quoted in *Essays in Old Testament Interpretation*, p. 285. Psalm 69.22–28 provides another example in the personal laments, Psalm 137.5–9 in the communal laments. The attempt by H. J. Kraus, *Psalmen*, ad loc. and A. Weiser, *The Psalms* (English Translation in Old

Testament Library Series 1955) ad loc. to take verses 8–20 of Psalm 109 as the words of the accusers being quoted by the Psalmist, is not convincing. Even if it were, it would leave similar passages to be explained. There have been many attempts to explain away such vindictive passages in the Psalms or at least to provide them with some theological respectability; see e.g. C. S. Lewis, *Reflections on the Psalms*, London 1961, p. 131.

13. Cf. J. H. Eaton, 'The Psalms and Israel's Worship'.

14. Among the Psalms of personal lament we must include Psalms 3–7, 10, 13, 17, 22, 25, 26, 28, 31, 35, 38, 41–43, 51, 54–57, 59, 63, 66, 69, 71, 86, 88, 102, 109, 120, 139, 140–143.

15. P. R. Ackroyd, in *Tradition and Theology in the Old Testament*, p. 221. A. R. Johnson, op. cit., p. 217 believes that the frustrating vagueness of the language of some of the personal laments may stem from the fact that in the activity of the cultic prophets 'the language may have been kept vague quite deliberately in order that the work might be used over and over again in appropriate circumstances'.

16. *The Church Hymnary Third Edition (1973)*, introduction, p.x.

17. Any precise enumeration of the different categories of psalms runs into difficulties since certain psalms may have features of more than one type. The estimate of the psalms belonging to each type employed for the purposes of this analysis has been done on rigorous lines. Any psalms of mixed or doubtful category have been ignored.

18. C. Westermann, op. cit., p. 25.

19. J. M. Powis Smith, *The Religion of the Psalms*, Chicago 1922, pp. 2f.

20. J. M. P. Smith, op. cit., p. 73.

21. W. Brueggemann, 'From Hurt to Joy, From Death to Life' in *Interpretation* Vol. xxviii, 1974, p. 6, and more recently 'Psalms and the Life of Faith' in *Journal for the Study of the Old Testament*, 17, 1980, pp. 3–32.

22. D. E. Roberts 'Psychotherapy and the Christian View of Man', New York 1950, p. 71, quoted in M. E. Marty, op. cit., p. 207.

2. Worship and the Search for Enlightenment

1. The most balanced case for the activity and function of such cultic prophets is to be found in the work of A. R. Johnson, *The Cultic Prophet in Ancient Israel*, Cardiff 1944, 2nd Edition 1962, and *The Cultic Prophet and Israel's Psalmody*, Cardiff 1979.

2. See, for example, W. McKane, *Prophets and Wise Men* (Studies in Biblical Theology 44), London 1965.

3. See the discussion of this issue by J. L. Crenshaw in His Prolegomenon to *Studies in Ancient Israelite Wisdom*, New York 1976, pp. 1–35 (hereafter *Studies*). His own definition of Wisdom as 'the quest for self understanding in terms of relationships with things, people and the creator', suffers from the same kind of vagueness of which he accuses others. For the Wisdom Psalms see S. Mowinckel, 'Psalms and Wisdom', *Supplement to Vetus Testamentum* III (1955), pp. 205ff.: R. E. Murphy 'A Consideration of the Classification Wisdom Psalms', *Supplement to Vetus Testamentum* IX (1962), pp. 156–87, reprinted in *Studies*, pp. 456ff.: J. K. Kuntz, 'The Canonical Wisdom Psalms: Their Rhetorical, Thematic and

Formal Dimensions' in J. T. Jackson and M. Kessler (eds), *Rhetorical Criticism*, Pittsburg 1974, pp. 186ff. and 'The Retributive Motif in Wisdom Psalms', *Zeitschrift für die alttestamentliche Wissenschaft*, 89, 1977, pp. 223–33.

4. M. Dahood, *Psalms* (Anchor Bible 1966), ad loc. thinks that the wicked, denied access to the heavenly council, will be condemned *in absentia*. The way in which Dahood, however, uses Canaanite material to find in the psalms numerous references to eternal life and final judgment, raises serious questions of methodology.

5. Dahood, op. cit. translates 'whatever it produces is good' arguing that the subject is still the tree. The switch to man as subject, however, is neither – as he claims – abrupt nor unnecessary. The sole question is how far the simile extends, since man is the subject at the beginning of verse 3.

6. It has played, for example, a prominent part in the growth of the contemporary Buddhist reform movement in Japan, Soka Gakkai.

7. A. Weiser, *The Psalms*, (Old Testament Library) 2nd Impression, London 1965, p. 825.

8. A. A. Anderson, *Psalms* (New Century Bible), London 1972, comment on Psalm 1.3.

9. J. K. Kuntz, 'The Retributive Motif in Wisdom Psalms' distinguishes between traditional, realistic, and futuristic attitudes in the retributive motif.

10. The New English Bible transfer of 'his children begging for bread' to become part of the description of the wicked in verse 20 has little to commend it.

11. Dahood, op. cit., takes Hebrew *yqr* (pomp) to be a poetic name for the nether world, and translates

> For man in the Mansion will sleep indeed
> become like the beasts that cease to be.

12. J. B. Pritchard (ed.), *Ancient Near Eastern Texts Relating to the Old Testament*, Princeton 1950, p. 90.

13. Sheol has very much the negative connotation which surrounds the traditional Greek concept of Hades; cf. the vigorous protest of Achilles that he would rather be the meanest slave, in this world than king in Hades. (Homer, *Odyssey* XI, l. 498.)

14. J. K. Kuntz, op. cit., pp. 231f. argues strongly for the immortality interpretation; cf. Dahood, ad loc.

15. Weiser, *The Psalms* (Old Testament Library), ad loc., p. 390.

16. Cf. J. H. Kuntz, op. cit., p. 233; S. Mowinckel, *The Psalms in Israel's Worship* vol ii, p. 36. J. M. Ross, 'Psalm 73' in *Israelite Wisdom*, New York 1978, pp. 161–175, argues that such a distinction is foreign to the Psalm, that it is '*both* a wisdom psalm *and* a psalm of lament, trust and thanksgiving', p. 170 and that the psalmist solved his problem both by visiting the temple and by participating in the discussions of the nearby wisdom schools. Thus the plural 'holy places of God' in v. 17 is taken to refer to the temple and to its precincts where the wisdom schools met. Although wisdom themes are present in the Psalm I am not persuaded

that any wisdom discussions as such are necessary to account for the psalmist's response.

17. Retaining the traditional Hebrew reading 'to Israel' as against the New English Bible acceptance of the emendation 'to the upright', and Dahood's rendering 'O Israel'. Israel in this context may well have a theological meaning, God's faithful people, of whom the psalmist believes himself to be one.

18. J. I. Durham in *Proclamation and Presence*, London 1970, p. 276.

19. For example, H. Ringgren in *Vetus Testamentum* III (1953), pp. 265ff. suggests the New Year Festival. A Weiser, op. cit., argues for a theophany in the context of a covenant festival. M. Dahood, op. cit., believes that God's sanctuary refers to heaven and that 'the glaring inconsistencies in this life will become intelligible to the psalmist in the hereafter'. The twin emphasis upon the destruction of the apparently powerful and God's presence 'with you' would also be appropriate within the context of a communal celebration of Passover.

20. M. Buber, *Moses*, Oxford 1946, p. 88.

21. Cf. A. A. Anderson *Psalms*, ad loc.

22. S. Terrien, *The Elusive Presence*, p. 316.

23. A. Weiser, *Psalms*, ad loc.

24. This point is well made by A. P. Hayman in his articles on the problem of theodicy in rabbinic literature in *Scottish Journal of Theology* 29, 1976, pp. 461–76 and in *Transactions of the Glasgow University Oriental Society* xxvi, 1978, pp. 28–43. Of relevance to Psalm 73 is his comment in *Transactions* p. 41: 'Perhaps at this point the problem of theodicy dissolves into the much wider, and probably insoluble, problem of the nature of religious experience.'

25. This suggestive phrase is used by J. A. Sanders in his discussion of the canon, cf. *Torah and Canon*, Philadelphia 1972, where he claims that it is the very nature of Canon to be 'the mirror for the identity of the believing community', p. xiv.

3. *Faith on Pilgrimage – The Patriarchal Traditions*

1. For an excellent discussion of the methodological problems in handling the patriarchal narratives see W. McKane, *Studies in the Patriarchal Narratives*, Edinburgh 1979.

2. It is one of the marks of much contemporary Old Testament scholarship that it is again beginning to take seriously the final form of the narratives both in their literary and theological implications. Literary appreciation and imagination are as important to the understanding of the text as the dissecting scalpel.

3. Much of the relevant material is gathered together in L. Ginsberg, *The Legends of the Jews*, Vol. 1, Philadelphia 1909, pp. 185–216. A more critical, historical presentation will be found in G. Vermes, *Scripture and Tradition in Judaism*, Leiden 1961, pp. 67–126.

4. Appeals to the Nuzi wife-sister motif are largely irrelevant to the narratives in their present form since they hinge upon Sarai being Abram's wife, not his sister. For a recent discussion of the problems

raised by the similarities and differences between Genesis 12.10–20; 20 and 26 see R. C. Culley, *Studies in the Structure of Hebrew Narratives*, pp. 34–41, Philadelphia 1976.

5. J. Fitzmeyer, *The Genesis Apocryphon from Qumran Cave 1*, Rome 1971.

6. L. Ginsberg, op. cit., Vol. 1, pp. 221ff.

7. Cf. G. von Rad, 'Faith Reckoned as Righteousness' in *The Problem of the Hexateuch and Other Essays*, Edinburgh 1965, pp. 125–30.

8. This is how Genesis 15.6 is interpreted in Pauline theology in Galatians 3.6ff. and Romans 4. This must not, however, be regarded as merely a piece of early Christian polemical interpretation. The Targums know of no other interpretation on Genesis 15.6 though there is a tendency in later Judaism to explain righteousness in terms of merit; cf. Rashi's comment 'The Holy One, blessed be He, accounted it into Abraham as a merit because of the faith with which he trusted in Him'. M. Rosenbaum and A. M. Silbermann, *Pentateuch with Rashi's Commentary*, London 1929, ad loc.

9. Cf. R. le Déaut, *Targum du Pentateuque I Genèse*, Paris 1978 ad loc.

10. Cf. R. E. Clements *Abraham and David, Genesis XV and its Meaning for Israelite Tradition*, London 1967.

11. M. Freedman and M. Simon, *Midrash Rabbah, Genesis I*, London 1939, p. 369, cf. Rashi, ad loc.

12. *Midrash Rabbah* III, Exodus, trs D. M. Lehrman, London 1939, p. 101.

13. See p. 60.

14. For example, W. Zimmerli, *Old Testament Theology in Outline*, Edinburgh 1978, p. 147.

15. The concept of 'order, morally intelligible order, is not of course confined to Israel. It is prominent in the Egyptian concept of *ma'at*. For a discussion of a universe of moral principles drawn from a consensus view of society, see J. Barton, 'Natural Law and Poetic Justice in the Old Testament', *Journal of Theological Studies* 30, 1979, pp. 1–14.

16. See pp. 66ff.

17. Cf. R. le Déaut, op. cit., ad loc.

18. J. L. Crenshaw, 'Popular Questioning of the Justice of God in Ancient Israel', *Studies*, p. 294.

19. See *Midrash Rabbah*, ad loc. It soon became evident in Israel that not all the people descended from Abraham were able or willing to fulfil their calling 'to conform to the way of the Lord'. There was always, however, a nucleus of the true people, not always easily identifiable, yet of vital importance for the future. Abraham's question then takes the form 'What is the relationship between this remnant and the community as a whole, how large must it be to be effective'.

20. Behind the varied uses of the verb *y'l* in the Old Testament, here translated 'presume' by the NEB, there seems to lie the idea of a willingness to do something (e.g. Exod. 2.21, Judges 17.11) or more positively a determination to do something, well illustrated in Hosea 5.11, which the NEB translates, Ephraim is an oppressor trampling on justice, *doggedly pursuing* what is worthless (cf. Judg. 1.35). There are

passages in which it is used to indicate God's willingness to do something for his people (e.g. I Sam. 12.22; II Sam. 7.28). Job uses it ironically in the context of expressing the hope that God will be willing to crush him and thus put an end to his suffering (Job. 6.9). Genesis 18, however, is the only passage where the word is used of a man's attitude to God. It indicates Abraham's determination to push an awkward question, in spite of the fact that he recognizes the fact that he is mere dust and ashes. This idea is better conveyed by the Good News Bible translation 'Please forgive my boldness in continuing to speak', although 'Please forgive' is not a necessary implication of the introductory *hinne-na*, which might rather underline the speaker's determination. Rashi, ad loc., takes the phrase to mean that Abraham is willing to speak, comparing Exod. 2.21, but this is too weak in context.

21. Wiesel, *Messengers of God*, New York 1977, p. 86.

22. See pp. 140ff. The sociological factor is being taken with new seriousness in recent Old Testament Study, e.g. P. D. Hanson, *The Dawn of Apocalyptic*, Philadelphia 1975; G. E. Mendenhall, *The Tenth Generation*, Baltimore 1973; R. R. Wilson *Prophecy and Society in Ancient Israel*, Philadelphia 1980; N. K. Gottwald *The Tribes of Yahweh*, London 1980.

23. Bruce Vawter, *On Genesis: a new reading*, London 1977, p. 256.

24. One of the best discussions of this passage is to be found in E. Auerbach, *Mimesis*.

25. For the Targumic evidence see R. le Déaut, op. cit., and Rashi, op. cit., p. 93. Varied material is collected in L. Ginsberg, op. cit., vol. 1, pp. 271–86, and discussed in terms of its historical and theological development in G. Vermes, op. cit., pp. 193–227.

26. D. C. Miller ed. *Exegesis*, Pittsburg Theological Monograph Series 21, Pittsburg, pp. 348f.

27. *Midrash Rabbah*, Vol. 1, p. 483.

28. The link between Genesis 12.1 and 22.2 in the repetition of the *lekh-lekha* 'go' is noted in the *Midrash Rabbah* I p. 487. More recent approaches to the narrative in terms of structuralism e.g. in *Exegesis* and R. Lack 'Le sacrifice d'Isaac – Analyse structurals de la couche élohiste dans Gen. 22', *Biblica LVI*, 1975 pp. 1–12, do not in my opinion add much depth to our understanding of the narrative.

29. Elie Wiesel, *Messengers of God*, p. 87.

30. Auerback, *Mimesis*, p. 12.

31. See pp. 140ff.

32. See Terrien, op. cit., p. 84.

33. G. W. Coats 'Abraham's Sacrifice of Faith. A Form Critical Study of Genesis 22', *Interpretation XXVI*, 1973, pp. 399f.

34. Vawter, *On Genesis*, p. 244.

35. Wiesel, op. cit., pp. 123f.

36. The identity of the assailant is variously given in later tradition, e.g. Esau's guardian angle (*Midrash Rabbah*) the angel Michael (Targum Jonathan), Sariel (Neofiti 1, R. le Déaut, op. cit.).

37. The need for the assailant to disappear at dawn may go back to a form of the story in which he was a night demon. Jewish tradition naturally sought for other explanations. Targum Neofiti 1 identifying the

assailant as an angel claims that he had to return to heaven since he was
leader of the celestial choir who each day praised God. Targum Jonathan
makes Michael depart with the words 'I am one of the angels of praise,
but from the day the world was created my time to praise Him has not
come until now'.

38. Rashi, op. cit., p. 159.

39. For Jewish and early Christian interpretations of the name see L.
Ginsberg, op. cit., vol. V, note 253, pp. 307f.

40. Cf. Rashi, op. cit., ad loc.

41. Cf. H. W. Wolff, *Hosea* (Hermeneia Series), Philadelphia 1974, ad
loc.; P. R. Ackroyd, 'Hosea and Jacob', *Vetus Testamentum* 13, 1963, pp.
245–59.

42. Ackroyd, op. cit., p. 259.

43. See p. 62.

44. See pp. 121ff.

4. *The Burden of Leadership – The Mosaic Traditions*

1. Cf. G. Widengren, 'What do we know about Moses' in *Proclamation
and Presence*, ed. J. I. Durham and J. R. Porter, London 1960, pp. 21–47.

2. The NEB translation assumes certain modifications to the traditional
text. It would be equally possible to translate the first two lines:

> If there is a prophet in your midst,
> I the Lord make myself known. . . .

This, however, does not alter the central theme of the passage, which is
to stress the uniqueness of Moses in his relationship with God.

3. M. Noth, *Überlieferungsgeschichte des Pentateuch*, 2nd edition, Stuttgart 1966, pp. 186ff.: English translation, *A History of the Pentateuchal
Traditions*, Hemel Hempstead 1972.

4. M. Buber, *Moses* Oxford 1946. For a cautious assessment of the
historical and literary problems involved, see G. Widengren, op. cit. and
S. Herrmann, *Israel in Egypt* (Studies in Biblical Theology, Series 2, No.
27), London 1973, pp. 38–50.

5. B. S. Childs, *Exodus* (Old Testament Library), London 1974, p. 54.

6. Cf. pp. 43f.

7. B. S. Childs, op. cit., p. 56; cf. M. Buber, op. cit., p. 47.

8. S. M. Lehrmann, trans., *The Midrash III Exodus*, London 1939, pp.
62–3.

9. B. S. Childs, op. cit., ad loc.; U. Cassuto, *Commentary on Exodus*,
English translation, Jerusalem 1967, ad loc.: cf. J. Calvin, *Harmony of the
Pentateuch II*, English translation, Edinburgh 1852, ad loc.

10. Two other passages use the expression 'Who am I that' (Heb. *mî
anōkhî kî*). In Sam. 18.18 it introduces David's response to Saul's
suggestion that he marry Saul's daughter. Since the narrative has just
commented on Saul's increasing jealousy of David and has recounted his
attempts to kill him, it is natural for David's response to be one of
surprise, tinged no doubt with underlying suspicion. II Sam. 7.18 is more
germane to the Exodus passage in so far as David's words are addressed

to God. The words mark the beginning of David's response to Nathan's oracle that he is destined under God to found an everlasting dynasty. David begins by expressing his surprise that God has brought him back so far in life, a surprise all the greater in the light of the further promises that have now been made to him. I am unconvinced by the argument (see e.g. U. Cassuto, op. cit., ad loc.) that such passages express merely humility and unworthiness.

11. B. S. Childs, op. cit., ad loc. *Notes on the New Translation of the Torah*, Philadelphia 1969, takes the sign to the immediately preceding words 'that I (God) will be with you'.

12. See pp. 56ff.

13. B. S. Childs, op. cit., p. 76.

14. See chapters 5 and 6.

15. See pp. 209ff.

16. S. Terrien, op. cit., p. 119.

17. It is noteworthy that God's speech to Moses is lengthy: in contrast Moses' objections are stated tersely and briefly. The situation is the reverse: in the so-called 'Confessions of Jeremiah' where the prophet's complaint and protest tend to be lengthy and the divine reply brief (see chapter 7).

18. See e.g. J. Calvin, op. cit., ad loc: U. Cassuto, op. cit., ad loc.

19. To find a prophetic parallel in Jer. 1.6 is tempting, but ought to be resisted. Both the prophetic objection to the call and the divine reply are concerned with a different issue from that raised here. Jeremiah's problem is not that of lack of oratorical finesse, but that of youthful inexperience which has had no prior acquaintance with the prophetic word.

20. Calvin, *Harmony of the Pentateuch*, ad loc.

21. See e.g. *Notes on the New Translation of Torah*, p. 156.

22. This is disputed by U. Cassuto, op. cit., who claims that reiteration is frequent in narratives of this kind, a reoccurence of a situation that existed before but in a different degree.

23. See R. le Déaut, *Targum des Pentateuque 2, Exode et Levitique*, Paris 1979.

24. NEB translates prophet (Heb. *nābhî*) as spokesman. As in chapter 4 the Targums replace 'god' by 'master' and prophet or spokesman by 'interpreter' (*meturgeman*).

25. Multiple objection is also characteristic of another call experience related to leadership role, that of Gideon in Judges 6.11–24. He raises three objections before acquiescing in his call.

26. For an excellent analysis see G. Vermes, *Scripture and Tradition in Judaism*, pp. 178–92.

27. B. S. Childs, op. cit., ad loc.: J. P. Hyatt, *Exodus* (New Century Bible), London 1971, ad loc.: M. Noth, *Exodus* (Old Testament Library), London 1962.

28. U. Cassuto, op. cit., pp. 58–61: 'The Lord met him' (Heb. verb *paghash*) is, however, unparalleled elsewhere in the Old Testament meaning 'he fell ill'. B. S. Childs' approach is hardly more enlightening.

This is one of the sections in Exodus where he is unable to provide any real theological comment.

29. See pp. 53ff.

30. M. Buber, op. cit., p. 58.

31. *Midrash*, op. cit., ad loc.; cf. L. Ginsberg, *The Legends of the Jews*, vol. II, pp 336–41.

32. Calvin, *Harmony of the Pentateuch* II, p. 124.

33. U. Cassuto, op. cit., p. 74.

34. B. S. Childs, op. cit., pp. 557–58.

35. B. S. Childs, op. cit., ad loc.; U. Cassuto, op. cit., ad loc. comments that Moses 'discerns that also in the Lord's mind there is an element of doubt as it were, and that even in the moment of his anger God feels love for his people and hints at the possibility *not to let* his anger continue to burn'.

36. *Midrash III, Exodus*, ad loc.

37. E.g. I Kings 13.6, II Kings 13.4; Jer. 26.19; II Chron. 33.12; Mal. 1.9. It is equally true of other passages which Brown, Driver and Briggs, *Hebrew Lexicon* classifies simply as asking for God's favour. It is God's favour against the background of a situation where there is no sign of such favour, e.g. I Sam. 13.12; Zech. 7.2; 8.21, 22, and where there is need for a change in God's attitude. The word, therefore, carries a more specific and restricted meaning than the more general words for praying or 'seeking the face of the Lord'.

38. *Midrash III, Exodus*, ad loc.

39. J. P. Hyatt, op. cit., p. 357, comparing, for example, Jer. 18.5–11.

40. Like its Exodus counterpart, the Deuteronomic expression is only applied to God in this passage. It is used in Judges 11.37 where Jephtha's daughter, after agreeing to her father's vow, requests permission to be left for two months to mourn her virginity.

41. Philo, *De Vita Mosis* II xxxi, 166 (trans. F. H. Colson), Harvard 1966.

42. There is no apodasis to the 'if' clause in Hebrew. The Septuagint, Targum Jonathan, and the Samaritan texts add 'forgive'. It would be equally impossible to supply 'well and good' cf. *Notes on the New Translation of the Torah*, p. 197.

43. See L. Ginsberg, *The Legends of the Jews*, Vol. III, p. 131.; B. S. Childs, op. cit., p. 586.

44. J. Calvin, op. cit., III, p. 359.

45. 'The Intercession of the Covenant Mediator (Exodus 33.1a, 12–17)' in *Words and Meanings*, ed., P. R. Ackroyd and B. Lindars, Cambridge 1968, p. 168.

46. Op. cit., p. 176.

47. 'I have chosen you' is the meaning of 'I have known you by name'. It is characteristic of this passage that the word 'know' occurs no less than six times in five verses with a wide variety of shades of meaning. Likewise the expression 'find favour in your eyes' occurs five times.

48. See chapter 8.

49. See B. S. Childs, op. cit., ad loc.; S. Terrien, *The Elusive Presence*, p. 140: J. Muilenburg, op. cit., p. 170.

50. Cassuto, *Commentary on Exodus*, ad loc.

51. S. Terrien, op. cit., p. 140.
52. S. Terrien, op. cit., pp. 142f.
53. B. S. Childs, op. cit., ad loc. S. Terrien's attempt to see in the present form of the text northern theological tradition defining the essence of a theology of presence through 'the name' in opposition to a southern theology of presence centring upon 'glory' raises more questions than it solves in my opinion (see *The Elusive Presence*, pp. 144ff.).
54. A. C. Welsh, *Kings and Prophets of Israel*, London 1952, pp. 45–67.
55. Welch, op. cit., p. 51. Although we have confined our study to the Exodus narrative the same emphasis is apparent in the Numbers tradition, see especially Num. 11.11–23; 14.

5. The Changing Word – Prophetic Narratives

1. See pp. 16f. above.
2. Much contemporary discussion of prophetic literature has been concerned with such reshaping and adaptation: e.g. E. W. Nicholson, *Preaching to the Exiles*, Oxford 1961; R. P. Carroll, *When Prophecy Failed*, London 1979; R. E. Clements, *Isaiah and the Deliverance of Jerusalem*, Sheffield 1980.
3. For a general discussion of this issue, see e.g. M. Noth, *A History of the Pentateuchal Traditions* (English translation B. W. Anderson), Englewood Cliffs, New Jersey 1972; R. E. Clements, *Prophecy and Tradition*, Oxford 1975, pp. 47ff.; J. Gray, *I and II Kings* (Old Testament Library Series), 2nd ed., London 1970, p. 39.
4. G. von Rad, *Studies in Deuteronomy*, London 1953, pp. 89ff.; J. Gray, op. cit., p. 9.
5. D. B. Macdonald, *The Hebrew Philosophical Genius*, Princeton 1936.
6. D. B. Macdonald, op. cit., p. 26.
7. R. P. Carroll, op. cit.
8. See p. 47.
9. See p. 72.
10. In addition to the discussion in the standard commentaries e.g. J. A. Montgomery and H. S. Gehman, *I and II Kings* (International Critical Commentary), Edinburgh 1951; J. Gray, op. cit., this chapter has been extensively discussed in the increasingly voluminous literature on 'true' and 'false' prophecy in the Old Testament: e.g. J. L. Crenshaw, *Prophetic Conflict*, Berlin 1971; J. A. Sanders, 'Hermeneutics in True and False Prophecy' in *Canon and Authority*, ed., G. W. Coats and B. O. Long, Philadelphia 1977, pp. 21–41.
11. Numerous parallels have been noted between the man of God at Bethel in the reign of Jeroboam I and Amos the prophet at Bethel in the reign of Jeroboam II. Attempts to identify the two, however, are far from convincing, and whatever plausibility they have depends upon stressing similarities and ignoring differences; cf. J. L. Crenshaw, op. cit., pp. 40ff.; J. Gray, op. cit., p. 322; P. R. Ackroyd, 'A Judgement Narrative between Kings and Chronicles? An Approach to Amos 7.9–17' in G. W. Coats and B. O. Long, op. cit., pp. 78ff.
12. See p. 71.

13. K. Barth, *Church Dogmatics II/2*, Edinburgh 1957, p. 395.

14. K. Barth, op. cit., p. 399. W. E. Lemke, 'The Way of Obedience: I Kings 13 and the Structure of the Deuteronomistic History' in *Magnalia Dei, The Mighty Acts of God*, ed., F. M. Cross, W. E. Lemke, P. D. Miller, New York 1976, pp. 301–28 makes a strong case for seeing the narrative in its present form as a pivotal passage illustrating one of the central themes of the Deuteronomistic history i.e. the importance of unquestioning obedience to the divine will, but he does not tackle the ambiguities which such obedience may have to face. H. B. Huffmon, loc. cit., p. 183 similarly argues that the story 'seems to reflect a test to persevere in the revelation one has received in spite of contrary claims by other prophets'; but in certain cases this might mean persevering in an inauthentic revelation.

15. Cf. Jer. 8.10–11; 23.9ff.; 28.5ff.; Ezek. 13–14.

16. H. St Thackery and R. Marcus, *Josephus V* (Loeb Classics Library) Harvard 1934 *Antiquities* VIII, sections 401–9.

17. J. Gray, op. cit., p. 449.

18. Micaiah's vision has strong formal and functional links with other prophetic visions e.g. Isa. 6.1–11; Ezek. 1–3.

19. Cf. T. W. Overholt, *The Threat of Falsehood*, London 1970. Overholt's analysis of *šeqer* in Jeremiah with its emphasis upon the false sense of security which it engendered in the minds of the people has obvious relevence to the message of the four hundred prophets.

20. *The Prophetic Faith* (English translation C. Witton Davies) New York 1949.

21. For a discussion of the usage of the same verb in Jer. 20.7 see p. 136, and note 17 to Chapter 7.

22. Cf. W. Zimmerli, *Ezekiel* (Hermeneia Series), Philadelphia 1979.

23. J. A. Montgomery and H. S. Gehman, op. cit., ad loc.

24. Contrast I Sam. 24.1 with I Chron. 21.1 where Satan takes the place of the Lord.

25. R. Davidson, 'Orthodoxy and the Prophetic Word', *Vetus Testamentum* 14, 1964, pp. 407–16.

26. J. Bright, *Jeremiah* (Anchor Bible 21), New York 1965, ad loc.

27. J. A. Thompson, *Jeremiah* (New International Commentary), 1980, p. 501.

28. Cf. J. P. Hyatt, *Jeremiah* (Interpreter's Bible 5), ad loc.

29. Cf. T. W. Overholt, op. cit., p. 64; H. J. Kraus, *Prophetie in den Krisis*, Neukirchen 1964, pp. 47ff.

30. For a general discussion of this passage see H. H. Rowley, *Men of God: studies in Old Testament History and Prophecy*, London 1963, pp. 37–65. For a more specific study of the key passage in I Kings 19 see E. Wurthwein, 'Elijah on Horeb: Reflections on I Kings 19.9–18' in *Proclamation and Presence*, ed., J. I. Durham and J. R. Porter, London 1970, pp. 152–66.

31. J. A. Montogomery and H. S. Gehmen, op. cit., ad loc.

32. For a fuller discussion of meanings of the phrase in I Kings 19.12 see R. Davidson, 'Some aspects of the theological significance of doubt

in the Old Testament' in *Annual of the Swedish Theological Institute* Vol. VII, 1970, pp. 41–58.

33. S. Terrien, op. cit., p. 232. M. Buber, *The Eclipse of God*, London 1953, p. 119, describes the phrase as 'A bold visual metaphor for an acoustical sound. It is silence, but not a thick and solid one, rather one that is of such veil-like thinness that the Lord shines through it'.

34. This is one of the reasons why E. Wurthwein's handling of the passage is unsatisfactory. Verses 9.14 cannot, in my opinion, be meaningfully discussed in isolation from the rest of the Elijah tradition; nor is it convincing to argue that verses 11–13 are a late addition to underline the parallelism between Elijah and Moses.

35. S. Terrien, op. cit., p. 229.

36. G. von Rad, *Old Testament Theology* Vol II, Edinburgh 1965, p. 20.

6. *Authority and Authenticity – A Prophetic Problem*

1. R. E. Clements in *Canon and Authority*, ed., G. W. Coats and B. O. Long, Philadelphia 1977, p. 49.

2. For a variety of views see J. D. W. Watts, *Vision and Prophecy in Amos*, Leiden 1958; E. Hammershaimb, *Amos*, Copenhagen 1966; H. W. Wolff, *Joel and Amos* (Hermeneia Series), Philadelphia 1977; B. S. Childs, *Introduction to the Old Testament as Scripture*, London 1979, ad loc.; R. B. Coote, *Amos among the Prophets: Composition and Theology*, Philadelphia 1981.

3. See e.g., S. Terrien, 'Amos and Wisdom' in *Israel's Prophetic Heritage*, ed., B. W. Anderson and W. Harrelson, New York 1962, pp. 108–15; H. W. Wolff, op. cit.

4. H. W. Wolff, op. cit., p. 96.

5. Translation by T. H. Robinson in Hebrew *qinah* lament style: see *The Poetry of the Old Testament*, London 1947.

6. Attempts, e.g. by H. W. Wolff, to assign this passage to a theological outlook later than that of Amos seem to me misguided. The passage fits in well with Amos' bitterly ironical approach.

7. Cf. R. Smend 'Das Nein de Amos' in *Evangelische Theologie* 23, 1963, pp. 404–23.

8. The explicit reference to the Exodus in this passage may be redactional, though the case for regarding it as such is not wholly convincing cf. H. W. Wolff, op. cit., ad loc.; J. L. Mays, *Amos* (Old Testament Library Series), London 1969. Even if we omit the explicit reference to the Exodus in verse 1b, the election theme stands.

9. J. L. Mays, op. cit., ad loc. Verse 8b which introduces a qualification into the statement of total destruction should probably be regarded as a later modification of Amos' stance.

10. J. L. Mays, op. cit., p. 159.

11. For differing views see S. Mowinckel, *He that Cometh*, Oxford 1956, pp. 125ff.; L. Cerny, *The Day of Yahweh and Related Problems*, Karlovy 1948; G. von Rad 'The Origins of the Concept of the Day of Yahweh', in *Journal of Semitic Studies* 4, 1959, pp. 97–108; J. D. W. Watts, op. cit., pp. 64–84.

12. J. Barton, *Amos' Oracles Against the Nations: A study of Amos 1.3–2.5*, Cambridge 1980.

13. A considerable literature has grown up around these doxologies e.g., J. L. Crenshaw, *Hymnic Affirmations of Divine Justice: The Doxologies of Amos and Related Texts in the Old Testament*, Missoula 1975; W. Berg, *Die sogennanten Hymnenfragmente im Amosbuch*, Frankfurt 1974; C. I. K. Story, 'Amos Prophet of Praise' in *Vetus Testamentum* 30, 1980, pp. 67–80.

14. It is the merit of C. I. K. Story's article that it does stress the need to take context seriously; but it seems to interpret context too narrowly.

15. W. Brueggemann, 'Amos iv. 4–10 and Israel's Covenant Worship' in *Vetus Testamentum* 15, 1965, pp. 1–15 attempts not wholly successfully to set the whole section against the background of a covenant renewal ceremony.

16. For the problems of the text see H. W. Wolff and J. L. Mays op. cit.

17. Cf. H. W. Wolff, op. cit., ad loc. P. R. Ackroyd in *Canon and Authority*, ed., G. W. Coats and B. O. Long, pp. 71–80 has interestingly argued that Amos 7.9–17 provides the link in tradition between I Kings 13 and II Chronicles 25.14–16, all of them touching upon the question of authority for religious faith. Thus I Kings 13 centres upon an unnamed prophet and Jeroboam I, Amos 7.9–17 upon Amos and the priest Amaziah who reports to Jeroboam II, while II Chronicles 25.14–16 has an unnamed prophet and King Amaziah. Ackroyd admits that the narratives function on different levels, that in Amos stressing the authority of a prophet commissioned by God, the validity of the word being undergirded by the proclamation of doom against the man who opposed it. He makes little attempt, however, to see the narrative in inter-relationship with the visions.

18. J. M. Ward, *Amos and Isaiah: Prophets of the Word of God*, Nashville 1969, p. 53.

19. Cf. E. Würthwein, *Amos Studien* in *Zeitschrift für die alttestamentliche Wissenschaft* 62, 1950, pp. 10–52.

20. H. W. Wolff, op. cit., p. 296, *per contra*, argues that the visions represent the challenging impact of insights which came to Amos before he began his ministry in the north. He claims that there is no evidence that Amos ever proclaimed anything but doom concerning Israel. But is there any evidence of Amos' insights before he began his ministry in the north?

21. For the Lord 'relenting' or 'changing' his mind see p. 83.

22. For a similar use of 'pass by' (Heb, *'br le*) meaning to forgive see Micah 7.18.

23. H. W. Wolff, op. cit., p. 113.

24. Among the issues considered on purely grammatical grounds are whether we understand 'was' or 'is' in this statement, whether the negative *lo* is to be taken as an interrogative or as an emphatic particle. For recent discussions of the issues see Z. Zevit 'A Misunderstanding at Bethel. Amos vii 12–14' in *Vestus Testamentum* 25, 1975, pp. 783–90; Y. Hoffmann 'Did Amos regard himself as a Nabi', in *Vetus Testamentum* 27, 1977, pp. 209–12.

25. See H. W. Wolff, op. cit., p. 308 for this view. A much more

reasonable approach is to be found in G. M. Tucker 'Prophetic Authenticity: A Form Critical Study of Amos 7.10–17', in *Interpretation* 27, 1973, pp. 423ff.

26. T. W. Overholt, '*Commanding the Prophet: Amos and the Problem of Prophetic Authority* in *Catholic Biblical Quarterly* 41, 1979, pp. 517–32; cf. B. O. Long, 'Prophetic Authority and Social Reality' in *Canon and Authority*, pp. 3–20.

27. T. W. Overholt, op. cit., p. 531.

28. For a balanced study see A. R. Johnson, *The Cultic Prophet in Ancient Israel* (second edition), Cardiff 1962.

29. For a survey of critical study of Habakkuk see P. Jöcken, *Das Buch Habakuk*, Bonn 1977.

30. A comparison of the NEB and the Good News Bible translations will highlight the problem for the English reader.

31. For the use of this passage by the Qumran community see W. C. Brownlee, *The Dead Sea Scrolls*, New York 1963.

32. For a good brief discussion of the root-'*mn* in the Old Testament see W. Zimmerli, *Old Testament Theology in Outline*, Edinburgh 1978.

33. For the hymn in Habakkuk 3 cf. W. F. Albright, 'The Psalm of Habakkuk' in *Studies in Old Testament Prophecy*, Edinburgh 1950, pp. 1–18; J. H. Eaton, 'The Origin and Meaning of Habakkuk 3' in *Zeitschrift für die alttestamentliche Wissenschaft* 76, 1966, pp. 144–71.

34. See pp. 32ff.

35. See pp. 22f.

36. For an excellent recent study of Habakkuk which combines sound critical judgment and sensitive spirituality see D. E. Gowan, *The Triumph of Faith in Habakkuk*, Atlanta 1976.

7. *Vocational Crisis – The Witness of Jeremiah*

1. For example, H. G. Reventlow, *Liturgie und prophetisches Ich bei Jeremia*, Gütersloh 1963, E. Gerstenberger, 'Jeremiah's Complaint: Observations on Jeremiah 15.10–21' in *Journal of Biblical Literature* 82, 1963, pp. 393–408; R. P. Carroll, *From Chaos to Covenant*, London 1981, arguing that 'The overall impression of the confessions illuminates the condition of the community in exile, and shows how the construction of the Jeremiah tradition utilized many elements from the life of the community in its presentation of the life of a prophet', p. 123. *Per contra*, J. Bright, 'Jeremiah's Complaints: Liturgy or Expressions of Personal Distress' in *Proclamation and Presence*, ed., J. I. Durham and J. R. Porter, London 1970, pp. 189–214; S. Blank, 'The Confessions of Jeremiah and the Meaning of Prayer' in *Hebrew Union College Annual* xxi, 1948, pp. 331ff.: J. Skinner, *Prophecy and Religion: Studies in the Life of Jeremiah*, Cambridge 1922.

2. J. Bright, op. cit., p. 190.

3. J. Skinner, *Prophecy and Religion*, p. 209.

4. For a recent survey of the problems surrounding the date of the beginning of Jeremiah's ministry see J. A. Thompson, *The Book of Jeremiah* (New International Commentary on the Old Testament), Grand Rapids 1980.

5. J. L. Crenshaw, *Prophetic Conflict*, Berlin 1971.

6. See Chapter 8. For Jeremiah's attitude to the Deuteronomic reform movement see H. H. Rowley, *From Moses to Qumran*, London 1963, pp. 184–208.

7. J. P. Hyatt, *Interpreter's Bible*, Vol. 5, ad loc.

8. P. L. Berger, *A Rumour of Angels*, Penguin Books 1971, p. 32.

9. D. Bonhoeffer, *Letters and Papers from Prison*, third ed., London 1967, p. 32. This book provides many valuable modern parallels to the Jeremianic confessional material.

10. Jer. 12.2 is similar in thought and imagery to Psalm 1.3–4 but it must remain uncertain whether there is any dependence, and if so in which direction.

11. See W. Rudolph, *Jeremia*, third ed., Tübingen 1968, p. 78; J. A. Thompson, op. cit., pp. 354–55.

12. G. Manley Hopkins, Sonnets, No. 50, *The Poems of Gerard Manley Hopkins*, ed., W. H. Gardiner and W. H. Mackenzie, Oxford 1967.

13. Cf. J. Bright, 'A Prophet's Lament and Its Answer: Jeremiah 15.10–15', *Interpretation* xxviii, 1974, pp. 59ff.

14. Skinner, *Prophecy and Religion*, p. 213.

15. A Confession of Jeremiah, *Union Seminary Quarterly Review* IV, 1949, p. 17.

16. It is hard to see the justification for the NEB variation in the translation of 15.20b and 1.19.

17. D. A. Clines and D. A. Gunn, ' "You have tried to persuade me" as Violent Outrage in Jeremiah xx 7–8' in *Vetus Testamentum* 28, 1978, pp. 20ff. argue that the verb *pitta* means 'to persuade' or 'to attempt to persuade', and that it is the theme of Yahweh's domination over the prophet which runs through this section; the prophet's 'Violence and Outrage' being directed against Yahweh who has committed him to being a prophet. The linguistic evidence, however, hardly seems conclusive, and the parallel to 'lying spirit' In I Kings 22 makes 'deceive' more likely. If their interpretation is correct the passage still expresses a violent protest by the prophet against the way the Lord has used his power to the detriment of the prophet, this same power which must be the source of the prophet's ultimate confidence.

18. Cf. R. Davidson, 'Orthodoxy and the Prophetic Word' in *Vetus Testamentum* 14, 1964, pp. 407–16.

19. G. Manley Hopkins, Sonnets, No. 16.

20. *Manchester Guardian Weekly*, Feb. 12, 1959, p. 6.

21. G. Manley Hopkins, Sonnets, No. 18.

8. Jerusalem – Symbol or Snare?

1. M. Buber, *The Prophetic Faith*, (English translation C. Witton Davies) New York 1949, p. 183.

2. See pp. 6ff.

3. See pp. 19ff.

4. *The Church Hymnary Third Edition*, Oxford 1973, Hymn 406.

5. See J. C. L. Gibson, *Canaanite Myths and Legends*, Edinburgh 1978.

6. M. Dahood's attempt, Psalms 1–50 (Anchor Bible 16), New York 1966, to reshape these verses and link the river with the picture of threatening cosmic upheaval is neither necessary nor convincing.

7. *Interpreter's Bible* 4, 1955, ad loc.

8. Compare the vision of the new Jerusalem in Revelation 21.9ff. associated with which in Revelation 22.1–5 there is the river of the water of life and the tree of life. Again we are dealing not with physical realities but with religious symbols.

9. Genesis 14 raises difficult questions concerning the origin and the historicity of this tradition. For a brief introduction to some of the issues involved see R. Davidson, *Genesis 12–50* (The Cambridge Bible Commentary), Cambridge 1979, pp. 32–40.

10. For a discussion of the early associations of Jerusalem with David and the subsequent development of its religious significance see M. Noth, 'Jerusalem and Early Israelite Tradition', in *The Laws of the Pentateuch and Other Essays*, Edinburgh 1966, pp. 132–44.

11. For the Assyrian account see J. B. Pritchard, *Ancient Near Eastern Texts* (third ed.), Princeton 1969, p. 288.

12. B. S. Childs, *Isaiah and the Assyrian Crisis*, London 1967; R. E. Clements, *Isaiah and the Deliverance of Jerusalem: A Study of the Interpretation of Prophecy in the Old Testament*, Sheffield 1980; J. Bright, *Covenant and Promise*, Philadelphia 1976, pp. 49–77.

13. I am not convinced that we should translate '*al* in verse 4 as 'against' and thus see it as an authentic oracle of judgement from Isaiah of Jerusalem, with verse 5 as part of the Josianic redaction, see R. E. Clements, op. cit., p. 32.

14. For the title Yahweh of Hosts see e.g. B. N. Wambacq, *L'Épithète divine Jahve Sabaoth*, Paris 1947; F. M. Cross, 'The Divine Warrior in Israel's Early Cult' in *Biblical Motifs*, ed., A. Altmann, Cambridge, Mass. 1973; W. Eichrodt, *Theology of the Old Testament* Vol 1, London 1961, pp. 192–94.

15. A strong theological apologetic for the Davidic dynasty and the southern kingdom of Judah, as opposed to the northern kingdom of Israel is to be found in Psalm 78 which has been well described as 'a charter myth explaining how Judah was the rightful heir of the exodus movement and therefore could claim the leadership of the people of Israel' R. P. Carroll, 'Psalm lxxxviii, Vestiage of a Tribal Polemic' in *Vetus Testamentum* 21, 1971, pp. 113–50. The quotation is from p. 150.

16. Cf. J. Muilenburg, 'Baruch the Scribe', *Proclamation and Presence*, pp. 215–38.

17. See p. 104.

18. This is likewise the emphasis in Jeremiah 18.1–11, so often misinterpreted as proclaiming a theology of hope.

19. Cf. H. H. Rowley, *From Moses to Qumran*, London 1963, pp. 184–208. The fact that there is scant biographical data for the early period of Jeremiah's ministry may indicate no more than that prior to the Temple Sermon (chapters 7 and 26) Jeremiah had no ready scribe. Baruch may indeed have been a convert of the Temple sermon.

20. See G. Lisowsky, *Konkordanz zum hebraischen Alten Testament*, Stuttgart 1958.

21. Cf. Jer. 5.14; 9.7.

22. For studies of the theological significance of Lamentations see N. K. Gottwald, *Studies in the Book of Lamentations*, London 1956; B. Albrektson, *Studies in the Text and Theology of the Book of Lamentations, With a Critical Edition of the Peshitta Text*, Lund 1963.

23. Cf. N. W. Porteous, 'Jerusalem and Zion: The Growth of a Symbol', in *Living the Mystery*, Oxford 1967, p. 107 where it is suggested that the 'I' may be intended to represent the bitter experience of the young king Jehoiakim.

24. The origin and the precise significance of the acrostic form has been much, and inconclusively, debated, cf. N. K. Gottwald, op. cit.

25. See S. N. Kramer, *Lamentation over the Destruction of Ur*, Chicago 1940.

26. Text in J. B. Pritchard, op. cit., pp. 455ff.

27. A. Toynbee, *The Study of History*, revised ed., London 1972.

28. Cf. N. K. Gottwald, op. cit., and B. Albrektson, op. cit.

29. D. R. Hillers, *Lamentations* (Anchor Bible 7A), New York 1972, ad loc. The NEB similarly avoids the question in verse 22 by translating:

> For if thou hast utterly rejected us,
>   then great indeed has been thy anger against us.

30. Cf. p. 9.

31. Cf. p. 126.

32. The 'full seventy years' of Jer. 29.16 should probably be taken as a round number, indicating an unspecified time in the future, but not during the lifetime of the present generation.

33. There are parallels elsewhere in the Old Testament between 'comfort' and 'fear not' e.g. Gen. 50.21 which suggest that the meaning conveyed by the verb *nhm* translated 'comfort' in Isa. 40.1 is probably that of bringing new hope into a situation of apparent tragedy.

34. Cf. N. W. Whybray, *Isaiah 40–66* (New Century Bible), London 1975, ad loc.

35. See B. S. Childs, *Memory and Tradition in Israel*, London 1962.

36. Neither the deletion of the question in verse 19b nor its transference into an emphatic statement cf. C. Westermann, *Isaiah 40–66* (Old Testament Library Series), London 1969 are necessary. It makes perfectly good sense as a challenging rhetorical question.

37. The literature on the 'Servant', his identity and mission, is enormous and has gathered apace since C. R. North's survey *The Suffering Servant in Deutero Isaiah* 2nd edition, Oxford 1965. The assumption taken here is that the servant is Israel or the community of faith within Israel which is the true Israel in the theological sense.

38. See C. Westermann, op. cit., and R. N. Whybray, op. cit., for different approaches to a passage which is not devoid of textual and interpretative difficulties. Isaiah 29.15–16 uses the same imagery in a different paradoxical context.

39. W. Zimmerli, *Old Testament Theology in Outline*, Edinburgh 1978,

p. 218 thinks that this passage may have been composed 'in answer to protests from the ranks of his own people who found the unorthodox message of Cyrus as the "anointed" unseemly'. 'Unseemly' seems to me a rather weak word to use in this context.

40. For discussion of the difficulties which verses 10 and 11 raise as to content and in particular as to the identification of the 'you' in verse 10 and the contrasting 'you' in verse 11 see C. Westermann and R. N. Whybray, ad loc. I see no reason to doubt that the contrasting 'you's refer to different sections within the exilic community; those prepared to take the risk in responding in faith to a hitherto unparalled situation, and those who wanted a greater security rooted in the past and God's ways of acting in the past.

9. Rewrite or Rethink

1. See P. R. Ackroyd, *Exile and Restoration*, London 1968.
2. R. E. Clements, *Isaiah and the Deliverance of Jerusalem*, Sheffield 1980.
3. J. Bright, *A History of Israel*, London 1960, pp. 288–93.
4. S. B. Frost, 'The Death of Josiah: a Conspiracy of Silence', in *Journal of Biblical Literature* 87, 1968, pp. 369–82.
5. For recent discussion of the outlook of the Chronicler see P. R. Ackroyd, 'The Theology of the Chronicler', *Lutheran Theological Quarterly* viii, 1973, pp. 101–16; J. M. Myers, *I Chronicles and II Chronicles* (Anchor Bible), New York 1965; H. G. M. Williamson, *Israel in the Book of Chronicles*, Cambridge 1977.
6. Cf. J. M. Myers, op. cit., ad loc.
7. *Apocalypse of Baruch* 64, see R. H. Charles, *The Apocrypha and the Pseudepigrapha of the Old Testament* vol II, Oxford 1913.
8. L. Ginsberg, *The Legends of the Jews* vol IV, Philadelphia 1909, p. 280.
9. I am deliberately excluding from the discussion that rewriting of history and theological revision which takes place in Apocalyptic, since once we move into the ethos of apocalyptic radical doubt disappears.
10. P. Weiss, in N. H. Glatzer, *The Dimension of Job*, New York 1969, p. 181.
11. The more prominent casualities of the literary and theological dissection of Job have been the prologue and epilogue (1–2; 42.7ff.), the hymn to wisdom (28), the Elihu speeches (32–37) and sometimes the divine speech in 40.6–42.6. Many recent studies, however, have insisted on respecting the integrity of the book in its present form e.g. the essays by J. A. Baker, 'The Book of Job: Unity and Meaning' and J. F. A. Sawyer 'The Authorship and Structure of Job' in *Studia Biblica* I, Sheffield 1978, pp. 17–26 and 253–57. See also R. Gordis, *The Book of God and Man*, Chicago 1967; M. Greenberg, J. C. Greenfield, N. M. Sarna, *The Book of Job*, Philadelphia 1980.
12. Cf. W. G. Lambert, *Babylonian Wisdom Literature*, Oxford 1960, pp. 15ff. For a powerful statement of the tension this theological position produces see A. Camus, *The Plague* where Father Panelaux' pulpit defence of the theory breaks down in the face of the painful death of a child.

13. See Chapter 2 above.

14. M. Pope's translation of Job 5.3 in *Job* (Anchor Bible 15), New York 1965:

> I have seen the fool strike root,
>   Then his abode suddenly accursed (cf. RSV)

is preferable to the NEB which eliminates the contrast within the verse by rendering 3a 'I have seen it for myself: a fool uprooted'.

15. There is widespread agreement that 24.18–24 are misplaced on the lips of Job, and probably form part of the lost third speech of Zophar. R. Gordis, op. cit., argues that Job is here quoting the conventional wisdom of the friends only to refute it.

16. The second half of this chapter likewise sits uneasily on the lips of Job and ought probably to be attributed to Zophar.

17. The certainty of vindication is the only thing that seems clear in the much discussed passage in Job. 9.25–26. Who the vindicator or redeemer is, how and when vindication will come are questions impossible to answer with any certainty because of the state of the text, as the wide divergence in English translations acknowledges cf. NEB with the Good News Bible. For a brief discussion of different approaches to the problem see H. H. Rowley, *Job* (New Century Bible), London 1970, ad loc.

18. See S. Terrien, *The Elusive Presence*, New York 1978, pp. 360ff.

19. R. P. Carroll, 'Postscript to Job', in *The Modern Churchman* (New Series 19), 1975–76, p. 166.

20. See M. Tsevat, *The Meaning of the Book of Job and Other Biblical Studies*, New York 1980.

21. R. Gordis, op. cit., p. 156.

22. Cf. H. H. Rowley, op. cit., pp. 18–21; M. Pope, op. cit., pp. lxxviif. For a recent interpretation of the divine speeches see J. G. Gamme, 'Behemoth and Leviathan: On the Didactic and Theological Significance of Job 40.15–41.26 in *Israelite Wisdom*, ed., J. G. Gammie et al., New York 1978.

23. H. H. Rowley, op. cit., p. 19.

10. The Radical Conservative

1. We shall throughout refer to the author as Qoheleth without attempting to adjudicate between the different interpretations and translations which have been proposed for this Hebrew word.

2. C. D. Ginsburg, *The Song of Songs and Coheleth* (The Library of Biblical Studies), New York 1970.

3. For example, O. Eissfeldt, *The Old Testament, an Introduction* (trans. from third German edition) Oxford 1965, lists as later additions 2.26; 3.17; 7.18b, 26b; 8.5, 12b, 13a; 9.9b; 12.7b and 12.12–14.

4. For a recent discussion of the theological significance of this passage see G. T. Sheppard, 'The Epilogue to Qoheleth as Theological Comment', *Catholic Biblical Quarterly* 39, 1977, pp. 182–89.

5. R. Gordis, *Koheleth, the Man and his World*, third ed., New York 1968.

6. Cf. R. B. Y. Scott, *Proverbs and Ecclesiastes*, Anchor Bible, New York 1965.

7. C. D. Ginsburg, op. cit., pp. 102f.

8. This tradition has its roots in the language of 1.12, and the heading in 1.1, though neither of these verses necessarily carry this meaning.

9. R. B. Y. Scott, *Proverbs and Ecclesiastes* (Anchor Bible), New York 1965, p. 196.

10. Cf. W. Zimmerli, *An Outline of Old Testament Theology*, Edinburgh 1978, pp. 161–63, and *Das Buch des Prediger Salomo*, Stuttgart 1962.

11. Thus e.g. AV, RSV, Jerusalem Bible.

12. See Job 38–40, Prov. 8.22–31 for earlier positive wisdom attitudes to the world, and Ecclesiasticus for a later positive wisdom response.

13. See R. Gordis, *The Book of Man and God*, Chicago 1967, pp. 45ff. for a good account of this upper class ethos.

14. See Chapters 1 and 2 above.

15. See J. L. Crenshaw in *Essays in Old Testament Ethics*, ed., J. L. Crenshaw and J. T. Willis, New York 1971, p. 44.

16. See p. 185.

17. R. Gordis, *Koheleth the Man and His World*, ad loc.

18. For Qoheleth's attitude to death see J. L. Crenshaw 'The Shadow of Death in Qoheleth', in *Israelite Wisdom*, ed., J. G. Gammie et al., New York 1978, pp. 205–14.

19. For a recent discussion of this passage see J. L. Crenshaw 'The Eternal Gospel', in *Essays in Old Testament Ethics*, pp. 23–56.

20. R. Gordis, *Koheleth the Man and His World*, ad loc.

21. See G. von Rad's comments on the limits of wisdom in *Wisdom in Israel*, London 1972, pp. 101ff.; cf. R. N. Whybray, 'Qoheleth the Moralist', in *Israelite Wisdom*, ed., J. G. Gammie et al., pp. 191–204.

22. See e.g. the Epic of Gilgamesh, text in A. Heidel, *The Gilgamesh Epic and Old Testament Parallels*, Chicago 1946.

23. M. Fonteyn, *Autobiography*, London 1979, pp. 206, 272.

11. *The Courage to Doubt – The Old Testament Contribution*

1. In addition to the material collected in J. B. Pritchard, *Ancient Near Eastern Texts* (third ed.) Princeton 1969; W. Beyerlin, *Near Eastern Religious Texts Relating to the Old Testament*, London 1978; D. Winton Thomas, *Documents for Old Testament Times*, London 1958 see S. N. Kramer, *Sumerian Mythology*, New York 1961, *The Sumerians*, Chicago 1963. For Babylonian material see W. G. Lambert, *Babylonian Wisdom Literature*, Oxford 1960. For Egyptian material see M. Lichtheim, *Ancient Egyptian Literature Vol I The Old and Middle Kingdoms*, *Vol II the New Kingdom*, Chicago 1975, 1976.

2. For divergent views see H. Frankfort, *Kingship and the Gods*, Chicago 1948; A. R. Johnson, *Sacral Kingship in Ancient Israel* (second ed.), Cardiff 1967; S. Mowinckel, *He That Cometh* (English translation G. W. Anderson), Oxford 1956; J. H. Eaton, *Kingship and the Psalms*, London 1976; M. Noth, 'God, King and Nation in the Old Testament', in *The Laws of the Pentateuch and Other Essays*, Edinburgh 1966, pp. 145–78.

3. For the text see S. N. Kramer, *The Sumerians*, pp. 127ff.

4. 11.70–71, quoted S. N. Kramer, op. cit., p. 128.

5. 11.102f., quoted S. N. Kramer, op. cit., p. 128.

6. Cf. S. N. Kramer, op. cit., pp. 117ff.

7. See W. G. Lambert, op. cit., p. 27 who suggests it would be more appropriately called 'The Babylonian Pilgrim's Progress'. The poem is datable in the early Cassite period circa 1500–1400 BC.

8. Tablet II lines 34f. cited W. G. Lambert, op. cit.

9. G. Widengren, *The Accadian and Babylonian Psalms of Lamentation as Religious Documents*, Uppsala 1937, pp. 181ff.

10. W. G. Lambert, op. cit., pp. 63ff. dates the document circa 1000 BC, though he admits that any date between 1400 BC and 800 BC is possible.

11. This volume reflects the Scandanavian patternist approach to Ancient Near Eastern religion and culture.

12. G. Widengren is particularly critical of G. R. Driver's sharp distinction between Hebrew and Babylonian psalm expresses in *The Psalmists*, ed., D. C. Simpson, Oxford 1926, chapter vi. A much more balanced study of the material is to be found in R. G. Castellino, *Le Lamentazioni individuali e gli inni in Babilona e in Israele*, Rome 1939.

13. Cited in G. Widengren, op. cit., p. 94, cf. Psalm 13.2.

14. G. Widengren, op. cit., p. 94.

15. For a useful survey of the Egyptian material see M. Lichtheim, op. cit. For the text of the Dispute see W. K. Simpson ed. *The Literature of Ancient Egypt*, Yale 1973, pp. 201–209; D. Winton Thomas, op. cit., pp. 162–167.

16. See p. 91.

17. R. de Vaux, 'The Revelation of the Divine Name YHWH' in *Proclamation and Presence*, pp. 48–75. For a discussion based on the syntax of Exod. 3.14 see B. Albrektson in *Words and Meanings*, ed., P. R. Ackroyd, Cambridge 1968, pp. 15–28.

18. See p. 71.

19. G. von Rad, *Wisdom in Israel*, London 1972, p. 110.

20. M. Buber, *The Eclipse of God*, p. 00.

21. Cf. J. Barr, 'Some Semantic Notes on the Covenant', in *Beiträge zur Alttestamentliche Theologie, Festschrift fur Walter Zimmerli*, Gottingen 1977, pp. 23–38.

22. For a stimulating discussion of the theological significance of the land in Old Testament thought see W. Brueggemann, *The Land*, London 1971.

23. M. Buber, *Moses*, Oxford 1946, p. 128.

24. A. M. Greeley in *Journeys*, ed., G. Baum, New York 1975, p. 202.

INDEX OF BIBLICAL REFERENCES